C000181416

The War of the Three Gods

'By some strange fatality, we find the gods more propitious
when we are at war than when we are at peace.'

Lucius Quinctius Cincinnatus (Livy, *Ab Urbe Condita* III.19)

'Worst book ever.'

Niall Harrigan (18:19, Tuesday, 2 November, 2010)

The War of the Three Gods

Romans, Persians and the Rise of Islam

PETER CRAWFORD

Pen & Sword
MILITARY

First published in Great Britain in 2013 by
PEN & SWORD MILITARY
An imprint of
Pen & Sword Books Ltd
47 Church Street
Barnsley
South Yorkshire
S70 2AS

ISBN 978-1-84884-618-0

A CIP catalogue record for this book is available from the British Library.

Typeset by Concept, Huddersfield, West Yorkshire, HD4 5JL.
Printed and bound in England by CPI Group (UK) Ltd, Croydon CR0 4YY.

Pen & Sword Books Ltd incorporates the imprints of Pen & Sword Aviation, Pen & Sword Family History, Pen & Sword Maritime, Pen & Sword Military, Pen & Sword Discovery, Wharncliffe Local History, Wharncliffe True Crime, Wharncliffe Transport, Pen & Sword Select, Pen & Sword Military Classics, Leo Cooper, The Praetorian Press, Remember When, Seaforth Publishing and Frontline Publishing.

For a complete list of Pen & Sword titles please contact
PEN & SWORD BOOKS LIMITED
47 Church Street, Barnsley, South Yorkshire, S70 2AS, England
E-mail: enquiries@pen-and-sword.co.uk
Website: www.pen-and-sword.co.uk

Contents

List of Illustrations

All Maps, Plans and Diagrams were drawn by Faye Crawford
(www.fayecreative.designbinder.com).

List of Plates

List of Rulers

Roman Emperors from Justinian I to Constantine V

527–565	Justinian I	685–695	Justinian II
565–578	Justin II	695–698	Leontius
578–582	Tiberius II	698–705	Tiberius III
582–602	Mauricius	705–711	Justinian II (restored)
602–610	Phocas	711–713	Bardanes
610–641	Heraclius	713–716	Anastasius II
641	Heraklonas	716–717	Theodosius III
	Constantine III	717–741	Leo III
641–668	Constans II	741–775	Constantine V Copronymus
668–685	Constantine IV		

Persian Emperors from Khusro I to Yazdgerd III

531–579	Khusro I	630–631	Buran
579–590	Hormizd IV	631	Azarmigduxt
590–591	Bahram VI Chobin	631–633	Hormizd V
590–628	Khusro II		Hormizd VI
628	Kavad II		Peroz II
628–630	Ardashir III		Khusro IV
630	Shahrbaraz		Khusro V
630	Khusro III	633–651	Yazdgerd III

The First Muslim Caliphs

632–634	Abu Bakr	644–656	Uthman
634–644	Umar	656–661	Ali

The Umayyad Caliphs

661–680	Mu'awiya I	717–720	Umar II
680–683	Yazid I	720–724	Yazid II
683–684	Mu'awiya II	724–743	Hisham
684–685	Marwan I	743–744	Al-Walid II
685–705	Abd al-Malik	744	Yazid III
705–715	Al-Walid I	744	Ibrahim
715–717	Sulayman	744–750	Marwan II

Acknowledgements

I would like to give thanks to those who have contributed in some way to the production and publication of this work.

To Phil Sidnell and Pen & Sword for placing their trust in a beginner to the world of publishing. I hope I have made sure that that trust was not misplaced.

To John Curran for not only having time to listen and offer advice, but for being the one to perpetuate my 'student' status by putting my name forward as a possible writer.

To all the staff, past and present, at Queens University, Belfast, and Dalriada School, Ballymoney for all the time and effort you have put in to help me get this far.

To all my predecessors and peers whose works have been consulted, digested and cited within.

To those artists and photographers, amateur and professional, whose images have been used to add depth to what would otherwise be a solid block of uninterrupted text. Not least my sister, Faye, who has lent her graphic prowess to produce all of the tremendous maps found within.

To all family and friends for putting up with me for so long and helping me stay sane with reminders that there is still a world beyond the confines of my computer desk and library.

Last, but by no means least, my mum, to whom I owe more than can ever be repaid.

gratias vobis ago

Introduction

The immense historical importance of the seventh century CE is much over-looked. It is in the period following the fifth-century collapse of the Western Roman Empire that is glossed over as the 'Dark Ages'. This is most definitely a misnomer for not only was this period not all that dark in Western Europe, the geographical limiter of the term, such cultural darkness certainly did not extend to the east. Despite some ups and downs, the Roman Empire was still the dominant force in the Mediterranean, while her most enduring foe, the Persian Empire of the Sassanids, continued to challenge her in the Middle East. How-ever, that does not mean that the seventh century was not a time of great change for the Eastern Mediterranean and Middle East. The first three decades might have started out like previous centuries with the Romans and Persians playing out another episode in the centuries-long east-west military dance that could trace its origins back to the conquests of Alexander the Great and even before. However, this would be a markedly different conflict and, as Fate would have it, this latest chapter of the Romano-Persian conflict would not only be the bloodiest, it would also be the last.

Romano-Persian wars had long been characterised as largely sterile affairs with only brief periods of intensive but largely indecisive fighting. This is best shown by the fact that after nearly 700 years of intermittent fighting between the Romans and the rulers of the Iranian plateau, the frontier had not moved all that far, east or west. Any conquests had been either limited in scale or ultimately ephemeral, with the two empires little changed by the experience. The war of 602–628 was to be very different. It would see immense territorial changes lasting the best part of two decades, political and religious intrigue, vast set-piece battles and sieges, and bring the Roman Empire to the very edge of extinction. Even though the territorial status quo would eventually be restored by the end of the war, both sides would be irrevocably altered by the length and brutality of the encounter; one side would not recover at all while the other would be so different that future historians would feel the need to identify it by a different name for the remaining 800 years of its existence. Such drastic changes can only be brought about on the battlefield, but it was not to be through renewed conflict between the Romans and Persians that these changes were to be fully realised. As devastating as the war between Heraclius and Khusro was, it did not represent even half of the story of the seventh century. While the two old foes were busy eviscerating each other, a sandy frontier land, long held to be made up of trading emporiums and temporary military nuisances, was experiencing a religious revolution.

That the seventh century marks the founding of Islam is probably its most well-known fact. However, the extent of the military conquests achieved in the name of this new religion by its skilled adherents is far less famous. Fuelled by their new faith, the Muslims would first unite the Arabian Peninsula and then not only challenge the traditional hegemony of Rome and Persia, but smash it to smithereens. Within a generation of the Prophet Muhammad's death, with a series of expertly conducted campaigns, monumental battles and shrewd use of political and religious tolerance, Islam and its adherents had taken the first massive strides towards severely altering the course of history not just for the Middle East but for the entire Mediterranean, Central Asia and the Indian subcontinent through one of the most spectacular military advances in all of history.

The seventh century brought about the end of the Ancient World.

Sources
As befitting a period of the utmost importance, there is a vast amount of surviving religious, secular and archaeological evidence for the seventh century from numerous sources, whether they are Roman, Persian, Muslim, western European or Chinese. From within the Roman Empire, there is the historical work of Theophylactus Simocatta, probably the last in the Procopian line of historians; the political poetry of George of Pisidia, an eye witness to the siege of Constantinople in 626; anonymously authored or fragmentary works such as the *Chronicon Paschale* or John of Antioch; the *Strategikon* of the emperor Mauricius, which highlights not just the organisation of the Roman army but also the forces of the Sassanids, Avars and Slavs; the later historians such as Nikephorus and Theophanes, who provide an account from hindsight; and regional histories such as the eye witness account of the Muslim invasion of Egypt by John of Nikiou, the Armenian *History of Khosrov*, wrongly attributed to Sebeos, or the much later *History of Caucasian Albania* by Movses Dasxuranci further enhance the picture of the seventh century.

From amongst the Persians, despite the predominance of oral traditions, the flowering of late Sassanid literature under Khusro I presents numerous works on philosophy, theology, medicine and statesmanship. Khusro II furthered this by collecting together the stories of Iran's national history in the *Book of Lords*. Of course, its strands of moral, social and political lessons on top of myths, legends, history and general entertainment mean it should be treated with a delicate touch.[1] It is also worth noting that much of the knowledge of the Sassanid state and its religion comes from places, temples, coins and most importantly the inscriptions and reliefs of Shapur I, Narses, the high priest Kirdir and Khusro II.[2]

Arabian culture also relied heavily on oral transmission of history, but by far the most well-known and important text from the seventh century not just for the Arabs but for the world as a whole is of the written variety – the Qur'an. As well as being the foundation of the religion of Islam, much like the New Testament can be used to illuminate early-first-century Judaea, the Qur'an can be used to help establish the circumstances prevalent in Arabia at the time of Islam's foundation. There is a substantial gap between the writing of the Qur'an and the other surviving written sources such as Ibn Ishaq, Baladhuri and Tabari, which is likely due to the Arabs only coming to fully appreciate the usefulness of written history after the advent of their world empire.

This expansion of Islam and the continued Roman involvement in Italy meant that sources from the eastern and western peripheries can provide some extra information. Chinese sources shed some light on the last decades of the Sassanid Persian dynasty and the early conflicts between Muslim and Chinese forces, while religious records like the *Liber Pontificalis* and Paul the Deacon can highlight the interaction of the western states with the Romans and then the Islamic conquerors in the late-seventh/early-eighth centuries.

However, despite the large amount of information that survives for the seventh century, its study suffers greatly from the lack of a standout contemporary historian of the calibre of Tacitus, Ammianus Marcellinus or Procopius. This deficiency is perhaps best seen in the Romano-Persian wars, where the series of events is largely established but elaboration on many of the major battles is conspicuous by its absence. Some of this slack is picked up in later decades by the Muslim sources, but these bring with them a different set of problems. While the great battles such as Yarmuk and Qadisiyyah are recorded in far more detail than the victories of Shahrbaraz, Shahin and Heraclius, the non-contemporary nature of these sources and their reliance on oral traditions undermine their accuracy, especially when it comes to chronology, making the understanding of the series of events increasingly difficult.

This tendency of early Muslim historians to veer towards tales of personal aggrandisement, drama and repetitive scenarios in order to plug many of the gaps in their knowledge further damages their reliability and forces any student to look for independent corroboration from elsewhere. Unfortunately, the same accusations of jumbled timelines can be levelled at the later Roman sources. The probable cause for this was a reliance on the Arab sources and oral transmissions for their information. There is also something of a dumbstruck undercurrent to much of the later Roman writing, as if even decades and centuries later they were still at a loss to explain the dire circumstances and fatalism that had afflicted the Empire. Unsurprisingly, Sassanid literature also suffered during the seventh century, being either lost during the Muslim conquests, or appropriated by Arab scholars and diluted through translation. However, such problems should not obscure or cast unnecessary doubt on the information contained within these sources and several modern historians –

Donner, Kennedy, Howard-Johnston – have gone to great lengths to demonstrate that they are usable in reconstructing the last Romano-Persian war, the rise of Islam and the seventh century as a whole.[3]

Spelling and Nomenclature
As a period of such monumental change where the clash of several cultures is recorded in several different languages – Latin, Greek, Armenian, Middle Persian and Arabic to name but a few – the seventh century presents the need to establish conventions with regards to spelling and place names. To that end, I have retained the more traditional Latinised style of Roman names over their Greek equivalents, such as 'Heraclius' rather than 'Heraklios' and 'Mauricius' rather than 'Maurice' or 'Maurikios'. Persian and Arab names present a more difficult problem as the transmission of many of these names into Greek and Latin can change them greatly. This is perhaps best seen with the Persian emperor, Khusro, whose name has been spelled in myriad different ways – Khusrow, Khusrau, Khosrau, Chosroes, Xosro and Xosrov amongst others. As I freely admit to not having even a passing knowledge of the languages, instead of attempting to apply any sort of linguistic convention I have endeavoured to maintain a consistency in spellings that hopefully does not create any difficulty in the identification of the individual or place.

As I take the view that the Roman Empire remained essentially Roman structurally, if not necessarily linguistically, until after the Arab conquests, I will refer to it as the 'Roman Empire' instead of the 'Byzantine Empire'. The only exceptions will be in a direct quotation from another writer. I also do not wish to become embroiled in the discussions regarding the exact ethnicity of the tribal confederacies that appear from the Eurasian steppe to the north of the main theatre. Therefore, when such peoples first appear in the narrative, a brief note on their origins will be made and then the more traditional or general terms such as Avars and Turks will be used. I have taken an even more general approach to the tribal make-up of the Muslim caliphate. In the early stages of Muslim expansion, there will be some mention made of the different Arab tribes, but once the armies of Islam move into the main theatre I have treated them as a more or less homogenous group.

As for city and region names, on many occasions, I have presented the ancient name and accompanied it with its modern equivalent or where it is near to aid in the identification; although some more famous ancient names will prevail over the modern, such as 'Constantinople' over 'Istanbul'.

Of course, I take full responsibility for any mistakes and resulting confusion.

Chapter 1

The Participants and Their Road to 600

From Gibraltar to Gaza, the inhabitants shared with the eastern provinces a common loyalty to the Roman emperors, a common piety, a common idiom in ornament, a common stable coinage.

Brown (2006), 158

The Persian nation is wicked, dissembling, and servile, but at the same time patriotic and obedient. The Persians obey their rulers out of fear, and the result is that they are steadfast in enduring hard work and warfare on behalf of their fatherland.

Mauricius, Strategikon XI.1

For it yields very little and uses up vast sums.

Cassius Dio, Roman History, LXXV, 3.2–3
(on the Romano-Persian conflict)

The Roman Empire in 600

The map of the Roman Empire had changed remarkably little between the first and fifth centuries CE. It stretched from Mesopotamia to the Atlantic and the highlands of Scotland to the sands of the Sahara. However, the reality was very different. Despite appearing to be united, there was a growing divide between East and West. Each had their own capital and senate, at Constantinople and Rome respectively, and after 395 each had its own emperor in Arcadius and Honorius. The Empire had been run by multiple emperors before but, as both the new *Augusti* were youths – Arcadius was 17 and Honorius was 10, it was left to their ministers to take command. With the East coming to rely more on a civilian government and the West being more under the sway of the military, these fraternal halves began to view each other as a rival.

This left the Romans less capable of dealing with the unfolding chaos beyond its frontiers sparked by the arrival of the Huns in Europe. While the East was far from immune, the West was particularly vulnerable, with its extended Rhine and Danube borders, to the 'migration of peoples' known as the *Völkerwanderung*. While the collapse of the Roman West is beyond the purview of this work and far more complicated than it being washed away by the barbarian tide, by the end of the fifth century Roman rule in the West was at an end. Britain was a battleground between Britons, Angles, Saxons and Jutes; Spain was home to Suebian and Visigothic kingdoms; Gaul was dominated by Franks

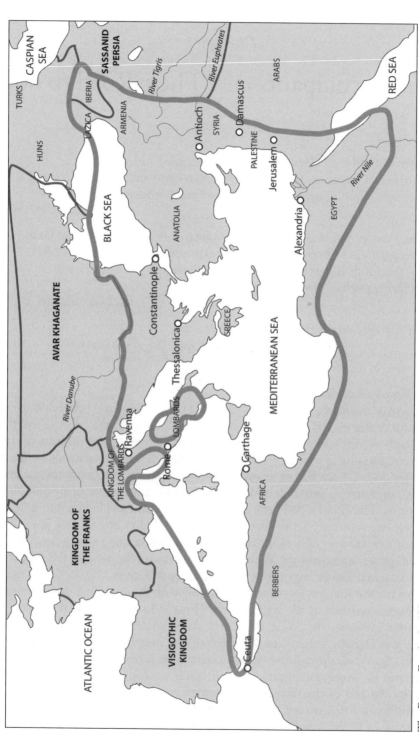

The Roman Empire in 600.

and Burgundians; Africa had fallen to the Vandals; and Italy was controlled by the Ostrogoths.

However, so large had the empire been that, even with these losses, the eastern half still represented the largest and most advanced state of the ancient world. Strong political leadership at Constantinople held the military largely at bay. Diplomacy and bribery were to be the new defensive weapons, along with the Great Walls of Constantinople and other cities, rather than an enlarged army. Despite the unpopularity of such a passive and un-Roman strategy, it helped the Eastern Roman Empire resist the 'turmoil of semi-serious wars, feints, intrigues, attempted coups, treaties, betrayals and counter-betrayals' that came with a resurgence of the military and the activities of the Ostrogoths and the Isaurians throughout the second half of the fifth century.[1] This solid base was built upon by the 'economic ingenuity' of the emperor Anastasius I, who, through tax remissions and abolitions, efficiency drives to reduce waste and professional reforms, nursed the Empire's tax base back into good health.[2] By 518, it was claimed that Anastasius left the treasury with a reserve of 320,000lb of gold.[3]

The man to take most advantage of this financial and military stability was the emperor Justinian. Across the empire, he embarked on a building pro- gramme of monumental scale.[4] Whether it was San Vitale in Ravenna with its famous mosaic of the emperor himself, the churches dotted across the Mediterranean from Morocco to Jerusalem, the cutting-edge technology applied to frontier fortresses, or the Sangarius Bridge in Bithynia, all demon- strated the continued brilliance of Roman art and architecture. However, it was upon his capital that Justinian lavished the most attention. He commissioned the rebuilding of the Church of the Holy Apostles and the Great Palace, while the Column of Justinian was erected to celebrate the substantial victories achieved in his name. However, the most awe-inspiring of his buildings was the Church of the Holy Wisdom of God, better known as Hagia Sophia. Designed and constructed by a mathematician and a physicist, it was to be the biggest church in the world for nearly a millennium. Its grandeur continues to astonish even in the modern day, particularly the immense pendentive domes that were also to be unmatched in scale until the Renaissance. Even Justinian himself seems to have been overawed by the accomplishment of his architects, declaring: 'Solomon! I have outdone thee!'[5]

However, Justinian did not use his Anastasian inheritance just to beautify the Empire. He spent vast amounts of cash in building an army capable of achiev- ing his military ambitions. After testing it against the Persians, Justinian turned his attention to the barbarian kingdoms that had carved up the Roman West. The first target was the Vandal kingdom of Africa. Providence shone on the Romans as Belisarius won the Battle of Ad Decimum, captured Carthage and then defeated a second Vandal army to deliver the entire kingdom by 534.[6] Such an unexpectedly swift conclusion saw Justinian allow himself to be dragged into war with the Ostrogothic kingdom of Italy. Once again, through good fortune and strong leadership from Belisarius, by 540 all of Italy south of the Po River was under Roman control.[7] A decade later, part of southern Spain was lifted from the Visigoths, virtually restoring the Mediterranean as a Roman lake.

However, while Justinian's conquests had gotten off to an impressive start, their consolidation was more testing. The resources they required were only sustainable so long as there was peace elsewhere. Once war with the Persians broke out in 540, priorities changed drastically. Belisarius was recalled before finishing off the Goths and it would be another twelve years before Italy was subdued, and, while Vandal resistance had ended in 534, fighting continued against indigenous tribes until 548 and the Visigoths wasted little time in challenging Roman Spain. On top of that, the Kutrigur Huns were putting increasing pressure on the Danube frontier.

The Empire of 540 might have dealt with these problems were it not for Fate dealing a cruel hand. In 541, at the height of the Empire's military deployment, bubonic plague erupted in the Mediterranean. Appearing first at the Egyptian port of Pelusium but likely originating in the upper reaches of the Nile or even further south, once it reached the flea-laden rodents of the Roman grain ships, it spread like wildfire.[8] Before the end of the year, it was playing a part in the lack of a decisive battle between Belisarius and Khusro I in the east. By early 542, it had reached Constantinople where Justinian himself became infected; by 543 it was in Italy and Gaul and had perhaps reached Ireland by 544. The horror story of Constantinople demonstrates the intensity of the pandemic as 'the tale of dead reached 5,000 each day, and again it even came to 10,000 and still more than that' with over-flowing cemeteries and mass graves.[9] To make matters worse, 541 was only the beginning of an infection cycle that was to repeat every generation for the next two centuries. Such prolonged reoccurrences may help explain the failure of the Roman and Persian Empires to stem the tide of Islam, for it is suggested that the plague left Arabia and its population relatively untouched.

In the Shadow of Justinian

Despite the outbreak of plague, with its achievements in architecture, technology and literature through the works of men like Procopius and the legal system with the publication of the *Codex Justinianus*, the age of Justinian is certainly one of the most colourful periods of Late Antiquity. Despite this, it is its military conquests in the western Mediterranean that really stand out. However, whether they represented a strengthening of the Roman Empire is an altogether different matter. They did not represent the establishment of a lasting peace in either Spain or Africa, as the Visigoths and Berbers began encroaching on Roman territory almost immediately. In Italy, the long war with the Goths had left much of its urban and rural infrastructure and its population as a whole in a rather sorry state. As war continued with the Persians after 540, Justinian's government had little time to invest in rebuilding the defences and infrastructures of these regained provinces. This in turn left them unable to look after themselves financially or militarily, so quickly becoming substantial drains on imperial resources. And once those resources were diverted to the core eastern provinces, unpaid wages saw to it that military effectiveness in these areas dwindled and mutinies became increasingly frequent. And worse was to come.

While the Goths, Vandals and Persians had been dealt with, the Danube erupted into chaos with the arrival of the Avars in the 550s. Who exactly these people were is disputed but it is likely that they were a polyethnic group of Mongolian, Turkic and Hephthalite tribes fleeing the emerging Turkic Khaganate of Central Asia. Justinian quickly employed them to subdue those Huns and Slavs who had been raiding the Balkans before encouraging them to intervene in the conflict between the Gepids and Lombards. The subsequent Avar victories over both left them as the undisputed masters of the Danube and the biggest threat to the Roman Balkans since Attila the Hun. However, the more immediate Roman problem was the reaction of the Lombards. Unwilling to accept the Avar yoke, they migrated to Italy in 568, where the Romans had no army that could defeat them. This led to Italy rapidly degenerating into a quagmire of continuous fighting that proved to be a ruinous black hole of imperial manpower and resources.

The diplomatic skills of Justinian might have stabilised the situation but he died in 565 before the true extent of the Avar/Lombard debacle had come to fruition. That is not to say that Justinian's successors were duds but it became increasingly obvious as the sixth century wore on that Justinian had not only been diplomatically gifted, he had also been fortunate to be able to call upon a large cadre of skilled generals and administrators throughout most of his reign – Belisarius, Narses, John Troglita, Germanus, John the Cappadocian and Tribonian to name a few. As the stream of skilled bureaucrats and generals dried up, Justinian's successors found that there was little imperial infrastructure to fall back upon. Mauricius and Heraclius soon had to campaign in person and rely on members of their own families and the imperial court to govern the Empire, regardless of whether they were suited to the job or not.

The military difficulties along the Danube, in Italy and against the Persians, as well as the strains of government, seem to have cost Justin II his sanity. Tiberius and Mauricius quickly prioritised the eastern frontier and, while the bulk of the imperial army was deployed successfully in Mesopotamia, local forces in Italy and the Balkans were left to fend for themselves. This allowed the Lombards to carve out not just a kingdom in northern Italy but also two independent dukedoms in the centre and south of the peninsula, while the

Visigoths reduced Roman Spain to a coastal strip. Most alarming though was the collapse of the Danube frontier. By the accession of Mauricius in 582 the Avar threat had been firmly identified and largely contained by annual tribute. However, what the Romans could not deal with was the vast southern movement of the Slavs. Escaping the control of their erstwhile Avar masters, the Slavs spread throughout the Balkans in such numbers that the Illyrian and Thracian armies had no chance of stopping them.

Thoroughly distracted by Avars, Slavs and Persians, Mauricius took decisive action with regards to the western provinces in establishing the Exarchates of Italy and Africa in 584 and 590, respectively. These were essentially devolved governments with their rulers, the exarchs, acting as the emperor's representatives at Ravenna and Carthage in both civil and military matters. The extent of these exarchate powers was something of an admission that the central government at Constantinople was unwilling or unable to provide prolonged assistance to its outliers. However, there was to be at least one positive to emerge from these exarchates as the son of the Exarch of Africa would lead a rebellion that was to change imperial fortunes in the seventh century.

There is Only One – Late Roman Religion

In the sphere of Roman religion, the fourth century saw the triumph of monotheistic Christianity over its polytheistic pagan rival. The pace of this victory was remarkable for at the outset of the century the Christian Church was still a small minority and faced concerted imperial persecution. However, with the victory of Constantine at Milvian Bridge in 312 and his attributing of it to the support of the Christian God, everything changed. Suddenly Christianity was not just legalised but promoted as the faith of the ruling Constantinian dynasty. By the end of the century, it was unimaginable that the emperor would be anything other than a Christian. In many ways, the organisation of the Christian Church mirrored that of the Empire itself, as is still seen today with the use of Roman terms in the Catholic hierarchy such as vicar, diocese and curia. The Bishop of Rome was essentially a religious emperor at the top of a hierarchy of bishops spread throughout the provinces. However, as power disseminated throughout the Empire, the Church hierarchy had to adapt accordingly. By the late-fourth century, with the divide of imperial power between East and West, the Pope was forced to accede to a similar arrangement. In 381, the patriarch of Constantinople was elevated to a position second only to the Pope and, by the time of Justinian, Antioch, Alexandria and Jerusalem were recognised as part of a Pentarchy that provided governance for the Roman Church.

However, this arrangement did not put an end to the power struggles involving the Church. As Rome and Italy declined in temporal importance, Constantinople continued its ascent in religious affairs backed by the presence of the emperor. By the sixth century, Justinian was not only building numerous churches across the Mediterranean and attempting to force religious unity upon heretics, Jews and pagans, he was also imposing what he saw as the right of the emperor to influence church doctrine. Should a Pope decide to go against imperial wishes, he could find himself deposed by force and the Papacy became a pawn of Constantinople. However, as the Lombards eroded imperial power on the Italian peninsula, the Pope found himself with increasing independence.

Christianity itself was also far from a united faith. There were various views dissimilar to the official Nicene/Chalcedonian Creed, with most stemming from the dispute over the nature of the Trinity and in particular about how Jesus of Nazareth could be both the divine Son of God and the human son of Mary. The major controversy of the late-sixth century was Monophysitism, which held that Jesus had only one divine nature in opposition to the official Christology, expressed by the Council of Chalcedon in 451, which stated that He held two natures within His one person. All of this seems unnecessarily pedantic to the modern reader but throughout late antiquity such disputes enflamed religious passions. It was therefore potentially very dangerous for an emperor or the Church to attempt to force Christological uniformity across the Empire, as it would almost certainly antagonise large sections of the Roman population. This was especially true of Monophysitism, which had numerous followers across Egypt, Syria, Mesopotamia and Armenia; areas that provided the vast proportion of the Empire's manpower and tax bases. Indeed, Heraclius and his successors would find out just how divisive and disruptive such doctrinal disputes could be, particularly in Egypt and Armenia, with the attempted enforcing of the compromise doctrine of Monothelitism, which stated that Jesus had a dual nature within His single being but only a divine will throughout the first half of the seventh century.

However, there were other religious groups within the Roman Empire. Under the guidance of their Patriarch at Tiberias, the Jews represented a rather large proportion of the Roman population.[10] The Diaspora and the Christianisation of the Empire saw the Jews treated with a suspicion that was to become all too common and unjustified as the centuries wore on. Influenced by past revolts, Romans saw these Jewish communities as a potential 'fifth column' always on the verge of rebellion and one that 'openly rejoiced at the calamities of the empire'.[11] As a result, Jews were not allowed to marry Christians, make a will, inherit, testify in court and were 'barred from seeking entrance to the imperial service', and there is some evidence of forced conversion on a local level.[12] However, the Romans did have some justification for their wariness towards the Jewish community. While the insidious nature of the Diaspora was illusionary, the potential trouble posed by those Jews who remained in Palestine was not. Roman fears would be somewhat borne out in the seventh century as the Jews invited the Persians to take Palestine, joined them in the siege of Jerusalem, and later welcomed the Muslims.

The brief reign of Julian the Apostate and the lack of long-term consequences proved just how far the collection of cult superstitions that came
under the umbrella of paganism had fallen behind Christianity.[13] However,
even with imperial opposition and Justinian relegating them to the same legal
position as Jews and heretics and subjecting them to heavy confiscations and
even exile, paganism continued to exist. This survival within the Empire was
aided by the paganism of many of its neighbours, such as many pre-Muslim
Arabs, Berbers, Avars, Slavs, Huns, Alans, Bulgars and Turks. However, it is
difficult to find evidence of Roman pagans causing as much trouble or disruption as heretical Christians or Jews; disruption that could affect their
military deployments.

The Late Roman Army

As the Roman Empire had changed over the centuries, its army had too.
Reforged in the cauldron of the third century and reinforced by the reforms of
Diocletian and Constantine, the classic 5,000-strong Roman legion was
replaced by divisions of 1,000 men. Supported by specialist cavalry and *auxilia*
units raised from non-Roman tribes, this new model army rebuilt and defended
the Empire throughout most of the fourth century. However, by the turn of the
fifth, the large-scale casualties incurred through civil wars and against barbarian
tribes and the increasing unwillingness of the citizenry to enlist made it
increasingly difficult to fill the ranks with Roman-trained infantry. This led
to the army relying more on barbarian soldiers, who grew increasingly independent as their numbers grew. While that alone did not cause the end of the
Western half of the empire, it did contribute heavily.

Geography, civilian government and a smaller army allowed the East to
avoid a similar fate. The overall composition of the Eastern army remained
remarkably consistent from the fourth to the seventh century. It continued to
be made up of field armies in Thrace, Illyricum and the East, and two in the
presence of the emperor at Constantinople, with additional field forces in
Armenia, Africa, Italy and Spain being added under Justinian. These armies
maintained a largely Roman core, bolstered by allied barbarian tribesmen and
supported by the *limitanei* deployed on the frontiers. Much of the equipment,
organisation, tactics and logistics of the army also remained recognisable to
that of the past. Martial emperors like Tiberius II, Mauricius and Heraclius did
command the army in person but it was more usually members of the imperial
family or talented non-imperial individuals like Belisarius and Philippicus.

The lack of detailed information on Roman manpower makes drawing any
firm conclusions about the size and composition of the army at the turn of the
seventh century difficult. It is possible that the field armies in the eastern
provinces remained of a similar size. The *Notitia Dignitatum*, a document that
recorded the Roman military establishment in both East and West in the
late-fourth/early-fifth centuries, suggests 104,000 field troops for the East

while the army of the mid-sixth century contained 95,000 men. The Eastern army of the early 530s was very similar to that of the *Notitia* and the Illyrian army of 548 was 15,000 strong and around 17,500 in 395.[14] Furthermore, given the conquests of Justinian and the stationing of extra field armies within them, the field forces of the mid-sixth century may have been larger.

	395	559
Praesental I	21,000	20,000
Praesental II	21,000	20,000
East	20,000	20,000
Thrace	24,500	20,000
Illyricum	17,500	15,000
Armenia	–	15,000
Italy	–	20,000
Africa	–	15,000
Spain	–	5,000
Total	104,000[15]	150,000[16]

These figures were almost certainly reduced by the attacks of Lombards, Goths, Avars and Slavs; although the recruiting of a 15,000-strong force called the *Tiberiani* may have replaced many of those lost forces.[17] Therefore, the Roman field armies at the turn of the seventh century may have been made up of a similar figure as that at the end of Justinian's reign – 150,000. However, such figures should only be seen as a paper strength and most likely did not reflect the forces on the ground. This is further borne out by the recommendations of Mauricius, who thought that an army of 5,000–15,000 was well proportioned and 15,000–20,000 to be large.[18] Few numbers are known for the 590s aside from the Roman force of perhaps 30,000–40,000 that was sent to help Khusro II regain the Persian throne.

There was also change in the tactical make-up of these armies. The organisation of the Roman army had always been complex but perhaps that of the *Strategikon*, with its appreciation that 'all nations do not fight in a single formation or in the same manner, and one cannot deal with them all in the same way', was the most elaborate yet.[19] Its combined-arms theory also highlighted the changes in ancient warfare. Perhaps the biggest change was the decline in effectiveness of infantry, particularly against the powerful bows and manoeuvrable steeds of the steppe peoples who had become increasingly prevalent since the end of the fourth century.[20] In response, the Romans began to hire steppe nomads and train their own horse-archers; however, the continued opposition of the Persians and Germanic tribes, the need to take fortifications and the rugged terrain of Italy, the East, and the Balkans meant that disciplined infantry still had a prominent role to play. To that end, whilst the proportion of cavalry and other specialist forces continued to rise to provide the Romans with the necessary flexibility and striking power, it was still infantry that remained the core of the Roman army, even if it had been 'long neglected and almost forgotten in the course of time'.[21]

The infantry of the *Strategikon* was divided into three separate types – heavy, light and missile. Each soldier was to sport short hair, a cloak and tunic and shoes with thick nail-studded soles for greater durability. This successor of the legionary was armed with sword, spear, short javelin and lead-pointed darts, and armoured with a helmet and large oval shield. Mail and greaves were expected for those men who occupied the exposed front and flanks of the formation. The light infantry were similarly equipped and armed with small javelins, spears, lead-pointed darts, and slings, although they were less well armoured. The infantry also contained a large proportion of archers, trained either in the bow or the crossbow. However, their training in the use of a shield, javelin and sling suggests that they were as much a skirmishing arm as a static missile battery.[22]

The infantry also continued to be heavily subdivided tactically. The basic unit was a *lochagiai* of sixteen men. Four of these units made up a sixty-four-strong *allaghion*; two *allaghia* a *hekatonarchia* and two *hekatonarchiai* an *arithmos*. On the battlefield, these 256-strong *arithmoi* would be deployed in an infantry square sixteen by sixteen. The *Strategikon* encouraged the infantry to be divided into three or four groups as well as altering the proportion of light to heavy infantry depending on the size of the force. If it was over 24,000 strong then up to half of the infantry was advised to be light-armed troops. If it was under 24,000 then the ratio was to drop to a third. On top of that, one of every nine heavy infantry was to be set aside to provide a reserve force.[23] The reformed cavalry served in a *bandon* of 300 soldiers and was subdivided into three *hekatonarchiai* of 100 men each; each *hekatonarchia* into two 50-strong *allaghia* and each *allaghion* into five *decharchia* of 10 men. That there were mechanisms in place for groups of up to 21,000 cavalry demonstrates the increased role of cavalry by the seventh century.

As well as tactical formations, divisions within the army could represent different sources of recruits. Not only did the army recruit Romans from across the Empire, it also recruited non-Romans to serve directly in 'Roman' units or be grouped together as *foederati*. Originally tribesmen serving under treaty obligations that implied submission, by the sixth century the *foederati* were described as those who served not because they had 'been conquered by the Romans but on the basis of complete equality.'[24] With that, *foederati* infantry and cavalry were seen as a permanent fixture in the Roman army, paid and trained as regular soldiers. Another class of soldiers were the *bucellarii*, who were originally the bodyguards of non-imperial individuals – the name, meaning 'biscuit-eater,' came from the idea that the employer would provide them with basic sustenance. As their make-up mirrored that of the regular army, a *bucellarius* could be from almost any walk of life: a local landowner could arm his slaves and tenants while a top-ranking general like Belisarius could collect an eclectic cabal of barbarians and experienced army officers. This also meant that the size of *bucellarii* could range in size from a few dozen to several thousand depending on the status, position and financial clout of the individual commander. Rather than let it get out of hand, the government at Constantinople incorporated these forces into its military, which saw the *bucellarii* emerge as an elite foreign legion.[25]

There were other elite units in the Roman army. The *scholae* and *protectores* still survived in the late-sixth century but they had degenerated into ceremonial units; so much so that when Justinian proposed sending them on campaign it elicited such terror that they willingly surrendered their pay.[26] The actual elite military units were the *excubitores* and the *optimates* – literally 'those out of bed' and 'the best'. The former was created by Leo I in the early 460s as a palace guard of about 300, originally made up exclusively of Isaurians. These men became increasingly influential in the sixth century with Justin I, Justin II, Tiberius II and Mauricius all relying upon their support to secure their accession. Indeed, both Tiberius and Mauricius had served as *comes excubitorum* to their predecessors. There is some dispute about the origin of the latter. The *optimates* may have appeared as early as the third century or been the creation of Tiberius II, but by the seventh century they were an elite corps of up to 5,000 men.[27]

A far less elite section of the Roman army was the *limitanei*. While originally an extension of the regular forces stationed on the frontiers, lesser privileges and status had reduced them to little more than a regional police force or peasant-soldiery.[28] So far had they declined that Justinian deprived them of their pay and status as soldiers.[29] However, this bleak outlook on the *limitanei* appears to be overly pessimistic: 'If the *limitanei* were so useless then at least one emperor between Constantine and Justinian would have noticed.'[30] They served in field armies throughout the sixth century and were used to garrison strategic forts and river crossings, and, despite his ill-treatment of them, Justinian appears to have maintained a concentration of *limitanei* on every frontier, even re-establishing them in Africa in 534.[31]

Despite the retreat from foreign manpower in the fifth century, the Roman army was forced by the extent of the Justinianic conquests to make increasing use of non-Roman forces. Just how integral such extramural forces became was highlighted at the Battle of Busta Gallorum in 552 where the Roman force contained almost as many non-Romans as it did regulars, while Justin II's reluctance to employ non-Romans saw the Empire's position in the east seriously undermined; a position not restored until Tiberius II initiated the widespread recruitment of men from beyond the frontiers. Financial constraints forced Mauricius to reduce the number of foreign recruits by 600 but circumstances would dictate that Heraclius employ barbarians en masse. This willingness to employ foreigners would continue throughout the existence of the Roman Empire and a list compiled from the sources includes every people with which the Romans were in contact – Huns, Slavs, Gepids, Lombards, Bulgars, Avars, Franks, Burgundians, Arabs, Goths, Vandals, Berbers, Armenians, Caucasians, Turks and Persians.[32]

Such reliance on non-Romans might suggest that there was some trouble finding Roman recruits. However, even with recurrences of plague, it is difficult to prove any significant reduction in population and so vast had the Roman advantage been over its contemporaries that, even in decline, Roman demographic superiority would have been maintained.[33] Instead of a lack of Roman manpower, the prevalence of non-Romans is coupled with the instances of desertion, disloyalty and apathy, and might suggest that the conditions of military service were not attractive enough for citizens to enlist. Even then, throughout the late-sixth and early-seventh centuries when there were sufficient funds available, there were sufficient recruits available to provide good armies.

All of this meant that in spite of territorial losses, political and religious fracturing, financial and administrative decay, and strategic and tactical problems, the Roman Empire at the dawn of the seventh century was still the leading state in Europe and the Middle East, with a multifaceted population of various origins, faiths and skills and an army that was still capable of defeating any of its foes.

Sassanid Persia

While most have heard of the Roman Empire, the name of its seventh-century opponent, Sassanid Persia, is not so famous. Some may know Persia as the state once ruled over by the Shah that became the Islamic Republic of Iran in 1979. Others may even have a fleeting knowledge of the Achaemenid Persian Empire that was stalled by the 300 Spartans at Thermopylae and conquered by Alexander the Great. Even amongst many students of ancient and early medieval history, Sassanid Persia is merely one of the myriad military opponents of the Roman Empire: an occasional annoyance that lay prostrate before the might of the legions any time an emperor sought the glory of an Alexandrian campaign. However, it was much more than that.

Racially, these Sassanids were of Aryan stock like their Parthian predecessors but were more likely an earlier offshoot that had settled in Persis, the modern Iranian province of Fars. The Sassanids claimed descent from the Achaemenids, with whom they shared the same homeland in Fars. While it is more likely that this was an attempt to ascribe more legitimacy to their regime, the Romans thought them the descendants of the sixth-century BCE King of Kings, Cyrus the Great.[34] The Sassanid state appeared in the early-third century CE as the central authority of the Parthian monarchy crumbled under

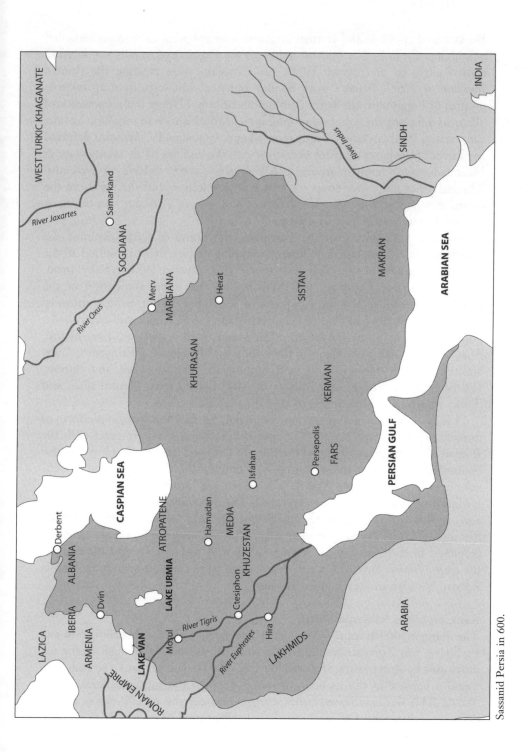

Sassanid Persia in 600.

the strain of civil war and Roman invasion. The eponymous Sasan is recorded as a high priest in Persis; a position that his son Papak used to rally support and seize control of the region. While the Parthians were tackling the Roman invasion of 216/7, Papak's sons, Shapur and Ardashir, were fighting for sole control of Persis with the latter coming out on top. Having built a network of alliances amongst the other petty kingdoms, Ardashir rose in rebellion against the warring Parthian kings, Vologaeses VI and Artabanus IV. Ardashir defeated the forces of the latter on three occasions with the decisive battle taking place at Hormizdagan probably in around 224. Vologaeses seems to have survived until 228 and other petty kingdoms were to hold out longer, but the reality of the situation was that, following his defeat of Vologaeses, Ardashir was the most powerful man on the Iranian plateau.[35]

With this supplanting of the Parthians, the house of Sasan assumed the mantle of the Achaemenid's continent-spanning empire that had united all the major civilisations of the Near East in the sixth century BCE – Babylonian, Median, Assyrian, Egyptian, and Lydian with the added dimension of the Hellenism introduced by the conquests of Alexander. While large sections of Achaemenid territory had never been recovered, the Sassanids still controlled a population of many nationalities, dialects and races – Iberians, Laz, Albani, Alans, Armenians and Medians in the Caucasus, Elymaeans, Characenes, Arabs and Persians in Mesopotamia and around the Persian Gulf and Surens, Kushans, Sakas, Yuezhi and Indians in Asia. Later Huns, Hephthalites and Turks would have been added to this already eclectic mix.

This gave the Sassanids an economic, social, cultural and foreign platform of immense diversity and scope. Not only did Sassanid Persia interact with the Roman Mediterranean, through the Persian Gulf and the Silk Road, it was also connected with the Arabian Peninsula, Central Asia, China, the Indian sub-continent and South East Asia. It was very much located on the cultural and trading crossroads between east and west. The Sassanids were well aware of this and went to great lengths to retain this rich and vibrant multiculturalism throughout the 400 years of their rule. Middle Persian might have been the language of the Zoroastrian priesthood, but it was not strictly imposed as the *lingua franca*. Several Persian inscriptions were carved not only in Middle Persian but also in Greek and Parthian.

Religion in the Sassanid State
The religion of Sassanid Persia, as it had been with the Achaemenids and Parthians, was Zoroastrianism. By the time of Sassanids, this dualist religion, developed by Zarathustra or Zoroaster from the Iranian sky and war gods, had found a balance in the worship of moral truth of the supreme deity, Ahura Mazda. This was manifested in the struggle between the angelic *ahuras* and the demonic *daevas* with the world as their battleground. As the only combatant capable of choosing a side, man could therefore influence this battle. Due to its

age and its teachings of 'individual judgment, Heaven and Hell, the future resurrection of the body, the general Last Judgment, and life everlasting for the reunited soul and body'[36] becoming integral parts of the Abrahamic religions of Judaism, Christianity and Islam, Zoroastrianism may have had 'more influence on mankind, directly and indirectly, than any other single faith'.[37] Given these ancient roots, the Sassanids took special care to associate their regime with Zoroastrianism, basing much of their legitimacy on a divine right to rule through their 'propitious relationship with the gods'.[38] In return for promoting and restoring the purity to the cult of Ahura Mazda, polluted by the Parthians, Sassanid kings claimed to be virtual god-kings due to the relationship, but were careful to emphasise their inferiority to the gods themselves.

Under the Sassanids, the Zoroastrian priesthood became more structured and organised across the empire. By the sixth century, each province or region had a chief priest tasked with maintaining spiritual and ecclesiastical harmony, while a Priest of Priests oversaw the whole of the Zoroastrian hierarchy, much like the Patriarchs and Popes of Christianity. There were also priestly groups charged with looking after the empire's numerous fire temples and religious life on a more local level. However, Zoroastrianism was far more than a religion in Sassanid Persia. Its ethics provided the legal framework of the empire, meaning that the clergy were not only responsible for religious well-being, but were present at all levels to dispense justice. Despite this organisation and state backing, in the face of Christianity and Islam, Zoroastrianism was 'burdensome, devoid of persuasive power and lacking in open-mindedness or readiness to reform'.[39]

The Sassanid state played host to a vast number of other faiths.[40] Christian beliefs had been spreading into Persia since the second century but adherents had remained scarce in number until the carrying off of thousands of Roman prisoners by Shapur I. Instances of persecution in the late-third century under Bahram II could suggest that the Christian community in Persia had grown to a size that saw it viewed as a potential threat. When the Roman Empire embraced Christianity, these Persian Christians were open to accusations of being 'fifth columnists', spying for the Romans, offering aide to any incursion or undermining the Sassanid state. However, there appears to have been little for the Sassanids to worry about as Persian Christians established their own identity separate from that of the Roman Church. By the time they held a synod at Seleucia-Ctesiphon in 410 they had their own ecclesiastical organisation headed by the Katholikos-Patriarch. This independence was further highlighted when a second synod at Jundaisabur in 484 renounced the Nicene Creed in favour of that of Nestorius, who emphasised the disunion of the human and divine natures of Jesus. This might seem like another petty argument of semantics but, when it is coupled with the anathematising of the Nestorian Creed by the Councils of Ephesus and Chalcedon in 431 and 451 respectively, it marked the final split between the Roman and Persian churches.

This encouraged the Sassanids to embrace these Christians with Khusro II taking a Christian wife, employing a Christian finance minister and claiming the protection of Christian saints.

Jews also played a not insignificant role in the Sassanid state. Despite periods of repression, the Sassanids were happy to incorporate Jews into their infrastructure as traders and tax officials and in return granted them some autonomy. Perhaps surprisingly, Persian Jews played a more important role in the Romano-Persian War of 602–628 than Persian Christians, particularly in regard to the Persian attack on Jerusalem. Despite occasional persecution, the Sassanids seem to have continued the religious tolerance of their predecessors. This may not have been out of any inherent benevolence but more because this array of different beliefs could pose a threat to the peace either through rebellion or, in the case of the Christians, a pretext for a Roman invasion. Therefore, it was more politically expedient to tolerate rather than persecute. That the Sassanids enjoyed financial, infrastructural and even military benefits from Judaeo-Christian participation in tax-collecting, trade and building work can only have further soothed any persecutory fervour within the Sassanid establishment.

Sassanid Society

Like the emperor of Constantinople, ultimate Persian civil and military authority lay with the King of Kings, which he dispensed through the court officials gathered around him. The territory he presided over was divided largely into two categories – kingdoms and provinces. The petty kingdoms that survived from the Parthian era were entrusted to Sassanid family members, local kings and dynasts, and may have enjoyed a certain amount of autonomy, sometimes problematically, as they could have their own agenda that contrasted with that of the king. The provinces were established on the territory that the Sassanids gained control of but which had no existing form of government that could be subsumed as a vassal kingdom.

The social divisions in the Sassanid state were even more varied. There were four somewhat distinct estates – the warriors, the priesthood, farmers and artisans – but even these were further subdivided and did not incorporate the entire population. The most important group with regards to the temporal power of the king were the aristocracy of the warrior class, which included the extended Sassanid family, local dynasts and noble families. All of these were linked to the King of Kings through 'a network of mutual obligations, interdependencies, and also common interests', although this did not stop them causing repeated problems for Persian kings.[41]

Perhaps because of these continued problems, throughout the sixth century attempts were made by Kavad I and Khusro I to alter the social structure of the nobility and the army.[42] Prestige and rank were to be conferred by the King rather than inherited, raising a lower administrative and military nobility to run the empire as a counterbalance to the power of the established warrior classes. However, despite these reforms, the last century of Sassanid Persia was plagued by rivalry between the king and the aristocracy, and even the most successful of late Sassanid kings, Khusro II, was not immune. Another major problem for the internal security of the Sassanid state was the struggle for power between the warrior classes and the other influential group of Sassanid Persia, the priesthood. Such internecine struggles between the Sassanid clan, the warriors and the clergy ultimately led to the fragmentation of the Persian state as many were more willing to fight each other rather than to fight for the Sassanid state.[43]

However, despite being the most important groups to the running of the empire, the upper classes were by far the least numerous of the Sassanid state. Urbanisation may have been prevalent in Sassanid Persia – Mesopotamia may have contained the highest urban population density in the pre-modern period[44] – but as with almost all ancient states, agriculture was the main driving force of Sassanid economics. This placed a huge burden on the farming classes to feed the Persian state, one that was only increased by having to provide the vast majority of its tax income. The artisan and merchant classes were held in even lower esteem, probably encouraged by the clergy due to the prevalence of non-Zoroastrians in those professions. However, this somewhat obscures their importance as the builders, doctors, craftsmen and merchants of the Sassanid state. They built the likes of the Band-e Kaisar dam bridge at Shushtar and the city of Bishapur, while Persian merchants sold their wares to India, China, south eastern Asia and even Malaysia or acted as middlemen in transporting silk, jewellery, spices, scents, hides, slaves and animals from east to west and vice versa. The importance of this trade is demonstrated in peace negotiations with the Romans and in Roman attempts to subvert the Persian trading position by reaching out to the inhabitants of Ethiopia, southern Arabia and the Turks of the Eurasian steppes.[45]

Even the masses, which were by far the most numerous of the population, were subcategorised into those poor that Zoroastrianism taught should be protected and the insolent troublemakers, who could cause trouble for their landlords. Another large group of Sassanid Persia was the slave population, which was involved in all manner of activities including agriculture and religion. Despite being perceived as a 'thing', a Sassanid slave was seen as a human being, something that distinguished him from the other possessions of his master and protected him from cruel treatment. Whether the Sassanid slave population was of the same order of magnitude as that in the Roman Empire, which was perhaps anywhere between 10 and 20 per cent, is unknown.[46]

The Sassanid Army
The Sassanid army largely resembled the traditional Iranian force; commanded by the King of Kings, a member of the royal family or a leading noble and made

up of aristocratic cavalry, light horse-archers from the minor nobility and nomadic allies, and the bulk of the infantry being forced into service. However, there is enough information from Roman sources like Ammianus Marcellinus, Procopius and Mauricius, as well as some useful archaeological evidence to present a more complete picture. 'Soldierly virtues were always part of the Iranian ruler's proof of legitimacy' so a Sassanid king might be expected to demonstrate their right to rule and the favour of the gods in battle.[47] However, should the King of Kings not be available or militarily skilled, the leadership of a Sassanid army could fall to a *spahbed* or a generalissimo from the royal or a leading noble family. There were also provincial military commanders and commanders of border districts, suggesting that there were some permanent units in the Sassanid army as well as a military hierarchy. Khusro I extended this hierarchy by dividing the Sassanid military into four separate forces based on Mesopotamia, the Caucasus, the Persian Gulf and Central Asia, each placed under the command of a *spahbed* – general. This made the Persian army more capable of sustained conflict on multiple fronts whilst reducing the reliance on local dynasts and nobles to provide troops. However, this division led to more revolts rather than fewer as *spahbeds*, removed from the gaze of the king, began to follow their own agendas. This was most apparent in the rise of Bahram Chobin, who not only challenged the Sassanid dynasty but sat on their throne as 'King of Kings' between 590 and 591.

Despite these reforms, the backbone of the Sassanid army remained the heavy cavalry provided by the nobility. Rider and steed were equipped with 'horse's armour, a coat of mail, a breast-plate, greaves, a sword, a lance, a shield, a cudgel... an axe or a club, a quiver and two bows with strings on them and 30 arrows, and finally 2 turned strings.'[48] The lance was the main charging weapon, which when used in conjunction with the horse at full charge 'had impetus enough to pierce through two men at once', while the sword, cudgel, axe or club would be used should the cavalry find itself in a melee.[49] The reflexive composite bow of sinew, wood and horn was the ranged weapon of choice and provided good penetrating power against even the best Roman armour.

Sassanid armour itself was not inconsiderable. While the 'grotto of Khusro II at Taq-i Bustan represents the culmination of the advancement in Sasanian armor',[50] it still bares a resemblance to the description of Ammianus from 363, who records how 'the whole man was clothed in metal scales.'[51] This idea of being fully encased in armour is reflected in the names given to the Sassanids' heavy cavalry by their enemies. The Graeco-Romans knew them either as cataphracts, meaning 'covered over,' or *clibanarii*, which was either a derivation from the Persian *grivpan*, meaning 'warrior' or, perhaps more attractively, the Latin name for a field oven, *clibanus*, in a joking reference to how these troopers must have sweltered in the desert heat. From amongst the cavalry, and inspired by its Achaemenid predecessor that came to grief so spectacularly at

Thermopylae against Leondias' Spartans, 'the Immortals' would be chosen to serve as an elite corps on the battlefield and as a bodyguard.

The Sassanids also made heavy use of cavalry raised from the numerous peoples that inhabited and surrounded their empire – Arabs, Turks, Kushans, Huns, Hephthalites and Armenians. Most of these were light-armed horse archers who would be deployed to harass an enemy formation with a shower of arrows but rarely to engage in melee as their lack of substantial armour made them extremely vulnerable. Another part of the Persian 'cavalry' was the elephant corps. Ammianus declares that their appearance on the battlefield in 363 'inspired almost unbearable fear' and that their 'noise, smell and strange appearance terrified [the] horses even more'.[52] He also recalls the potential danger these mammoth beasts posed to both sides should they run amok, and how the elephant rider was ordered to kill his mount by driving a blade or stake into the beast's neck. The grotto of Taq-i Bustan shows elephants in the army of Khusro II, while the forces of Yazdgerd III would use them against the Muslims.

The complementing of heavy and light cavalry with bows had long been a critical component of Iranian battlefield tactics. The firepower afforded by the reflex composite bow allowed the mounted archers to cause the enemy a constant drip of casualties or coerced them to break their defensive formation in a vain attempt to engage, providing the heavy cavalry with an opening for a decisive charge. Despite the suggestion that the Persians did 'not know how to wheel about suddenly against their attackers, as do the Scythian nations', they must have retained the ability to discharge a volley of arrows backwards while they pretended to flee, known to history as the 'Parthian shot' – something the Roman infantry was wary of.[53]

While mounted forces were the main offensive arm of the Sassanid army, the vast majority of it was made up of infantry. Sassanid archers, protected by long, curved shields of wickerwork and hide and armed with composite bows, were held in high regard as 'by highly skilful finger-work the shafts flew with a loud hiss, dealing deadly wounds.'[54] The peasant levies were a motley crew of unpaid foot-soldiers recruited from the rural population. While they were armed with a spear, shield and sword, they usually did not feature in any Sassanid battle plan, serving mostly as attendants for the cavalry, guarding the baggage train and taking part in sieges. This paucity of heavy infantry meant that the Romans identified the Persians as being susceptible to close-quarter fighting.[55]

Despite this weakness in infantry, the Romans were wary of Sassanid military organisation and planning. Mauricius goes to great lengths in the *Strategikon* to explain their 'calmness and determination, marching step by step in even and dense formation... [as] they draw up for battle in three equal bodies, centre, right, left'.[56] However, the most obvious example of Sassanid improvement on Iranian military organisation was in the art of siege warfare. Learning siege craft techniques from Roman prisoners of war, the Sassanids became increasingly adept at taking even the largest of settlements, perhaps even more so than the Romans themselves. Indeed, Sassanid military science in general seems to have reached a sophisticated level with detailed manuals on organisation, horses, riding, archery, tactics and logistics surviving in fragments.[57]

Even with this organisation, the lack of reliable testimony makes the size of the Sassanid military difficult to gauge. Their long-term stalemate with the Romans suggests that they could raise significant forces. Up to 40,000 Persian infantry and cavalry plus 10,000 reinforcements from Nisibis attacked Belisarius at Dara in 530 while 30,000 men, including a sizeable contingent of foreign auxiliaries, were detached to attack Nicopolis.[58] Perhaps half of Khusro's 60,000-strong Romano-Persian force deployed at Blarathon in 591 came from his Sassanid supporters while Bahram had a force of 40,000, suggesting that the Persian state could field at least 70,000 men at any one time.[59] The Persians may have had an even larger military establishment than these field armies suggest with it likely that, like the Romans, some forces had to be deployed along the frontiers against not just the Romans but the Caucasians, Arabs, Turks and Indians.

Despite Ardashir's aim of moving away from the rule of petty kings that characterised the Arsacid dynasty and the building of a more centralised state, the Sassanid state remained heavily influenced by its Parthian predecessors – the rule of a single clan, the division of the aristocracy into classes, the interdependence of that nobility with the king and the general make-up, layout and running of the empire were all established long before the advent of Sassanid rule. Not only did the Sassanids find these practices too deeply entrenched to remove but their continuity brought added stability. These roots were still present when the Muslim Arabs conquered Iran and they had little option but to follow many of them as well. However, the Sassanids were able to improve upon their Parthian inheritance in the military sphere and by the end of the sixth century the Persian state was in a position to take advantage of any Roman weakness.

Back to the Starting Point: The History of Romano-Sassanid Interactions

It is unsurprising that the relationship between the Romans and the Sassanids would be one punctuated with military conflict. As both empires were essentially militaristic states, they saw each other as a target. Therefore, at any given time, a ruler could overturn years of peaceful relations in favour of a 'glorious' campaign of conquest should he need to distract his population from internal problems or add legitimacy to his rule. Almost immediately after defeating the Parthians, in order to consolidate his grip on power, Ardashir led his forces against Roman Mesopotamia, supposedly boasting that 'he would win back everything that the ancient Persians had once held, as far as the Grecian Sea, claiming that all this was his rightful inheritance from his forefathers'.[60] While there was little in the way of enduring conquests in this first engagement, it told the conquered peoples and the Romans that this new Sassanid state was not to be taken lightly.

However, in spite of this warning and the presence of eleven legions in the eastern provinces, it would appear that the Romans were slow to fully appreciate the threat posed by their new neighbour. Ardashir's second invasion made deep in-roads into Mesopotamia and Syria, and his son Shapur would put the Romans under such pressure that their eastern defences virtually fell to pieces. Throughout the 240s and 250s the Persians captured cities like Dura-Europus and even Antioch, won stunning victories at Barbalissus and Edessa and carried off thousands of Roman prisoners, including the Roman emperor, Valerian, who would end his days as a stool for Shapur to mount his horse.[61] Further Persian conquests were only forestalled by a fighting retreat in the Taurus Mountains but the Roman position was only recovered by the increasingly independent actions of Septimius Odenathus, the ruler of the caravan emporium of Palmyra. Not only did Odenathus force the Persians to retreat from Syria, he recaptured Nisibis and Carrhae before marching on Ctesiphon. However, such success led to the revolt of the Palmyrenes against the Romans and this along with the instability caused by the death of Shapur quelled Romano-Persian hostilities. With both empires facing internal struggles, peace largely prevailed in the last decades of the third century, punctuated only by the sack of Ctesiphon by Carus in 283.

It was only in the last years of the century that hostilities broke out again, with the Persian king Narses attacking Armenia and defeating the Romans outside Carrhae. However, a counter-attack by Emperor Galerius resulted in a crushing Roman victory and their annexation of virtually all of Northern Mesopotamia in 299. This situation remained unchanged until the late 330s when Shapur II launched a series of attacks on Roman territory in response to a military build-up by Constantine aimed at helping Persian Christians. However, despite several Persian victories, the defensive strategy of Constantius II prevented them from making any decisive gains. Shapur II's next attack came in 359, which culminated in the siege of Amida, an event captured in detail by the Roman historian Ammianus Marcellinus, who took part in and survived the siege. This defeat led to a major Roman expedition in 363 under the last pagan emperor, Julian, who won his battles but was unable to capture Ctesiphon and was subsequently killed during his retreat. Only major concessions on behalf of his successor, Jovian, surrendering all Roman territory beyond the Tigris, Armenia, Nisibis and Singara, allowed what was left of Julian's army to return home. A more conclusive treaty was signed in 387 with the Romans and Persians agreeing to partition Armenia, which essentially removed the major flashpoint between the two empires.

For the next century, the Romano-Persian frontier was remarkably quiet as both were distracted by large-scale barbarian raids and migrations along their northern frontiers. Only two brief and largely unsanguinary wars are recorded throughout the entire fifth century. By the time war broke out in 502, both states were markedly different from those of Julian and Shapur II. The western half of the Roman Empire had been lost to the tide of Vandals, Goths and Franks, while the Persians were paying the Hephthalites a huge indemnity to remain the 'masters' of the Iranian plateau. Given these circumstances, it is unsurprising that this Anastasian War resembled past contests, with the initial in-roads of the Persians at Amida and Edessa soon rebuffed by the Roman army, leaving the frontier back where it had started.

Despite Armenia being removed as a flashpoint, the Romans and Persians soon found other territories to squabble over – Iberia and Lazica. War broke out in the mid-520s when the Persian client state of Iberia defected to the Romans and by 530 the Persians had a clear upper hand. However, the reorganisation of Roman forces by the emperor Justinian and Belisarius stemmed the Persian tide with victories at Dara and Satala. A subsequent Persian victory at Callinicum in 531 continued the war for another year but by September, 532, with both sides tiring of conflict, what was optimistically called 'the Eternal Peace' was signed. It lasted eight years. Taking advantage of Roman preoccupation with Italy, Khusro I answered the pleas of Lazica, the eastern part of modern Georgia, and launched several large-scale attacks on the Roman East. The recalled Belisarius was only just able to contain Khusro's forces but, with the aid of the stout defences of several Roman cities and another victory at Dara, the Romans were able to once again recover their lost territory in Mesopotamia. The war seemed to have run its course by 545 but the Laz decided that they preferred their former Roman masters to Persian 'protection', leaving the Lazic War to meander on intermittently for another seventeen years with few results before another optimistic treaty was concluded in 561, this time to last for fifty years.

It lasted eleven. Conflicting trade interests sparked the latest round of fighting, with the Persians extending their influence in southern Arabia thereby threatening Roman trade links with India through the Gulf of Aden, while the Romans were negotiating with the Turks to subvert Persian influence along the Silk Road. In 572, a Roman invasion of Persian Mesopotamia stalled due to the untimely removal of its leader, Marcian, from command by the increasingly unstable Justin II. The main Persian army under Khusro then not only undid the Roman advances but raided Syria and captured Dara; a loss that is supposed to have unhinged Justin to the point that he abdicated. Buoyed by this success, Khusro launched a daring raid into Anatolia in 575. However, aside from Sebasteia, all the Roman cities he targeted withstood his attacks and the Roman army then dealt him a decisive defeat near Melitene. On the back of this failure, Khusro attempted to secure peace but died before it could be established and his successor, Hormizd IV, chose to continue the fighting. The focus of war returned to Mesopotamia and Armenia but neither side could gain the upper hand, trading victories throughout the remainder of the 570s and the entirety of the 580s.

In many ways, the war of 572–591 represented the previous 350 years of Romano-Persian warfare in microcosm. Both sides were capable of achieving large-scale victories, fighting proxy wars on the fringes, sending raiding parties and making in-roads into enemy territory, while the whims of individual kings or emperors or the wrangling of allies could quickly alter the overall situation or overturn years of peaceful coexistence. However, in the grand scheme of things very little actually changed. Client states might alter their allegiance and one side might briefly achieve the upper hand, but aside from some backwards and forwards in northern Mesopotamia, the Romano-Persian frontier at the end of the sixth century bore a striking resemblance to that of the early-third century. On the face of things, the outbreak of the Romano-Persian War of 602–628 was no different – a new Roman emperor had been crowned and his Persian counterpart felt duty-bound to test him with a military challenge in the now traditional battlegrounds of their shared frontiers. However, Khusro II, the Persian king who was to initiate and dominate much of the conflict, claimed much more gallant reasons than simple opportunism. The source of this gallantry was the culmination of the war of 572–591, for it had not ended in the more usual peace talks forced by years of attritional and unproductive warfare.

In 589, the military and strategic stalemate that had prevailed for over a decade was completely overturned by the Persian *spahbed* Bahram Chobin. Dismissed and humiliated by Hormizd IV for failing to defeat the Romans in the Caucasus, Bahram rebelled and quickly gained the support of a large section of the Persian army. In a panic, the Persian aristocracy overthrew Hormizd and replaced him with his son, Khusro II. However, Bahram was not to be placated. The forces loyal to Khusro were defeated and the young king was soon on the run, leaving the *spahbed* to be crowned as Bahram VI. This marked the first interruption in the Sassanid dynasty in its history, but of more importance was where Khusro fled to.

Before the end of 590, he found himself in Roman Syria and was quickly escorted to Constantinople and the court of the new emperor, Mauricius, himself a successful general on the eastern front. Seeing an opportunity to end the stalemate and make substantial gains, Mauricius agreed to send an army to help Khusro regain his throne. This Romano-Persian force defeated Bahram's men near Nisibis in early 591, claiming the Persian capital, Ctesiphon. The allies then contrived a pincer movement to finish off the usurper with Khusro and Narses, the *magister militum per Orientem*, approaching Bahram's position in Atropatene, modern-day Azerbaijan, from Mesopotamia while John Mystacon entered Persian territory from Armenia. The subsequent Battle of Blarathon saw the decisive victory of Khusro and his full restoration as ruler of Persia. This co-operation between Mauricius and Khusro marked a drastic change in the relationship between the Romans and Persians. It did not go as far as establishing a Roman protectorate over the Sassanid state but the vast number of cities and territories in Armenia, Iberia, Lazica and Mesopotamia ceded to Mauricius by Khusro – Amida, Carrhae, Dara, Martyropolis, Tigranocerta, Manzikert, Yerevan and Ani to name but a few – did mark a major shift in the balance of power in the Near East.

Or at least it should have; however, the 'apparently never-ending cycle of armed confrontations' that characterised the previous centuries of Romano-Persian conflict proved impossible to overcome and a decade later this co-operation between Mauricius and Khusro would provide the spark for the conflicts of the seventh century that would change both empires and the world forever.[62]

Chapter 2

The War of the Usurper and the Revolt of Heraclius

'Is it thus, O wretch, that you have governed the state?'
'No doubt you will govern it better'.

Heraclius and Phocas before the latter's execution
(John of Antioch, *Hist. FGH* V:38)

Persian Pretext: Rulers, Raiders and Rebels

The pretext for what was to be the final Romano-Persian war emerged not just from the end of the war of 572–591 but also from the military activities of Mauricius in the decade after his restoration of Khusro II. This closing down of the eastern front for the first time in nearly twenty years allowed Mauricius to turn his attention to a long overlooked problem for the Roman Empire – the Danube provinces. The sixth century had not been kind to these territories, in particular the three decades since the death of Justinian. As the Roman army was focused on the Persians and Italy, the rise of the Avar Khaganate and the southern movement of the Slavic tribes had gone largely unmolested. Indeed, with the capture of Sirmium, modern-day Sremska Mitrovica in Serbia, by the Avar Khagan mere months before Mauricius' accession in 582, the Danube frontier seemed irrevocably shattered. Afflicted by increasing financial paralysis and prolonged fighting in several theatres, the early years of Mauricius' reign did little to suggest any change as the Slavs raided with impunity and the Avars sacked Viminacium and Singidunum, modern Belgrade, in 584. The Romans could harass enemy raiding columns, threaten their homelands and set ambushes but, with an under-strength, underpaid and unmotivated army, Roman commanders could not force any kind of decisive victory as direct confrontation with larger enemy forces had to be avoided. This meant that whilst an individual raid could be disrupted there was little to prevent the Avars and Slavs from trying again.

However, Mauricius was determined to re-establish the Danube frontier, and the peace that came with the restoration of Khusro II saw him redeploy veteran soldiers from the east to the Balkans. This allowed the Romans to shift to a more pre-emptive rather than reactionary strategy, with armies deployed all along the length of the Danube. The barbarians still proved capable of driving deep into Roman territory – the Slavs attacked Macedonia in 593 while the Avars approached the walls of Constantinople in 598 – but by the turn of the seventh century Mauricius could look upon the Danube as a job well done. The frequency of raids dropped as the barbarians became less and less eager to confront the reinforced Thracian and Illyrian armies and as a result Roman forces began to cross the Danube and defeat the Avars and Slavs in their homelands. Such was the extent of these victories that the Avar Khaganate seemed on the verge of collapse as its constituent tribes took to fighting amongst themselves and the Slavs and Germans rose against their oppressors.

However, there was to be a reprieve for these transdanubian barbarians as the Roman position suffered a cataclysmic shift in late 602. The campaigning season had ended with Mauricius' brother Peter inflicting another heavy defeat on the Slavs across the Danube in southern Romania, and then receiving orders to winter his troops in enemy territory. The strategic, propagandist and financial benefits of such a move are plain to see – the continued harassment of the Slavs in their homelands, the kudos of a successful foreign campaign and saving the Empire money by having the army live off the land in enemy territory. However, the emperor had misjudged the situation. Throughout his reign, Mauricius had tried to reduce expenditure, with the army his main target as the most costly instrument of his government. Therefore, despite his military successes, Mauricius' financial reforms and military expectations made him very unpopular with the soldiery. His cost cutting had already caused two mutinies; the first in 588 had forced the abandonment of a plan to cut military pay by 25 per cent and the other in 593 from the Balkan army was only defused by its commander disobeying an order to winter north of the Danube.

However, in 602, familial loyalties saw to it that Peter did not disobey the emperor and he quickly lost control as the army mutinied and marched on Constantinople. Mauricius quickly found that he had little military support to stand up to the mutineers and he fled the capital, hiding in a monastery at Chalcedon. Before the year was out, the Balkan army had taken Constantinople and placed their leader, Phocas, on the imperial throne. This new emperor, eager to placate the army and remove a lingering if powerless threat, had Mauricius dragged from the sanctuary, forced him to watch the execution of his sons and then had him executed. Not only was this the first successful *coup d'état* to occur in Constantinople, it was the catalyst for a series of wars that were to consume the Eastern Mediterranean for the next generation as Khusro II would use the murder of his benefactor as the reason for renewing hostilities between Rome and Persia.

The Portrayal of the New Emperor
Very little is known about the man who emerged as *Augustus* in late-602. Phocas' family would seem to have been of Thracian origin, suggested by the names of his brothers, Comentiolus and Domentziolus, and it is possible that their father was a soldier in the Balkan army. However, aside from that,

virtually nothing else is known about Flavius Phocas before he appears in the narrative of the late-sixth century. He must have been a capable soldier for not only was he serving as a non-commissioned officer along the Lower Danube, Phocas was held in high enough regard by the rank and file to be chosen to serve on a deputation to submit the grievances of the army to Mauricius. However, this ordeal cannot have endeared the emperor and his government to Phocas for not only were the grievances of the army rejected and the ransom of prisoners taken by the Avars refused, leading to their massacre, but Phocas himself was seemingly humiliated and even physically abused by court officials. Unsurprisingly then, Phocas emerged as a leader of the mutiny in 602 and was ultimately chosen by his colleagues to replace Mauricius in Constantinople. It could easily be argued that Phocas was simply a common soldier in the right place at the right time; an illiterate figurehead swept into the highest office in the Empire by martial politics beyond his control. However, while there is little evidence for it, it cannot be ruled out that Phocas manipulated the situation for his own ends and that his popularity within the army had as much to do with his machinations as with his physical abilities.

However, no matter how it occurred, it is understandable that history should record Phocas' accession in an unflattering light. Not only was he a low-born usurper from the soldiery with no legitimate claim to imperial power, his reign inaugurated a period of calamity that almost brought the Roman Empire to its knees. However, the same could be said for his successor, Heraclius. The main differences between the two could simply be social rank and longevity of reign. As will be seen, Heraclius came from an established family of military ability and survived long enough to establish a new dynasty that had its own historians. The likes of Theophylactus Simocatta and George of Pisidia rarely mention their patron's predecessor but when they do they go for the literary jugular, hurling accusations of barbarian heritage and mythological comparisons with Gorgons, Centaurs, Cyclopes and a leviathan. Other later historians agreed that the reign of Phocas was a low point in Roman history.[1]

However, whilst united in their hatred, none of these historians gave any specific explanation as to how he caused the calamities that befell the empire aside from moral degradation. While there was a propagandist agenda and the need to find a scapegoat for the poor state of the Roman Empire from the contemporary sources, there is little excuse for the rather biased approach of many modern scholars. Even some of the most prominent Late-Roman historians are guilty of aiming this kind of vitriol at Phocas, referring to him as a monstrous tyrant who caused the dismemberment of the Roman Empire and the ascendency of the Arab Caliphate.[2] In more recent times, there have been attempts to look beyond such slanderous rhetoric and poor military record to see the politics behind Phocas and his usurpation, but the stigmata long attached to his reign will be difficult to discard even if Phocas was damned for events that he had little or no control over.[3]

It is also worth noting that the vilification of Phocas, past and present, was not universal in the early-seventh century as there were groups that welcomed his accession and policies. Clearly, large sections of the army supported him as he attempted to address their complaints. Some political leaders in Constantinople may have been happy to see the back of Mauricius while the Green circus faction may have been responsible for his acclamation as emperor. One part of the Empire in which Phocas was particularly popular was Italy. The new emperor's support of Pope Gregory I's agrarian reforms to combat corruption and exploitation was well received in letters from the latter.[4] Phocas' donation of the Pantheon in Rome to the Church saw his high regard continue under Gregory's successor, Boniface IV. This donation, his continued support for the Papacy in doctrinal disputes and perhaps also his restoration of the previously deposed Exarch of Ravenna, Smaragdus, in 603 saw the erection of the Column of Phocas in his honour. This was to be the last imperial Roman monument to be raised in the Forum Romanum and, despite originally supporting a now missing gilded statue of Phocas himself, it still stands today.

As well as having the support of large sections of the Church and the army, Phocas also bought the acceptance of large sections of the population as a whole by reducing the tax burden that had become immensely heavy under Tiberius II and Mauricius. However, despite this seemingly broad support, Phocas remained unpopular with those who saw him first and foremost as a creature of the army. In order to consolidate his hold on power, Phocas appointed his brothers Comentiolus and Domentziolus as *magister militum* and *magister officiorum* respectively, but was forced to employ increasingly populist and pandering policies and, when those did not bring security to his regime, he is reported to have killed thousands with increasingly barbaric cruelty. The treatment of Phocas by the sources makes these figures suspect but it is likely that he will have had to dispose of supporters of Mauricius.

Khusro's Reign: The First Decade
However, while the internal reactions to Phocas' usurpation were mixed at best, by far the most important reaction was external. Since being restored to the Persian throne, Khusro II had spent the next decade consolidating his power. Bahram Chobin had survived the battle of Blarathon, fleeing to the Turks of Ferghana, who he had campaigned against for Hormizd IV. However, in a similar way to how Phocas had to deal with Mauricius even after he had been driven from power, Khusro found it necessary to deal with the renegade *spahbed*. The re-enthroned King of Kings achieved this either by an assassin's blade or by exerting pressure to have the Turks deal with his rival. Khusro also faced some kind of revolt from his uncle Wistahm, who in the last years of the sixth century was minting coins in his own name in Media. It does not seem to have been an overly dangerous revolt and nothing is heard from Wistahm or his mint after 600. However, the circumstances are somewhat strange as Wistahm

had been prominent in putting Khusro on the throne in the first place. Perhaps Khusro did not like having a kingmaker in close proximity or perhaps members of the nobility targeted Wistahm as a threat to their influence. Due to this kind of intrigue and their notorious fickleness, Khusro treated the Persian nobility with respect but was careful not to overly rely on them. As a counterweight, Khusro cultivated links with the Christian population in his empire and continued the more meritorious promotion of individuals that had begun in the sixth century. He also continued the modernising reforms of his grandfather, Khusro I, perhaps most famously with the codification of the *Book of a Thousand Judgments*.

With such strong internal organisation and peace with the Romans, Khusro took a more hard-line approach to his other frontiers. As already suggested, the death of Bahram Chobin involved a more aggressive stance towards the Turks. He also looked to consolidate Sassanid influence in Arabia, influence which had long been established from the Persian Gulf through modern Qatar, Bahrain and Oman all the way to Yemen. However, for military and security purposes, the most important of the Arab tribes for the Sassanids were the Lakhmids, who lived south of the Lower Euphrates. For the most part, the Lakhmids were Sassanid allies who kept the other tribes in order, but this relationship was far from smooth and in the last years of the sixth century Khusro decided to impose his authority more directly. Due to some personal or political slight, the Lakhmid leader al-Nu'man III b. al-Mundir was deposed and murdered. This may have led to the Battle of Dhu Qar in around 609 where the Lakhmids tried to dislodge the Sassanids from Hira, the Lakhmid capital. While they were unable to get rid of Khusro's puppet, the Lakhmids did defeat the Sassanid army; a victory that was to be claimed retrospectively by Muslim sources as the first Arab victory over one of the major powers.

Having cowed his opponents within and without his empire, Khusro was now eager for some foreign conquest. Not wanting to risk conjuring up a Turkic storm from the Eurasian steppe and seeing no value in exploring the Arabian desert left him with only one option – the disputing of the settlement he had made with Mauricius. The usurpation of Phocas brought him the opportunity to do so whilst maintaining the veneer of avenging his benefactor.

Khusro *versus* Phocas

The specific spark that saw war break out between the Roman and Persian empires in the early years of the seventh century was the actions of Narses, the *magister militum per Orientem* who led the Roman contingent during Khusro's restoration. Remaining loyal to Mauricius, the general refused to recognise Phocas as emperor and used his forces to take possession of Justinopolis, more commonly known as Edessa, an important centre in Roman Mesopotamia. This rebellion against the usurper was further fuelled by rumours of the survival of Mauricius' eldest son, Theodosius. The story has it that, having bribed his way to freedom, Theodosius fled across Roman territory before, rather conveniently, dying in Lazica. These rumours were almost certainly not true but Narses exploited them to the fullest, producing a false Theodosius to add legitimacy to his rebellion. However, as powerful and symbolic as this figure was, he could not take the place of much-needed soldiers and Narses was soon besieged by forces loyal to Phocas under Germanus. The rebel and the imposter then turned to the one man willing to provide them with sufficient military aide in the name of Mauricius' heir – Khusro.

Unsurprisingly, the Persian king jumped at this chance to exploit Roman in-fighting and launched his armies across the frontiers. His initial assault on Armenia seems to have been beaten back at Elevard but Persian forces were more successful in Mesopotamia, defeating and killing Germanus near Constantia and relieving Narses at Edessa. However, despite being saved by the Persian king and possibly collaborating with him over the promotion of the false Theodosius, the hitherto rebellious general may have perceived Khusro and his armies as the greater threat to the Roman east. Therefore, Narses decided to extend the olive branch of peace to Phocas and travelled to Constantinople. This was an opportunity for reconciliation but instead Phocas took it as a chance to remove the rebel. After being promised safety, Narses was seized and killed, supposedly burned alive. In one ill-considered act of vengeance, Phocas removed perhaps his best hope for settling the eastern situation for not only was Narses his best general, he had an existing relationship with Khusro.

With the deaths of Narses and Germanus and the defeat of the Eastern field army at Constantia, it may be expected that the Roman position in Mesopotamia would have rapidly unravelled. However, with Roman forces garrisoned in numerous heavily fortified cities across Mesopotamia, Khusro was forced into the same inglorious warfare that usually characterised Romano-Persian conflicts with a series of time-consuming sieges. Indeed, the most important of Roman-held fortress, Dara, withstood an eighteen-month siege before succumbing in 604. Given the extended time taken for these sieges, it would be expected that the Romans could have brought together a force capable of challenging Khusro's advances. However, if the sources are to be believed, distracted by metropolitan factional politics, Phocas did very little in response to Khusro's aggression after the deaths of Narses and Germanus. There may be some truth to these accusations as Phocas faced at least two conspiracies in the first three years of his reign, both with involvement of the widow of Mauricius, Constantina, who had been sent to a monastery, and an influential senator called Germanus who had been a prime candidate to succeed Mauricius.

However, these domestic issues do not mean that Phocas was completely inactive in dealing with the Persian invasion. Lacking the time, money and perhaps the support to raise new recruits, he seems to have focused more on transferring armies from other frontiers to boost his eastern armies. The army that Phocas himself had led to Constantinople in 602 does not seem to have returned to the Lower Danube and other Danubian forces seem to have been removed east by 605. These forces may have curbed the rebellious Narses and the movements of Khusro in the short term but in the long term they do not seem to have been able to turn the tide on the eastern frontier.

Perhaps surprised at his early successes and smelling an opportunity for greater conquests, Khusro seems to have enforced a more wide-ranging military mobilisation. The resulting actions and their timeframe are not well recorded in the sources but it would seem that Khusro's generals were aiming to advance Persian control the length of the Euphrates and remove Roman influence from Mesopotamia altogether. The combination of Roman transfers and Sassanid mobilisation meant that attritional warfare still prevailed but the momentum was clearly with the Persians, and they were soon probing Roman Syria. It was not just in Mesopotamia that the Persian advance had been successful. Despite their initial defeat in 603, Persian forces soon gained the upper hand in Armenia throughout 604 and 605, with victories at Akanich, Basean and Taron leading to the recapture of all of Persarmenia ceded to Mauricius in 591.

Not only did the forces transferred from the Balkans not stop the Persian advance, they were not replaced along the Danube by any substantial numbers of newly raised recruits. Phocas may even have gone as far as to spend much needed financial resources on preventing the barbarians from raiding. This was to have drastic consequences for the Balkan provinces as the removal of so many troops relieved the military and fiscal pressure that Mauricius had built up on the Avars and Slavs. However, it was still another decade before barbarian pressure on the Danube frontier became a major problem for the Romans again. This should have allowed Phocas to focus solely on the increasingly alarming situation on the eastern frontier. However, there was to be another distraction for the embattled emperor; one that was to prove his undoing – the revolt of the Heraclii.

The Revolt of the Heraclii

Unlike Phocas himself, the revolt against him that began in 608 came from a far loftier position than a mere soldier. The patriarch of the Heraclii family in the early-seventh century was Heraclius the Elder, a military commander of Armenian origin active during the Romano-Persian War of 572–591.[5] Whilst he will have served elsewhere, the first historical mention of Heraclius the Elder was under the command of Philippicus, *magister militum per Orientem* between 586 and 588. He saw action at the battle of Solachon and the siege of Chlomaron and was instrumental in saving Philippicus' army from a Persian relief force by undertaking a dangerous scouting mission. He probably served briefly as *magister militum per Orientem* when Philippicus was ill or away at Constantinople. He also served at the Battle of Sisarbanon in 589 and may have played a major role in staving off a Roman defeat there too, although this could easily be the invention of a later source looking to glorify Heraclius' military record. In 595, Mauricius decided to make use of Heraclius' Armenian origins by appointing him as *magister militum per Armeniam*, although his tenure there would seem to have been brief.[6]

During the latter years of his reign, Mauricius promoted Heraclius to Exarch of Africa so the emperor must have trusted Heraclius, as he was putting him in command of a rich, affluent province complete with a sizeable military force. With such an appointment, Heraclius brought a large proportion of his family with him to Carthage. His brother, Gregory, and his family, including Gregory's son Nicetas, were present in Africa and would play a large role in the upcoming revolt. Heraclius' wife, Epiphania, seems to have spent a large portion of his exarchate by his side, although there will be one important moment when she was not in Africa that was to cause some consternation.[7] Their children also joined Heraclius in his new province – Maria, Heraclius and Theodore. There is some suggestion of a third son of Heraclius and Epiphania called Gregory but it seems as though this is an historical error.[8]

However, the most important of their offspring was their firstborn son, Heraclius the Younger, for it was he who was to ultimately emerge from the revolt as the Roman Emperor.[9] Born sometime around 575, Heraclius' early life is clouded by poor sources and no record of his early experiences, friends or religious persuasion survives. He will have almost certainly received a classical education and could probably speak both Greek and Armenian, with perhaps some Latin picked up from his time in Africa. By the time his father was serving with Philippicus, Heraclius may have been old enough to receive some military training and maybe even joined him on campaign. He certainly gained some valuable information and contacts from his father's links to Armenia and northern Mesopotamia and it is not completely unlikely that Heraclius gained some of that information personally in his formative years.

Heraclius was probably about twenty-five years old when he went to Africa and the surviving descriptions depict him as 'handsome, tall, braver than others and a fighter',[10] 'robust, with a broad chest, beautiful blue eyes, golden hair, fair complexion and wide thick beard'.[11] It is also suggested that Heraclius fought lions and wild boar in the arenas of Africa,[12] but while there is some suggestion that Phocas had reinstated these practices,[13] and it would have helped ingratiate Heraclius to the Africans, it is more likely that this is a literary device used to connect Heraclius to the deeds of his mythical namesake. Despite his age and the eight years he spent in Africa, it is unknown whether Heraclius had any official position. It is likely that he will have played some part in Heraclius the Elder's exarchate, even if it was merely as part of his council. Also, he did not marry during his time in Africa. However, perhaps to solidify local relations, he or his father did contract a match with Eudocia, also known as Fabia, the daughter of an African landowner, Rogas.

This match may have played a role in encouraging the Heraclii to revolt for at sometime around 608 Eudocia and Heraclius' mother, Epiphania, travelled back east, perhaps to the family estates in Armenia or Cappadocia. Whilst there Phocas ordered both women to Constantinople to force himself upon Eudocia.[14] This is likely just gossip and an attempt to further blacken Phocas' name whilst simultaneously giving the Heraclii a reason for their revolt. However, it would seem that both Eudocia and Epiphania did come under the control of Phocas during the revolt. It is also suggested that Phocas' *comes excubitores* and son-in-law, Priscus, contacted the Heraclii and encouraged them to revolt against the increasingly unpopular emperor, although this could also be a later embellishment and the sources do not agree as to whether this advice came before or after the Heraclii had revolted.[15] Another report suggests that Heraclius had harboured imperial ambitions since staying in an imperial residence in Constantinople sometime before leaving for Africa.

However, despite these more personal reasons for the revolt, the overriding reason was the unpopularity of Phocas. Not only were his armies losing battles to Khusro's forces in Mesopotamia but 'widespread reports of a tyrannical reign of terror with ruthless purges and displays of cruelty all added justification to any explanation for the very serious decision to rise in rebellion'.[16] No doubt after contacting associates across the Roman world, inquiring after the situation of the Empire and how well received they would be, and gathering together the forces and wealth of Africa, the Heraclii launched their rebellion against Phocas in 608 with Heraclius and his father proclaiming themselves consuls.[17] This somewhat arcane political gesture might seem like a strange move as the consulate had long been obsolete and Justinian I had allowed it to lapse after 541; however, as Justinian had also associated the consulate solely with the reigning *Augustus* and because the consulate had embodied civilian and military authority, the Heraclii were claiming imperial power without expressly saying so whilst giving due deference to Rome's glorious past.

The military side of the revolt was to be a two-pronged attack with Heraclius' cousin, Nicetas, travelling overland to secure Egypt, the breadbasket of Constantinople. As the distance from Carthage to Alexandria was some 2,000km (1,200 miles), it might appear peculiar that Nicetas did not take ship for Egypt rather than marching. However, the attack on Egypt may have been planned as something of a diversion to draw Phocan forces away from the centre of the Empire, leaving Phocas vulnerable to a naval strike. For this to work, Heraclius would need the vast majority of the naval and military strength of Africa under his control. Therefore, Nicetas may have marched overland to conserve the naval strength of the rebellion whilst finding alternative sources of manpower on the way. Whether this was the actual plan or merely a reading of the consequences is unknown but by the time Nicetas entered Egypt he had managed to gather 3,000 Romans and unrecorded numbers of local tribesmen from Tripolitana and Cyrenaica.

However, even if the attack on Egypt was meant as a diversion, that did not mean that the Heraclii were complacent regarding its planning. Not only did Nicetas gather forces en route, there had been a lot of ground work laid before his arrival. Taking advantage of the unpopularity of Phocas, bribery and secret agreements had brought the Prefect of Mareotis, Leontius, and a former Prefect of Alexandria, Theodore, over to the Heraclian cause.[18] There also seems to have been some contact with the populace of Alexandria as it quickly rose in support of Nicetas after he defeated the forces loyal to Phocas. Indeed, the ease with which Nicetas and his general Bonakis extended Heraclian control across Egypt suggests a real lack of support for Phocas. However, this rapidity of expansion may have bred some over-confidence, for Nicetas then divided his forces, sending Bonakis east to continue the conquest whilst he himself remained in the vicinity of Alexandria.

Once Bonakis encountered resistance at Semanud and Athrib, his advance slowed greatly and, while he was fully deployed at the latter, Bonakis was caught completely unprepared by the counter-attack of loyalist reinforcements under Phocas' general Bonosus. The subsequent battle saw Athrib relieved, Bonakis captured and killed and the remnant of the Heraclian force sent spinning back to Alexandria. Bonosus then lived up to his reputation for ruthlessness by exacting vicious retribution on those who had supported the Heraclian cause. However, such depredations came back to haunt him, for many Heraclian partisans retreated to Alexandria in the face of his advance. These extra bodies bolstered Nicetas' garrison and enabled him to resist two separate assaults by Phocan forces. Defeated before the walls of Alexandria, Bonosus had to fall back into the Nile Delta, where his depredations had reduced the resources available to him and made the Egyptian populace hostile. This forced the Phocan loyalists to retreat from Egypt altogether while Bonosus himself took ship from Pelusium for Constantinople in early 610 to report to Phocas that Egypt and its vital supplies of wealth and crops had been lost.

This was a great victory for the Heraclii and a major step in the overthrow of Phocas but, for the Roman Empire itself, Nicetas' conquest of Egypt contained many worrying signs. Heraclius' cousin had been able to wrest control of the most important province of the Empire from the central government with what was basically a scratch force made up of provincial forces and barbarian tribesmen. This highlights not only how the eastern frontier had sucked in so many of Phocas' forces but could also hint at the increasingly alarming state to which the Roman military had deteriorated overall; and with Romans fighting Persians, Avars and each other, the situation was to get worse before it got better.

Striking Off the Serpent's Head

With Nicetas campaigning in Egypt and perhaps encouraged by reports like that of Priscus, Heraclius was preparing for a strike at Constantinople that would hopefully bring a swift conclusion to the civil war. The exact timing or route of his naval expedition is unknown, as is the size of the force he brought with him, although Berber tribesmen are again thought to have contributed a sizeable proportion.[19] Whatever the route, Heraclius' forces penetrated the Dardanelle Straits sometime in late September 610. The failure of Phocas and his admirals to engage Heraclius before he reached the Sea of Marmara is curious. However, perhaps this is where Nicetas' invasion of Egypt bore strategic fruit for Heraclius as it may have diverted the naval forces of Phocas to the Eastern Mediterranean and the strategy may even have bolstered Heraclius' strength with the capture of parts of the Egyptian fleet, or at least denied them to Phocas. This allowed Heraclius to capture Abydos and Herakleia virtually unhindered and when the naval battle finally came somewhere off the coast of Sophia, the rebel forces were victorious.

Phocas' only hope now was to contest Heraclius' landing and drive him back into the sea before he could gain a beachhead near the capital. However, he did not know where Heraclius would try to force his landing and having control of the sea meant that the rebel could choose wherever he wished. Phocas decided to gamble on a Heraclian landing near the Land Walls and sent his brother, Domentziolus, with the majority of the forces available to him to guard against such an eventuality. However, this gamble did not pay off as Heraclius landed his vanguard at Hebdomon, a town named for the fact that it was at the seventh milestone from Constantinople, on 3 October 610. There may have been something symbolic about Heraclius' choice of Hebdomon besides its strategic position, for it was one of the main training bases of the Thracian field army and several Roman emperors had been elected through acclamation there, including Valens, Arcadius, Honorius, Theodosius II and perhaps even Phocas himself. The distance between the city walls and Hebdomon left Domentziolus powerless to prevent the Heraclian forces establishing a foothold. This lack of a victory over the enemy at the gates was a severe blow to what was a military junta and allowed Heraclius to watch from afar as Phocas' regime rapidly fell apart.

It would seem that, much like Nicetas had done in Egypt, Heraclius had made contact with many elements within Constantinople before he arrived. The desertion of many prominent senators including Theodore the Illustrious had already raised serious doubts about the future of the regime and when Heraclian forces landed at Hebdomon the extent of the discontent was revealed.[20] Even if his alleged communication with the Heraclii is a fabrication, Priscus aided Heraclius by pleading illness and gathering the *excubitores* and the *bucellarii*, the main constituents of the imperial bodyguard, at his mansion, keeping them out of any potential fighting. The Green circus faction also rose in support of Heraclius under the leadership of a charioteer called Kalliopas who freed Epiphania and Eudocia before Phocas could use them against Heraclius. The neutrality of Priscus, the neutralising of Domentziolus, and the death of Bonosus while trying to flee the popular uprisings in the capital, sealed Phocas' fate. Within two days of Heraclius' arrival at Hebdomon loyalist resistance in the city had collapsed.

The sources give varying accounts of Phocas' ultimate demise. Perhaps in an attempt to excuse the lack of imperial funds and attempt to shift the blame from the civil war initiated by Heraclius to Phocas, one source claims that Phocas was slain by a group of senators and military officials for throwing the remains of the imperial treasury into the sea. Another has Phocas captured at the Palace of Placidia and taken to Heraclius, who was still aboard ship, before being executed and dismembered with the pieces displayed around the city. However, the most famous depiction of Phocas' last moments has him dragged before Heraclius for a brief interrogation in which the deposed emperor shows remarkable spirit in questioning how well Heraclius will do as *Augustus* after having his own rule derided. The anger of Heraclius' response, having Phocas executed, dismembered, paraded through the streets and then burned suggests that the new *Augustus* knew that his condemned predecessor may have been right.[21]

With his forces and supporters victorious, Heraclius quickly organised his own coronation and on 5 October 610, after the traditional *refutatio imperii* – a deferential show of reluctance to accept imperial power when it is first offered – Flavius Heraclius was crowned as *Augustus* in the chapel of St Stephen by Patriarch Sergius. Straight after his coronation, Heraclius made good his promise and married Eudocia, who was then crowned *Augusta*.[22] Suggestions that Heraclius 'was proclaimed emperor by the senate and people'[23] would fit in with the traditional 'invocation of the role of the senate and people in providing some procedural stability and legitimation';[24] although it is entirely possible that this is simply a later addition to add legitimacy to a regime that had taken power as bloodily and illegitimately as its hated predecessor.

However, the execution of Phocas and the coronation of Heraclius was not the end of the transition of power. Supporters of Phocas were treated with brutality as Heraclius encouraged an outpouring of relief and revenge against those who had ruled the Empire with an iron fist since the overthrow of Mauricius. However, in order to differentiate his rule from that of Phocas, Heraclius was willing to exercise leniency where appropriate, including the sparing of Phocas' nephew, Domnitziolus, after the intercession of St Theodore of Sykeon. However, there was one member of the Phocan family who still posed a threat to the newly established Heraclian dynasty. Phocas' brother Comentiolus was in winter quarters with one of the few Roman armies not to be entirely chewed up by the Sassanids. Cleverly, he had chosen Ankyra as his base, a strategically important location between the eastern frontier and Constantinople. In recognition of the danger of this position, Heraclius sent an army under Eutychianus to prevent Comentiolus from threatening the capital. It is also possible that Nicetas had advanced as far north as Syria and together with Eutychianus will have had enough men to defeat Comentiolus. However, Heraclius was keen to avoid any further bloodshed given the trauma that had already rocked the Empire over the last decade and the likelihood of further conflict with the Persians.

Despite the sparing of his nephew, the grizzly ends of his brothers will have made Comentiolus wary of his fate should he surrender to Heraclius. He will also have known that his army was a useful bargaining chip and, despite their initial opposition to the regime of Phocas, it is likely that the Persians would have welcomed Comentiolus as a weapon to be used against Heraclius – a trick that Romans and Persians had used against each other for centuries. Therefore, to expedite a peaceful but rapid conclusion to this stand-off, the new emperor sent Philippicus to treat with Comentiolus. In an attempt to further his bargaining position, Comentiolus arrested Philippicus and threatened to execute him. However, this gambit was a complete failure. Not only was Philippicus a respected general but by arresting and threatening a man on a diplomatic mission, with all the inherent immunities, Comentiolus alienated any support he had within his own army and was soon assassinated by an Armenian commander called Justinus.

The elimination of Comentiolus removed the final obstacle to Heraclius' exercising of full authority over the Roman Empire. However, while his rise to power had been remarkably bloodless, Heraclius' accession did not solve all of the Empire's woes. Becoming emperor exposed Heraclius to an entirely different set of circumstances. He now had to deal with external enemies looking to take advantage of the weakened Roman state all the while settling internal disputes and rebuilding the imperial infrastructure that had suffered so much in the fifty years since the death of Justinian.[25] Indeed, the internecine struggle instigated by Heraclius may have played a pivotal role in extending the Romano-Persian war for the better part of two decades. With no civil war to divert resources and the Persian threat to galvanise his forces, Phocas and his generals could easily have forced a resolution with Khusro. It is quite possible that the Sassanid king chose to continue the war beyond 610 purely due to the opportunity that Heraclius' revolt presented him.

However, Heraclius had no time to second-guess his own actions and he will have quickly realised that winning the Empire had been the easy part; saving it was going to be a completely different story and even the great Heraclius was not going to save the Roman Empire overnight, something that Phocas clearly understood with his defiant final words to the new emperor.

Chapter 3

'It Has Come to the Triarii'

That kingdom belongs to me, and I shall enthrone Mauricius' son, Theodosius, as emperor. Heraclius went and took the rule without our order and now offers us our own treasure as gifts. But I shall not stop until I have him in my hands.

Khusro II
(Sebeos, *History*, ch.24)

The Collapse of the Eastern Frontier

Secure as emperor, Heraclius went about restoring the grandeur of the imperial office, rebuilding infrastructure, demonstrating that the rule of law would be fair and balanced, and establishing religious ceremony as an integral part of the imperial regime. Heraclius also understood the need to establish a lasting dynasty and on 7 July 611 he and his wife Eudocia welcomed their first child Epiphania, who was born in the palace of Hiereia near Chalcedon, and more importantly the following year, on 3 May 612, Heraclius Constantine was born in the palace of Sophianae in Constantinople, securing the succession of the Heraclian dynasty. However, any domestic bliss experienced by Heraclius was shattered later that year as Eudocia died of epilepsy on 13 August 612. The outrage caused by a recorded show of disrespect during her funeral procession and the subsequent burning alive of the offender 'denoted the jittery Constantinopolitan mood at the beginning of Heraclius' reign.'[1] The death of Eudocia and the visceral reaction will have snapped Heraclius and the general populace back into the grim reality of the Roman Empire's situation. From the glowing panegyrics of Heraclius and his depiction as the saviour of the Empire, one would think that the tide of the war with Khusro II turned as soon as he assumed command. The truth is considerably different. The military situation had not improved since the removal of Phocas and was to get far worse during the first decade of Heraclius' reign.

Aside from the usual Persian declarations of rebuilding the empire of the Achaemenids, Khusro's aims at the outset of the war are unknown but, realistically, he will have hoped for some gains in Armenia and Mesopotamia and then a peace treaty to confirm them. However, the war went better than Khusro could have possibly imagined. With the dissension Phocas' usurpation caused amongst the Roman ranks, a combination of sieges, diversionary attacks and probing raids kept the Roman army off balance, allowing Persian forces to

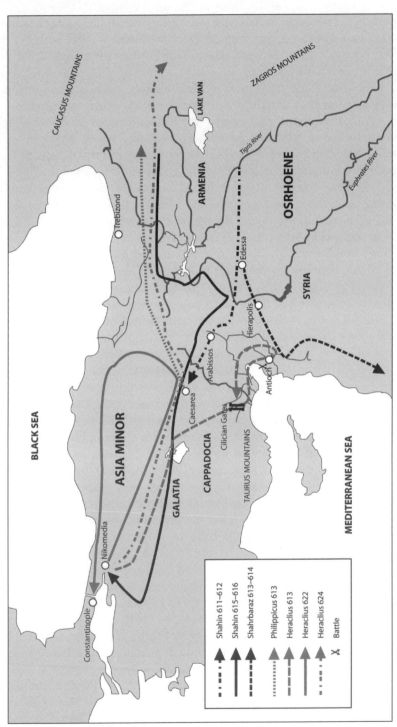

Legend

Shahin 611–612	
Shahin 615–616	
Shahrbaraz 613–614	
Philippicus 613	
Heraclius 613	
Heraclius 622	
Heraclius 624	
✗ Battle	

Romano-Persian Campaigns, 611–624.

make significant advances in Armenia and Mesopotamia, including the capture of Dara. Once Phocan forces were diverted to Egypt to deal with Nicetas' invasion, Khusro's generals were able to take further advantage of the mass mobilisation ordered by Khusro.

The subsequent Persian advances in Mesopotamia would not be categorised as spectacular but they certainly were consistent. As attritional warfare continued, significant damage was caused to the Roman army as the Mesopotamian maelstrom sucked in whatever forces were available, where they were either defeated or holed up behind city walls to suffer the steady drip of casualties until their inevitable surrender. Amida fell in 609 and when Edessa fell the following year the Romans were removed from Mesopotamia entirely. In Armenia, capitalising upon the momentum gained at Akanich, Basean and Taron, Ashtat Yestayar, perhaps with the aide of the imposter Theodosius, captured the main Roman stronghold in Armenia, Theodosiopolis, modern Erzurum in Turkey in 608. This was followed up sometime in 609–610 with a victory by the Persian general Shahin that left the Sassanids in control of almost all of Armenia.[2]

Unsurprisingly, given this military situation, one of the first things that Heraclius attempted when he came to power was to negotiate a cessation of the war with Khusro, reckoning that the removal of Phocas also removed the Sassanid *raison de guerre*. However, even less surprisingly, with his armies sweeping all before them, Khusro saw no reason to accept a negotiated settlement, especially when two months before Heraclius' coronation on 7 August 610 the Persian army had crossed the Euphrates into Roman territory and defeated the imperial forces defending the passes into Cappadocia. With Khusro's churlish rejection of peace and the continued advance of Shahin onto the Anatolian plain threatening the integrity of his Empire, Heraclius decided that his own personal involvement was needed on the front lines.[3] Few eastern emperors had led the army in person since Theodosius I in the last years of the fourth century so it may be an indicator of just how desperate the military situation had become. However, it may also suggest some wariness on the part of the emperor for his commander in the field was the same Priscus whose inactivity had proven so vital to the collapse of Phocas' regime.

By the time Heraclius arrived at the front the fighting had switched to Caesarea in Cappadocia, where Shahin had captured the city only to be surrounded and besieged by Priscus. If Heraclius was wary of Priscus, he was to be proven right for not only did the general fail to meet the emperor in person, again pleading illness, he also proved unable to bring the siege to a successful conclusion. The dispositions of the besieging Roman forces seem to have been more than adequate to force the capitulation of Shahin as Heraclius did not feel the need to take complete command but somehow Priscus allowed Shahin and his army to escape intact during the summer of 612, the Persian commander burning Caesarea as he left. This was a great humiliation for Heraclius and he moved swiftly to deal with Priscus. Under the pretext of being named the godfather to the recently born Heraclius Constantine, Priscus let his guard down and travelled to Constantinople where he was stripped of his command, forcibly tonsured and committed to the Monastery of the Chora, where he died in 613.[4]

That Priscus died so soon after could lend credence to the idea that he was unwell and that perhaps his neutralising was merely Heraclius' final step in establishing control over the army by removing a rival and liability from authority. The men that replaced Priscus in his numerous roles also suggest that Heraclius was looking for men he could trust. Heraclius the Elder's old comrade, Philippicus, was appointed to the military command in Anatolia; Heraclius' brother, Theodore, became *curoplates* and Nicetas was appointed *comes excubitores*. That Heraclius also took Priscus' *bucellarii* and gave them high positions and privileges could be seen as a placatory measure towards men who might have been provoked by the removal of their commander; although it is also possible that Heraclius simply needed skilled soldiers wherever he could find them.

Even if Priscus was made something of a scapegoat for the Caesarea debacle, the fact remained that the escape of Shahin had been deeply embarrassing. So far had the reputation of the Roman army fallen in the previous decade that it was now vital that Heraclius did something to demonstrate that Roman arms were still formidable. This led to the curious expedition of Philippicus into Armenia in mid-613. He penetrated as far as Theodosiopolis before retiring without a fight. The lack of direct confrontation was probably a major corner-stone of Philippicus' march as Heraclius could not afford any casualties. It also seems to have surprised the Persians for, while they quickly reoccupied the areas that Philippicus traversed, their pursuit of the Roman army seems to have been rather costly due to ill preparation.[5] It is also possible that Philippicus' march was a diversion, as Heraclius seemed to have already decided to challenge the Persian presence in Syria and any Persian forces diverted from there in a fruitless attempt to engage Philippicus would have helped that endeavour. However, even though the sources do not provide enough information to rebuild the exact events, what is clear is that the combined force of Heraclius and Nicetas suffered a serious defeat at the hands of Shahin near Antioch in 613. The presence in Syria of another of Khusro's skilled generals, Shahrbaraz, commanding another sizeable force would suggest that Heraclius' attempt to remove the Persians with one decisive encounter was foolhardy.

The folly of this failed attack was further revealed for not only were the Romans defeated in the field, they found their strategic position completely undermined. After the battle, Antioch, the third city of the Empire, fell as Shahin and Shahrbaraz drove to the coast of the Mediterranean. Not only was this a major loss in prestige and a psychological blow, it also saw the Roman Empire riven in two with the cutting of the land routes to the Egyptian, Palestinian and remaining Syrian provinces. Worse still, the army defeated at

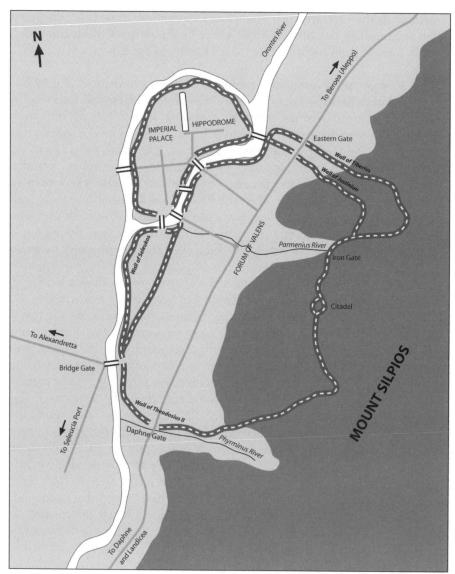

City Plans of Antioch.

Antioch was also split in two with Heraclius and Theodore retreating north into the Taurus Mountains and Nicetas having to retreat south towards Damascus. The former attempted to hold a defensive line in the mountains but were soon driven back to Anatolia with significant casualties, leaving the Persians to capture Tarsus.[6]

Nicetas fared no better. Outmatched by the pursuing forces of Shahrbaraz, by the end of 613 the Romans had to accept the loss of major cities such as

Apamaea, Emesa and Damascus. Shahrbaraz then won some sort of victory near Adhri'at that was significant enough for the Arabs to record it in the Qur'an.[7] Nicetas may also have won a victory near Emesa in 614, but despite the claims of some 20,000 casualties and the erection of an equestrian statue of Nicetas in celebration, there is little evidence to back up the claimed extent of this victory.[8] It also did little to stall the Persian advance, as by mid-614 Caesarea Maritima, Arsuf and Tiberias had surrendered on terms. However, there was one city that refused to surrender.

The Siege of Jerusalem, 614

As the Persians worked their way south, they entered the religious battleground of Palestine. The Zoroastrian Persians had little religious interest in the area but they do seem to have understood how deeply the split between Jews and Christians went and were fully prepared to exploit it to their strategic advantage. To that end, there is some evidence that Khusro had put a plan in place as early as 608 to capitalise on the good relations between the Sassanid state and the Jews as he placed the son of Hushiel, the Jewish Exilarch, Nehemiah, in a position of symbolic leadership within the army of Shahrbaraz. This overt demonstration of the Judaeo-Persian alliance along with a proclamation that the Jews were entitled to retake their historical homeland not only encouraged Jews from within the Sassanid state to join the Persian army but also many Jews from within the Roman Empire. As Shahrbaraz set out from Syria, he and Nehemiah were joined by large numbers of Jews, including a man of immense wealth called Benjamin of Tiberias who had raised a Jewish force from Nazareth and Galilee.

As they approached Jerusalem itself, they were also joined by Jews from further south, including a band of Jewish Arabs. It is suggested that by the time they reached the city walls Shahrbaraz and Nehemiah had gathered together thousands of Jewish militia; perhaps as many as 26,000. It is quite possible that, despite the presence of the Zoroastrian Sassanids, many Jews expected the coming of their Messiah, a role that Nehemiah began to be identified with after Jerusalem was delivered to the Judaeo-Persian army. Jewish riots in support of the 'liberation' of Palestine across the Middle East will also not have helped the Roman defensive effort.

The defenders of Jerusalem seem to have been made up almost completely of Christian priests and civilians. There is a mention of a 'Greek' force being summoned from Jericho by a monk called Abba Modestus but, upon approaching Jerusalem and viewing the size of the Persian army that had invested the city, they retired from the unwinnable battle. This 'Greek' force was likely either a garrison of Palestinian *limitanei* or part of Nicetas' rearguard. They may have approached Jerusalem thinking that they could have saved the great city if they were able to get behind its formidable defences. However, once they

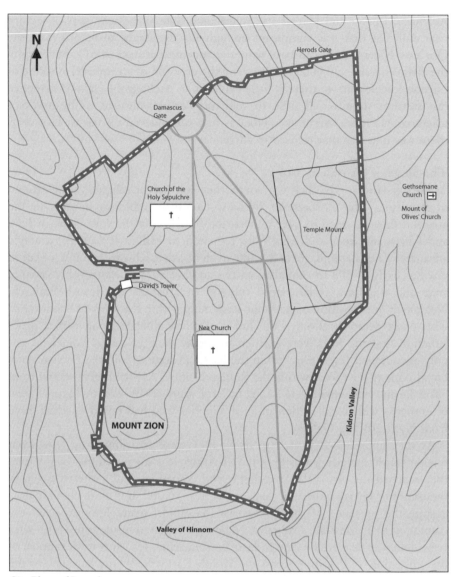

City Plans of Jerusalem.

saw the Persians already had the city surrounded, they retreated, as the Romans could not afford to lose more men in a futile endeavour.

For such an important event in the Romano-Persian War and with its religious importance, the sources for the siege of Jerusalem are scant on specific details. Not even the dates of the siege are firmly agreed upon. One start date for the Persian assault is given as 15 April 614.[9] While most agree that the siege lasted three weeks, the weight of the sources point to the Persian breakthrough coming between 17 and 20 May, rather than 5 May, which the mid-April start time would indicate.[10] With his forces arrayed in blockade, Shahrbaraz offered the defenders a peaceful capitulation, likely pointing out that any chance of relief retreated with Nicetas. However, his offer was rejected and both sides settled in for what was likely to be a fiercely fought siege, especially with Jerusalem's formidable fortifications.[11] While the accounts focus on the use of ballistas and other heavy equipment to bombard the walls, as skilled practitioners of siege warfare it is likely that the Persians will have made use of other techniques such as scaling ladders and siege towers or perhaps even undermining the walls with tunnels. There are even suggestions that the Sassanids had developed some form of chemical warfare for use during such undermining operations.[12] However, perhaps wary of fully committing his men to an assault in case the 'Greek' force or Nicetas was to return, Shahrbaraz decided to focus on destroying the walls through bombardment. Such a process would have been lengthy as Roman masonry techniques in the seventh century could produce very strong walls, as seen particularly at Constantinople. However, after twenty days of heavy bombardment it would seem that the walls of Jerusalem gave way and the Judaeo-Persian army took control of the holy city.

What happened in the aftermath is disputed; however, it is alleged that in response to anti-Semitic riots prior to the siege the Jews now vented their frustrations on the Christian population of Jerusalem and, with the consent of Shahrbaraz, contrived to commit a massacre. The account of Strategius in particular paints a picture of destruction and death on a vast scale with figures of up to 65,000 men, women and children killed along with buildings such as the Church of the Holy Sepulchre being burned. One particularly shocking tale claims that 25,000 captive Christians were butchered near the Mamilla Pool, one of the city's ancient reservoirs, after refusing to convert to Judaism. However, it was the Sassanids who were in full control of this situation and they had a long-established tolerance of other religions; an ideal that Khusro himself ascribed to. Therefore, even with the importance of the Jews to his success and evidence that the Holy Sepulchre was damaged around this time, it would be strange if Shahrbaraz allowed such a massacre to take place. He may have been angered by the resistance of the city and its inhabitants but some controlled looting, the deportation of up to 35,000 people and the removal of the True Cross, Holy Lance and Holy Sponge to Ctesiphon will have been seen as punishment enough and the Jews would not have carried out such a massacre themselves without the Persian commander's agreement.[13]

The archaeological record also seems to go against the suggestion of a brutal sack. While there was some evidence of a mass grave at Mamilla Pool, there is no general layer of detritus and rubble that would suggest mass destruction and, aside from the Holy Sepulchre, there is little to suggest the wide-ranging destruction of Christian churches from the period. There is also little to suggest the great demographic change that would have come with the massacre of vast numbers of Jerusalem's Christian population. A large number of Jews might have replaced the murdered but it seems more likely that a Christian presence was maintained throughout the decade of Judaeo-Persian rule.[14] Therefore, while there are certainly shreds of truth, such as the destruction of the Holy Sepulchre, the removal of the True Cross and deaths at Mamilla, they do not seem to have been in the order of magnitude suggested by the likes of Strategius. Instead, many of the Christian accounts of 'the Persian capture of Jerusalem in 614, of the circumstances which led to it, and of the consequences for the city and its inhabitants ... [were] carefully concocted with a view to shocking Christian readers, with much exaggeration of physical damage, inflation of casualty figures, and graphic illustrations of the sufferings of the deportees.'[15]

This seems more likely with the suggestion of an underlying current of anti-Semitism permeating most of the Roman Christian sources of the mid-seventh century potentially twisting the retelling of events, leaving the idea of a Judaeo-Persian massacre in 614 the work of post-war propaganda. Some of this bias might have been encouraged by the Jews siding with Khusro and the Persians but there was also ill feeling before the war started. It is even possible that anti-Semitic riots were one of the reasons the Jews of Palestine called for Khusro's aid, while the treatment of the Jews of Tyre when a Jewish force moved against the city where the authorities executed 100 of them for every church that was destroyed and launched their heads over the city walls at the besieging force indicates just how deep the ill feeling ran.[16]

The Invasions of Anatolia and Egypt and Further Collapse

Whatever the events at Jerusalem in 614, the loss of the holy city and the True Cross to a Judaeo-Persian regime of Nehemiah ben Hushiel and Benjamin of Tiberias had an extremely detrimental effect on the morale of the Roman Empire. Given the importance of Christian ceremony in the early reign of Heraclius, it caused not only great embarrassment but raised the issue of divine wrath.[17] However, this loss was not the end of the Empire's misfortunes. The defeat of Heraclius outside Antioch had drastic consequences not just for the south where Shahrbaraz chased Nicetas back to Egypt but also for Anatolia. With Heraclius' army retreating before him, Shahin probed what was left of the eastern defences and found their strength, organisation and morale wanting. In 615, the Persian army smashed through Roman Anatolia, advancing as far as Chalcedon, the city on the opposite side of the Bosphorus from Constantinople. That Shahin was able to advance this far into Roman territory without much opposition suggests just how bad the Roman military situation had gotten.

However, it must be pointed out that it is possible that Heraclius chose not to confront the advancing Shahin in an attempt to conserve his already depleted manpower. Even with the enemy literally on his imperial doorstep, Heraclius refused to deviate from this approach. Instead, demonstrating his under-standing of strategy, the emperor sent Philippicus on another raid into Persian territory. This threat to his supply lines caused Shahin to pull back from Chalcedon in the hope of catching and destroying Philippicus' army but the wily, old general was able to avoid such a fate and returned to Roman territory safely once again. However, he could not avoid the ravages of time. Seemingly, not long after his second diversionary action, Philippicus fell ill and died, depriving Heraclius of his most experienced general.

Given the loss of Jerusalem and the Persian advance to the Bosphorus, it is unsurprising that in 615 Heraclius made another attempt to negotiate a cessation of hostilities with Khusro. Learning from Khusro's previous refusal to recognise his authority as emperor, Heraclius sent the Praetorian Prefect, Olympius, the Prefect of the City, Leontius and Anastasius to deliver a letter to Khusro from the Roman Senate and people.[18] It is unlikely that such consti-tutional niceties meant anything to Khusro and his advisers and, with his armies advancing on all fronts, it is unlikely that the Persian king even entertained the idea of a negotiated settlement, perhaps seeing the chance 'to seize the Roman Empire completely'.[19] This embassy to Khusro may have been encouraged by Heraclius' interactions with Shahin when the Persian commander was resident at Chalcedon.[20] However, while Shahin himself was unable to negotiate with Heraclius and the embassy was unsuccessful, the precedent of a meeting between Heraclius and a Persian commander detached from his king would have important consequences a decade later.

However, the manoeuvrings of Philippicus that forced Shahin to retreat from Chalcedon did little to slow the Persian advances to the south. Using their capture of Jerusalem as a springboard, the Sassanids launched an invasion of what was perhaps their most valued target – Egypt. Once again, detailed infor-mation regarding this campaign is not available but Shahrbaraz seems to have begun his campaign with the attack and capture of the Egyptian border town of Pelusium in around 616. From Pelusium, the Persians moved to take control of the Nile Delta by capturing cities like Nikiou and the fortress of Babylon, which forms the oldest part of what is now Cairo. Persian willingness to negotiate settlements and capitulations almost certainly helped their thrust towards Alexandria while the willingness of the Egyptians to capitulate was likely influenced by the Judaeo-Persian treatment of Jerusalem or at least the exaggerated stories emanating from surviving Christians.

What exactly Nicetas did to organise the defence of Egypt is also unknown but he will have had to deal with being considerably outnumbered after his losses in Syria and an increasingly severe lack of resources. This will have meant that the Romans were unlikely to try meeting Shahrbaraz in open battle, relying instead on the defences of Alexandria. Nicetas' lack of resources also led to a dispute with Patriarch John the Almsgiver over the appropriation of church resources, something that foreshadowed Heraclius' later dealings with the

Church. Egypt was also a centre of religious unrest as the home to millions of Monophysite Coptic Christians who had little love for the imperial government and its Nicene/Chalcedonian Creed. Civil unrest in Cyprus further hindered Nicetas' defensive efforts by disrupting communications with Heraclius.

Despite these problems, Nicetas does seem to have been able to organise an effective defence at Alexandria as it is suggested that the Roman garrison resisted for up to a year before supposedly being betrayed in 619 by someone informing the Persian besiegers of a disused canal that bypassed the defences and allowed the Persians to storm the city. The subsequent sack of Alexandria seems to have been bloody but both Nicetas and Patriarch John escaped to Cyprus. However, Heraclius' cousin is not heard from again after this escape. There is not enough information to extrapolate a date or an explanation for Nicetas' death but it is clear that by 620 Heraclius had been deprived of another trusted and capable commander. With Alexandria secured, Shahrbaraz gradually brought the rest of Egypt under his control by 621 from the bases he had already established.

The Persians were not the only forces making vast inroads into Roman territory. With the Danube no longer well protected by Thracian and Illyrian field forces, between 613 and 616 the Avars overran large parts of Pannonia, Dacia and Dardania, forcing thousands to take refuge behind the walls of Thessalonica and Constantinople. This shattering of the Danube frontier proved irrevocable as Slavic tribes roamed further and wider than the Avars, settling throughout the Balkans and peninsular Greece; the latter would not be recovered by the Romans until the ninth century under Nicephorus I while the Danube was not the imperial frontier again until the reign of Basil II in the early-eleventh century. Also during this same period of adversity, Heraclius was forced to accept the loss of Roman Spain as the Visigothic king, Sisebut, retook Malaca and Assido in 615.[21]

In addition, there was further trouble in Italy as pressure from the Lombards and the increasingly confident and independent Papacy almost brought about the end of the Exarchate of Ravenna. The exarch himself, John, was murdered in around 615–616 and while the eunuch that Heraclius sent, Eleutherius, patched up relations with the Papacy, defeated a rebel army under John of Conza and struck something of an accord with the Lombards, he then rebelled in 619. While Eleutherius' bid for imperial power was quickly ended by Roman soldiers at Luciolis, such repeated warfare and unrest in the European provinces ensured that they continued to be a drain on the already strained imperial resources, or at least failed to provide anything of tangible value to Constantinople.

The ordinary Roman citizen would have been forgiven for thinking that he had replaced one ineffective emperor with another, for the first decade of Heraclius' reign had proven to be far worse than that of his predecessor. There may not be any record of the type of savagery that is attributed to Phocas but, militarily, it had been a disaster. In an empire that just half a century before controlled the entire Mediterranean there was now virtually nowhere that was safe from foreign interlopers, not even Constantinople, which was now under threat from both Persians and Avars. So despondent was Heraclius that he supposedly threatened to move the imperial capital to Carthage.[22] He was dissuaded from doing so but the sheer suggestion that the emperor was even considering the abandonment of the city that had been the imperial capital for nearly three centuries highlights how dire the situation had gotten for the Romans.

The State of the Empire
Since his defeat outside Antioch in 613, Heraclius had been directing the conflict from Constantinople, partly because the advances of the Avars and Shahin had brought them to the doorstep of the capital but also because the Constantinopolitan factions had been quarrelling. However, not only was Heraclius able to encourage the withdrawal of the Avars through payments made from precious metals from Constantinople's churches, including Hagia Sophia, and Shahin by raiding Persian territory, he was also able to bring these factions under control.[23] This was no mean feat given their disruptive conduct throughout the previous century and may be an overt sign that Heraclius was succeeding in re-establishing imperial prestige within the Empire. However, it was during this time in Constantinople, between 622 and 624, that Heraclius caused a scandal with his choice of a second wife – Martina, the daughter of his sister, Maria, and therefore his own niece. This familial link caused great controversy and Patriarch Sergius initially refused to conduct the service and investiture.[24] Not only did this incestuous union cause religious scandal, it also laid the foundations of later political trouble. While the offspring of Heraclius and Martina were to demonstrate signs of ill health possibly prompted by the consanguinity of their parents – five of the ten died while they were still young – the survival of others saw Martina determined to see her eldest surviving son, Heraklonas, succeed as *Augustus* rather than Heraclius Constantine.

However, in spite of these burgeoning religious and succession issues on top of the vast territorial, resource and prestige losses his empire had suffered, rather surprisingly Heraclius faced no serious internal challenge to his authority after the disposal of Comentiolus. It is also worth noting that Khusro and his generals do not seem to have heavily promoted the pseudo-Theodosius or any other potential usurper as the legitimate Roman emperor once Heraclius was firmly established. This lack of internal strife would allow the emperor to concentrate on rebuilding his position and bring together the remnants of his army for a counter-attack. Heraclius was also aided by the fact that after the Persian conquest of Egypt there seems to have been a lull in the fighting. Possibly caused by a recurrence of plague[25] and some war weariness on both sides, it allowed Heraclius 'to observe the Persians, to regroup his forces, and to try to obtain an accurate assessment of the current situation of his empire'.[26]

What the emperor would have found would not have brought him much relief. The financial consequences of the territorial losses had been colossal. There are several examples of the Roman government trying to cut back on spending whether it was the reduction in pay for many of its officials and the soldiery, or the restructuring of the currency itself with the reduction in weight of the copper *follis* or the introduction of the silver hexagram at Constantinople with the rather desperate-sounding inscription of '*Deus adiuta Romanis*' – 'God help the Romans'.[27] The territorial losses also had a vast impact on the imperial agricultural economy, particularly with the loss of Egypt. Not only was it the richest province of the Empire, it also provided the lion's share of its grain particularly for the larger cities, including Constantinople, which had to abolish its grain dole in 618.[28] The exact state of Heraclius' army at this time is unknown. There was almost certainly still a hangover from the financial and manpower problems that had plagued the Empire since the reconquests of Justinian while the defeats by the Persians, Avars, Slavs and in civil war will have left it in an increasingly sorry state, a state only exacerbated by the loss of experienced generals such as Nicetas and Philippicus.

However, Heraclius' observations will have brought some positive news to his attention. In spite of its vast extent and its talented leadership, the Persian advance was not without vulnerabilities. Perhaps the primary one was that so swift had their progress been that the Persians found their lines of communication and logistical support stretched. Despite there seemingly being little or no guerrilla resistance from Roman populations, the Persians would have faced a lack of popularity as the conquerors of a large and diverse number of peoples. The Persians also seem to have failed to build any infrastructure in their new territories, depriving them of revenue in terms of crops and taxes. This also meant that, aside from some Mesopotamians and Jews, there was little evidence that the Persians were able to recruit men. The Sassanid ranks also remained susceptible to their almost customary problems with internal cohesion. The army itself continued to lack professionalism, relying too much on mercenaries and lower class levies to maintain good discipline. The Romans also found diplomatic and espionage channels to be open and while the early contacts with Khusro, Shahin and Shahrbaraz were mostly fruitless, they did expose rivalries that could and would be exploited.

However, before Heraclius could capitalise on these weaknesses he had to devise a strategy that would continue the rebuilding of the morale and effectiveness of his beleaguered forces without risking them in an intense and attritional confrontation. With the closing down of the Egyptian theatre, the only remaining area of conflict with the Persians, aside from some limited naval engagements, was in Anatolia. Apart from their brief occupations of Caesarea and Chalcedon, the Sassanids do not seem to have permanently moved onto the

Anatolian plateau, leaving the Taurus Mountains as something of a makeshift and ill-defined frontier between the two empires. This saw the fighting become irregular and more limited to isolated raids than large set-piece battles. There does seem to have been a great deal of discussion between the emperor and his advisers about how to approach this change in the military situation, but Heraclius seems to have been convinced that not only did the army need to take the field and take advantage of this porous frontier, he felt it necessary for the morale of that army that the emperor himself should lead it.

Taking the Offensive – the Campaign of 622

To build an army capable of challenging the Persians, Heraclius shifted what remained of the Balkan field armies to Asia Minor to bolster the Roman forces already there.[29] This abandoning of the Balkans to their fate might seem pusil-lanimous but in reality it was a pragmatic and necessary move. The real threat to the survival of the Empire came from the Persians and, as the main provider of resources, Anatolia had to be prioritised. Furthermore, with the lack of skill in siege craft amongst the Avars and Slavs, the Romans could rely on the defences of the major cities such as Thessalonica and Constantinople to main-tain a Roman presence south of the Danube. With these forces transported across the Bosphorus and the regency of Martina and the *magister militum praesentalis*, Bonus, firmly established, Heraclius himself then crossed to Asia Minor with an icon of the Virgin Mary to great poetic fanfare on 5 April 622 to assume command.[30]

From there, Heraclius marched east through Bithynia into northern Anatolia, gathering together the scattered remnants of the Roman army. Whilst the size of the force that Heraclius brought together is not mentioned, the likelihood is that it was a multi-national entity, composed not just of what remained of the praesental, eastern, Egyptian, Armenian and Balkan armies but also whatever barbarian forces Heraclius had managed to coerce into serving, such as the Berbers he had brought with him from Africa or some Slavs, Huns or Germans keen to escape the Avar yoke.[31] Such diversity will have been of some military benefit to Heraclius in that so many different peoples brought different military skills making his army multi-faceted and adaptable but at the same time it will have brought with it problems with discipline.

The route that Heraclius traversed is much discussed. From northern Anatolia, he may have driven south-east into Cappadocia towards Caesarea; however, given that he will have not wanted to risk a confrontation with Shahrbaraz, who had just arrived from Egypt to take command in Anatolia, it is more likely that he marched east along the coast of the Black Sea. Somewhere along this route, there was a skirmish between the Arab scouts operating in both armies; an engagement that the Roman contingent won with the prisoners they took being persuaded to defect. Indeed, there is a story of one Persian soldier who defected to the Romans, only to soon flee back to the Sassanid ranks where he was executed as a deserter.[32]

Shahrbaraz, perhaps realising that Heraclius intended to raid Armenia, blockaded the roads and mountain passes that led east. However, Heraclius seems to have moved faster than Shahrbaraz predicted and having reached Hellenopontus, west of Euchaita, modern Beyözü in the Turkish province of Çorum, he was able to outflank the Persian lines somewhere near Ophlimos. Again, Shahrbaraz was quick to react and managed to counter-march around the Roman flank, putting himself in a position to launch a night attack that may only have been thwarted by a waning moon.[33] The new day demonstrated to the Persian commander that Heraclius had chosen his battlefield well, having taken up a position on a wide plain to the east. This will have forced the Sassanids to fight on an open field; something which Shahrbaraz will have wanted to avoid.[34] Therefore, despite the success of his counter-march and the subsequent night attack, Shahrbaraz retreated from a confrontation and Heraclius did not try to force what would have been a large-scale battle.

However, several days later, after further posturing and manoeuvring, Heraclius found the opportunity he was looking for. Through careful deployment of scouts, the emperor discovered that Shahrbaraz had laid an ambush and decided to follow the maxim that 'an ambush, if discovered and promptly surrounded, will repay the intended mischief with interest'.[35] To do so, he contrived a feigned flight by a small section of his army to entice the Persian to attack. For this to succeed, Heraclius will have chosen his best troops, as a feigned retreat can quickly become an actual one if the discipline and training of the men involved is not of the highest calibre. That Heraclius would even think of attempting such a risky manoeuvre demonstrates the confidence that he and his generals had in their men. Risky or not, the feigned flight worked perfectly for, as the Persians saw the small group of the Roman army fleeing, they charged after their quarry in a disorderly fashion, allowing the Romans, led by Heraclius' elite guard, the *optimates*, to counter-attack and force the Persians from the battlefield.[36]

Heraclius decided not to give chase as he could not take the risk of a Sassanid counter-attack or of falling into another ambush. However, as his reconstituted army made for its winter quarters in Pontus, Heraclius will have been happy that it had passed its first real test with flying colours. The strategic tête-à-tête with and limited victory over one of Khusro's foremost generals will have been enough to buoy the spirits of the Roman army and the Empire as a whole while, at the same time, it served as a timely reminder to the Persians that Roman arms were still a threat and that the emperor himself was a more formidable foe than his previous military outings at Caesarea and Antioch had suggested. The campaign of 622 would seem to be a rather straightforward affair with two armies marching and counter-marching to find the best strategic position before battle was joined to decide the winner. However, despite the positive outcome of a mostly bloodless, morale-boosting victory, it could be said that because the campaign had ended in battle it was something of a strategic defeat for Heraclius. It is entirely possible that he had hoped to avoid battle altogether and, despite the reverse suffered by Shahrbaraz, the Persians had prevented him from invading Persian or even Armenian territory.

However, Heraclius had learned some very valuable lessons. The fluidity that had so far characterised the conflict in Anatolia was present in the campaign of 622, making areas of control difficult to pin down and encouraging both sides to exploit 'the porosity of the military forces and the flux of loyalties'.[37] It also demonstrated the importance of effective scouting as it permitted the speed of movement and good judgement that was so crucial in such cat-and-mouse manoeuvres. With these lessons and his burgeoning success in reconstituting the army, Heraclius had taken the first steps in developing a strategy with which to turn the tide against the Persians.

The Grand Tour of 624–625

However, all of the ground work laid in 622 was almost completely undone in mid-623.[38] Having left his army in Pontus, Heraclius returned to Constantinople to deal with the Avar Khan, who had asked for a face-to-face meeting with the emperor. Under political, military and financial pressure to close down this front again, Heraclius agreed and travelled to Heracleia in Thrace on 5 June 623. Perhaps this pressure made Heraclius act hastily and without due attention to scouting the rendezvous, as the Avars used the diplomatic overtures to set a trap and Heraclius walked straight into it. The emperor managed to escape capture and return to the safety of his capital but in the confusion the Avars were able to penetrate right up to the main walls of Constantinople once more.[39]

Despite such overt duplicity, due to the war with Persia still rumbling on, Heraclius had little choice but to continue to negotiate with the Avars and was forced to swallow his pride in paying a ransom of Attilan dimensions, including 200,000 solidi and numerous high-profile hostages, as well as his own illegitimate son, John Athalarichos, his nephew Stephen and the illegitimate son of Bonus.[40] Yet Heraclius will have been well aware that this treaty with the Avars was not worth the paper it was drafted on. The moment that he crossed back to Asia, it would be almost expected that the Avars would violate the treaty in search of further financial gain and perhaps even because 'it was in their interest to prevent any overwhelming [Roman] military victory, because Heraclius might then turn victoriously against them.'[41] Clearly, the treaty with the Avar Khan was a calculated financial and political risk but one that Heraclius felt he needed to take due to the military adventure he was planning for 624.[42]

Heraclius had faced civil war, defeat and humiliation, the virtual dismemberment of his Empire and had taken his time in rebuilding, retraining and testing his army as well as his own strategic and tactical leadership, but by 624 he had

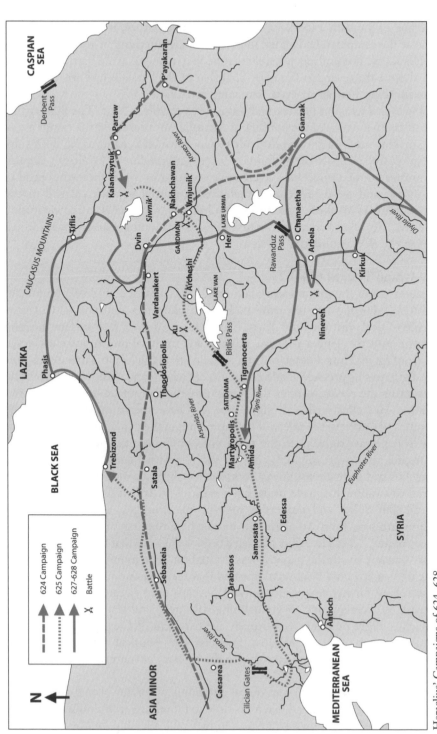

Heraclius' Campaigns of 624–628.

built up an 'appetite to penetrate into the innermost parts of Persia'.[43] Upon leaving Constantinople on 25 March 624, Heraclius would not return to his capital for four years. However, despite this poetic bravado, it is unknown exactly what Heraclius' hopes and aims were for his upcoming campaign. It is doubtful that he planned the extended invasion of Persian territory that was to come nor is it likely that he hoped for the kind of rapid, decisive strike against Khusro that had proven so successful in previous centuries. This was to be another campaign of movement and provisions, not a decisive stab at his opponent's heart. However, the success over Shahrbaraz in 622 will have made Heraclius and his soldiers more confident in seeking out an opportunity to defeat an enemy army again.

His initial march towards Caesarea might suggest that he hoped for a repeat of the 622 campaign by drawing Shahrbaraz out from his mountain strongholds to the Anatolian plains where Heraclius could out-manoeuvre and defeat him again. However, it may be that Shahrbaraz either did not respond to Heraclius' provocation or was caught unaware by the suddenness and audacity of the Roman march so that he could not follow. With the free rein that came with not being followed, Heraclius then made for the Armenian frontier and, once Shahrbaraz realised what the emperor now planned, instead of giving chase the Persian *spahbed* invaded Roman territory. This did nothing to halt Heraclius' advance and, once he reached Armenia, he sent another letter to Khusro hoping to bring about an end to hostilities. Once again the Persian king refused to treat with an enemy he felt was at his mercy and again replied with a haughty letter that not only called the Roman emperor 'our senseless and insignificant servant … [who had] collected an army of brigands' but also ridiculed the Christian God for not saving Jerusalem, Caesarea or Alexandria from the Persians and suggesting that if Christ could not save himself from the Jews, how could He save the Romans from Khusro?[44]

So religiously and patriotically inflammatory was the language of this letter that it would seem more likely that it was the product of the Heraclian propaganda machine to enflame the passions of soldiers, citizens and clergy rather than from the pen of the Persian king. That Heraclius also seems to have circulated dreams that he had had in which someone threw down the Sassanid king and proclaimed 'I have delivered him into your hands' could be another facet to Heraclian propaganda.[45] Had he invoked such religious patriotism and oneiromancy, it would give credence to the suggestion that Heraclius had initiated something akin to a medieval crusade, but, as religious zeal was only part of the conflict, 'crusade' would be an inappropriate term.[46] Furthermore, even if Khusro did write such a provocative letter, and he had already demonstrated that he was capable of such grandstanding, it did not accurately represent the situation unfolding in mid-624. The size of Heraclius' army may not have been in the order of magnitude of 120,000 as related by some ancient sources, or as large as some of the other expeditionary forces that Roman emperors had led against the Persians in the past,[47] yet his force of between 25,000 and 40,000 men posed a threat to hitherto unmolested Persian territory as Heraclius moved unopposed through Armenia.[48]

With Shahrbaraz and Khusro powerless to stop him, Heraclius invaded Persian territory on 20 April 624.[49] He encamped at Bathys Rhyax, north of Sebasteia, the modern city of Sivas, before passing Satala, modern Sadak in the Turkish province of Gümüşhane, Theodosiopolis, and Vardanakert before following the Araxes river to Horosan. Despite the distance covered, the invasion up to this point had been rather uneventful given the limited interaction with Persian forces; although this is a testament to how off guard Heraclius had caught the Sassanids and his subsequent rapidity of movement once the opportunity to take the fight to Persian lands demonstrated itself. However, it ignited, quite literally, when Heraclius arrived at the Armenian city of Dvin. Perhaps with a hint of religious vengeance or maybe just to draw out Khusro or one of his generals, Heraclius put Dvin to the torch, before moving south-east to Nakhchawan, which he may have reached by mid/late-June 624.[50]

Roused by the sack of Dvin, or maybe enough time had passed for him to gather his forces, Khusro himself approached Ganzak with a force of up to 40,000 men.[51] The intentions of the Persian king are unknown but the string of successes that his armies had won over the past two decades will have encouraged him to think that he could settle matters with this brash usurper as decisively as he had done with his predecessor. However, the reaction of Khusro to Heraclius' decisive move against him would suggest that a confrontation was not in the Persian plan. Once the Roman emperor got word of Khusro's approach, he sensed a great opportunity. Decamping from Nakhchawan, Heraclius crossed the Araxes and drove straight for the Persian army at Ganzak. The Arab scouts fought another skirmish and again the Romans were victorious, but before a definitive battle could take place Khusro retreated back to Dastagard. This allowed Heraclius to loot much of the countryside, including Ganzak itself and, in a crushing blow to the prestige of Khusro's regime, the great fire temple of Takht-i-Suleiman.

Deprived of his potentially climactic showdown, Heraclius now had a choice to make. He had the Persian king on the run and, should he be able to catch him, he could have ended the war before the end of the campaigning season of 624. However, there were also many factors against continuing on. It is unlikely that the Roman army had the provisions or logistical support for a prolonged invasion of Mesopotamia and the Iranian plateau in the oppressive heat of late summer, particularly as Khusro will have employed the usual Persian tactic of scorched earth. Also, driving deep into Persia at this point will have left Heraclius open to being caught between Khusro's force and those of Shahrbaraz and Shahin. Despite some division within the Roman leadership, common sense prevailed as Heraclius decided that he could not risk his army in such unfavourable circumstances and began a withdrawal north to the

Caucasian foothills to be near his Iberian allies, amongst whom he could winter and recruit more men.[52] Some were not receptive, such as the inhabitants of Partaw who abandoned their homes for the mountains rather than join the Romans. However, there were numerous Albanian, Laz and Iberian peoples who did take the emperor up on his offer and as 624 came to an end Heraclius will have been happy with his military successes.

Unfortunately, the emperor had unwittingly retired to a position where he could be easily surrounded. Khusro seems to have recognised his opportunity and by the beginning of 625 three separate Persian armies under Shahrbaraz, Shahin and Sarablangas were converging on the Roman position.[53] Through his continuing careful deployment of scouts, together with added intelligence from his Caucasian allies, Heraclius recognised his predicament before it was too late and left his camp at Kalankaytuk' and headed towards the ports on the Black Sea. However, as Shahrbaraz was approaching from the west to cut off this route of retreat and Shahin and Sarablangas were quickly reclaiming the towns Heraclius had passed through in 624 and seizing river crossings and mountain passes, the Romans were forced back to the region of Siwnik', around Lake Sevan. Shahin, with 30,000 men under his command and Sarablangas' force in close support, then attempted to force a military confrontation by driving Heraclius into the passes north of Lake Van and into the path of the advancing Shahrbaraz.[54]

Again, the exact movements of these four forces are unknown but it certainly appears that Heraclius had to act fast to prevent being completely surrounded. A series of manoeuvres and rapid marches kept the Roman force out of immediate danger, but Heraclius had realised that he would have to fight his way out before it was too late and addressed his soldiers with the promise of eternal life through death in the upcoming battle.[55]

Yet Heraclius was not resigned to fighting all three Persian armies at the same time on their terms. To achieve this, he sent false deserters to the Persian camps to spread word that not only were the Romans retreating but also that the other Persian armies were closing in. This may not seem like much but Heraclius was expertly exploiting the personal rivalries between the Persian commanders. Shahrbaraz, Shahin and Sarablangas will have had no wish to see each other claim a share in their victory and this made them impatient for battle. Using this Sassanid impatience, Heraclius lured first Sarablangas and then Shahin onto terrain of his suiting, a grassy plain near Gardman, where he defeated them both in turn, inflicting heavy casualties on both.

However, these victories had not extricated the Romans from the perilous strategic situation. Despite their defeats, Sarablangas and Shahin still had viable armies at their command and Shahrbaraz had yet to be confronted. From Gardman, Heraclius moved back towards the Araxes, perhaps hoping to set up a camp on the plains near Nakhchawan. Yet Shahin had kept pace with him and after the Romans had crossed the Araxes and set up camp near Vrnjunik' they found themselves obliged to give battle once more. Again, little is known about the subsequent confrontation except that Heraclius was once again victorious and that the integrity of Shahin's command was undermined to the point that he had to join his force to that of Shahrbaraz.[56] Despite this third victory in quick succession, the Roman withdrawal from the Caucasus and the continued presence of large Persian forces led to the desertion of Heraclius' Caucasian allies. This was a damaging loss not just in terms of manpower but also of local knowledge which would be so vitally important if the Roman army was to escape.

Despite these losses Heraclius does seem to have put marshy land between his army and the Persians, allowing him to steal away towards Archesh.[57] Moving west from Vrnjunik', Heraclius' continued diligence in posting scouts paid further dividends with news that Shahrbaraz was attempting to set a trap north of Lake Van. In doing so, he had split his forces, positioning 6,000 men near Archesh to ambush the Romans and another 6,000 along the Roman line of march at Ali, with a third section hovering in the Aliovit region to the north. Had it been successfully sprung, this trap would have seen Heraclius caught between three Persian armies and the northern shore of Lake Van. However, armed with foreknowledge, Heraclius not only avoided this ambush but again repayed its intended mischief by applying another of the strategies outlined in the *Strategikon* for use against the Persians – 'unexpected attacks at night against their camp are effective because they pitch their tents indiscriminately and without order inside their fortifications.'[58] The initial night strike seems to have all but annihilated the western prong of the Persian ambush but, instead of just escaping, Heraclius then immediately turned on the detachment at Archesh under Shahrbaraz's direct command. It would seem that the Persian commander got only the briefest of warnings – some accounts have it as a single survivor – before the Roman forces stormed his camp at Archesh. While probably not as bad as sometimes claimed, with Shahrbaraz arriving in the Persian camp to the north naked and barefoot, having lost his harem, all his men, baggage and personal effects,[59] the dual defeat north of Lake Van was certainly embarrassing.

With all three Persian commanders having faced defeat by late-February 625, Heraclius' route to the relative safety of Roman territory was now far clearer. However, the emperor still had a choice to make – he could take the easier but poorly provisioned pass of Taranta or go over the Taurus Mountains into north-eastern Syria, which was better provisioned but more dangerous. He decided on the latter and set off at a hectic pace. Mere days after breaking camp north of Lake Van, not only had Heraclius crossed the Yanarsu river near the proposed site of the ancient Armenian capital of Tigranocerta but he had also forded the Nymphios river, known today as the Batman river. However, possibly in mid-crossing, the Romans were caught by a pursuing Perso-Arab force and suffered casualties; although suggestions that the reverse was bad enough to warrant the celebrating of a great Roman defeat by the Arab poet, al-A'sha, and the Arab naming of the river as the Satidama – 'the blood-thirsty river' – seem to be exaggerated. The Romans do not seem to have slowed their pace any and only a week after leaving Lake Van behind they had reached Martyropolis, modern Silvan. Heraclius then forged on to Amida, from where he sent a progress report to Constantinople, before completing his retreat through Samosata and across the Ceyhan river.[60]

The regrouped Shahrbaraz shadowed Heraclius all the way and may even have forced another showdown near the Ceyhan, where Heraclius supposedly had to personally rally his men in the face of a Persian attack, although this is likely panegyrical posturing.[61] Once across the Ceyhan, the Romans stayed ahead of any pursuing Persian forces, passing through the Cilician Gates to once again return to Caesarea. So rapid had Heraclius' march been that it would appear that he arrived at Caesarea in April 625, meaning that a substantial part of the campaigning season remained. However, this return to more friendly territory gave Heraclius more strategic and tactical options. After a brief stand-off, the Persians seem to have recognised this as well and the armies disengaged, with the Persians returning south and the Romans heading north through Sebasteia and across the Halys river to enter winter quarters on the Pontic coast, perhaps somewhere near Trebizond.

The campaign of 624–625 had been a great success but the panegyrists could not agree for whom – unsurprisingly, the Sassanids magnified their holding off of Heraclius, forcing him to retreat rather than invade Persia proper, harassing him all the way back to Roman territory and highlighting defeats such as Satidama. The Romans played up the heroic distances covered by Heraclius and the repeated defeats of the best Sassanid generals and the running off of the Persian king himself. While there is truth in the Persian argument and the argument that neither side had been able to inflict the crushing defeat on their opponent, the sack of Ganzak and the destruction of the fire temple at Takht-i-Suleiman were major blows to the prestige of Khusro's regime and would play a major role in the Persian king's moves in the following year. The ability of Heraclius to inflict such blows represented a great swing in the progression of the war. After over two decades of Persian success, through a 'text-book execution' of the advice of the *Strategikon*, Heraclius had put his enemy on the back foot, winning victories for his beleaguered army and showing himself to be tactically and strategically astute.[62]

Chapter 4

'The Ram Has Touched the Wall'

I pursue and run after peace. I do not willingly burn Persia, but compelled by you. Let us now throw down our arms and embrace peace. Let us quench the fire before it burns up everything.

Heraclius' ultimatum to Khusro II, 6 January 628
(Theophanes, *Chron.* AM 6118)

The Siege of Constantinople, 626

By 626, the last Romano-Persian war was fast entering its final stages and, to a contemporary, the result seemed to be in little doubt with Khusro looking every bit the clear winner. Persian control over the conquered territories in Syria, Armenia, Palestine and Egypt was under no direct threat; Persian armies marched into what remained of Roman territory with impunity; while the Roman emperor had only one major army that stood between the Roman Empire and total collapse. However, under the surface, there were definite signs of a Roman revival. Not only had Heraclius traversed enemy territory for almost a year and emerged largely unscathed, he had inflicted psychological and physical damage to the Persian military by defeating all of its best generals in battle and destroying the fire temple at Takht-i-Suleiman. His position was still tenuous but there were more grounds for optimism than before the campaign had started.

Keen to avenge the humiliations of 624 and 625 and nip this Roman revival in the bud, in mid-626 Khusro directed his forces to attack the last bastions of the Roman Empire – Heraclius' army in northern Anatolia and the imperial capital of Constantinople. Despite the defeats suffered by Shahrbaraz, Shahin, Sarablangas and Khusro himself, Persian manpower does not seem to have been greatly compromised as Khusro was able to send Shahrbaraz against Constantinople and Shahin against Heraclius. The size of Shahrbaraz's army is not recorded but it cannot have been much different in size from the 50,000 men entrusted to Shahin. However, despite the continued power that Khusro was able to wield in the shape of these large forces, the fact that he was committing them both abroad at the same time suggests that he may have been feeling some pressure, personal or political, to bring an end to the war.

The forces of Shahrbaraz and Shahin were not the only Roman worry in 626, for despite the heavy ransom paid in 623, rather predictably, the Avars had proven untrustworthy. The Avar Khan had either made threatening moves

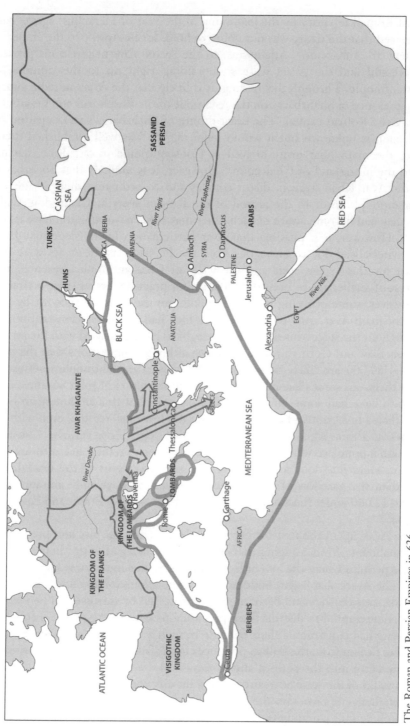

The Roman and Persian Empires in 626.

against Roman territory by the beginning of the year or Heraclius' agents had recognised that the treaty was not going to hold, for by April 626 the emperor had sent an ambassador, Athanasius, to the Avars. Any negotiations proved unsuccessful and the Avars were soon raiding right up to the suburbs of Constantinople. Through this raiding, it is likely that the Avars became aware of the presence of Shahrbaraz on the Asian side of the Bosphorus and his aim to capture the Roman capital. The exact timing of Shahrbaraz's reoccupation of Chalcedon is unknown but it would seem that he was well established there before the main Avar army arrived at Constantinople in late June, having raided the hinterland of Chalcedon.[1] However, it is unlikely that Shahrbaraz and the Avar Khan were in direct contact and co-ordinated their assault on Constantinople prior to the arrival of the Persian army at Chalcedon. Only once they had become aware of each other may some co-ordination have taken place.[2] However, it is possible that Avar participation in the siege may have only materialised due to entreaties from the Persians, as the Avars were not known for their siege craft and the walls of Constantinople presented the greatest of challenges to even the most skilful practitioners of siege warfare.

However, some planning must have gone into the Avar advance for by late June the main Avar army of about 30,000 men had arrived at Constantinople. Throughout the siege, this number is thought to have increased with the arrival of Avar, Slav and German reinforcements; although suggestions that the host reached 80,000 are likely to be too high.[3] With Constantinople now under threat there was some discontent centred upon the figure of John Seismos, who seems to have had some kind of political agenda, but this amounted to little more than a local riot and proved no threat to Heraclius' regime, even with his absence at a time when the capital was under siege. However, the Constantinopolitan populace was anxious for their emperor to return and, although he did not, Heraclius does seem to have sent reinforcements to the capital, but even then the garrison of Constantinople seems to have only amounted to around 12,000 under the command of the *magister militum* Bonus and Patriarch Sergius.[4]

The Avars spent the first fortnight of July investing the city and preventing the inhabitants from foraging, harvesting crops and gathering their animals. This is perhaps where the loss of Egypt and its grain supplies was most harshly felt.[5] The Avars also began building their siege engines, including a defensive palisade, siege towers and battering rams protected by tortoises.[6] The Roman garrison attempted to disrupt these preparations with sorties but it seems that the Avars had constructed their palisade in such a way that it directed Roman refugees fleeing from the Balkan provinces towards the gates of Constantinople and therefore into the path of any sorties.

The sight of the Avar host surrounding the city and defeating sorties with no sign of their emperor saw the inhabitants turn to religious ceremony, with Patriarch Sergius parading the icon of the Virgin along the city walls to bolster

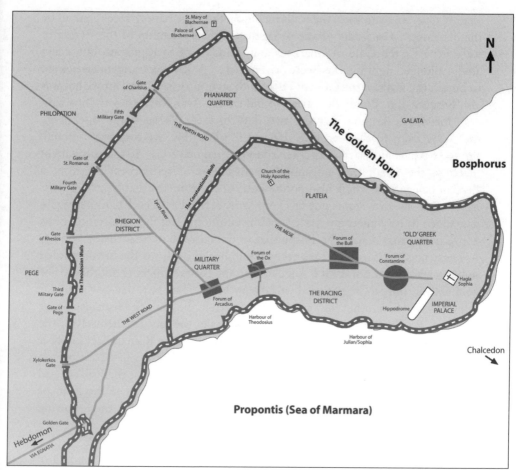

City Plans of Constantinople.

morale and the saying of several prayers for divine aid.[7] While these preparations were ongoing, there was continued diplomatic interaction between the
three interested parties. The Avars were in direct contact with Shahrbaraz by
late July and at around the same time Athanasius arrived back in the capital with
the Avar Khan's demands, which amounted to little more than the total surrender of Constantinople. This was, of course, refused. The Avar Khan himself
arrived at the siege on 29 July and after reviewing his dispositions and the
Roman defences, and perhaps receiving promises from the Persians, he ordered
the assault to commence.[8]

The Avars spent the following day bringing their battering rams into
position and on 31 July the first assault took place, with towers and trebuchets
also brought to bear against the walls. Despite the assault lasting until the
eleventh hour – 5.00pm – numerous assaults by both the Avars and the Slavs

against separate sections of the walls including the Pege region were repulsed by the defenders.[9] On 1 August the Avars turned their attention to the section of walls between the Gate of Charisius and the Gate of St Romanus, but, again after prolonged fighting, they were driven back.[10] A Slavic contingent attempted to breach the walls of the Golden Horn with an improvised naval attack but was also unsuccessful. Bonus then tried to induce the Avar Khan to withdraw with cash incentives, hoping that the two days of futile losses would discourage the Avars from further fighting. However, while this overture was rejected, the Avar Khan did ask for another round of negotiations. At the subsequent meeting, the Khan was galvanised by promises of reinforcements from a Persian delegation, which also pointed out to the Romans that 'your emperor has neither invaded Persia nor has your army arrived'.[11] The Khan then again demanded the complete surrender of Constantinople and the deportation of its entire population across the Bosphorus to the custody of Shahrbaraz.[12]

These negotiations may have taken a number of days, for the next recorded military action was not until 6 August, with the Avars launching another major land assault, only to be repulsed with heavy losses. The next day saw a similar assault as well as another Slav attempt to penetrate the Golden Horn also being defeated. Realising that the Avars could not take the city by themselves, the Persians attempted to wrestle control of the seas from the Roman fleet in order to allow them to take part in the siege. However, a Roman naval victory on 7 August would seem to have put paid to any pretentions that Shahrbaraz had of bringing any substantial aid to the Avar Khan, especially when the Romans foiled a Persian attempt to ferry 4,000 cavalry across to Europe the following day, perhaps suggesting that the naval battle of 7 August was something of a diversion or that this attempted crossing was a desperate last gambit.

The failure of the Persians to cross to Europe proved vital to the ending of the siege. The heavy casualties they had suffered during the major assaults of 6–7 August seem to have weakened the resolve of the Avars and as news filtered through that the Persians had been unable to force a crossing they began to withdraw. There is some suggestion that negotiations preceded the Avar retreat, raising suspicions that perhaps the financial incentive offered by Bonus a week previously was offered again and this time accepted. The argument for a cash incentive for the Avar withdrawal is further bolstered by Bonus' prevention of a sortie by the Roman garrison in retaliation for the destruction of the Churches of SS Cosmas and Damian in the Blachernae region.[13] The Persian reaction to the raising of the siege is unclear, as Shahrbaraz may have wintered at Chalcedon or withdrawn immediately. However, whatever their reaction, it will have been clear to the Persians that Constantinople was a step too far without control of the seas.

Despite the damage and casualties inflicted by the Avars, the Roman victory along the walls and waters of Constantinople was a great triumph for the

Empire. Notwithstanding his absence, Heraclius was praised for his planning for the defence of Constantinople. This transference of the plaudits from the actual commander, Bonus, to the emperor was a usual Roman ploy as it was considered that the victory had taken place under the emperor's auspices. However, on top of the personal praise of Heraclius, ultimate credit was given to the Virgin Mary for her watching over the city in its time of need. Even the Avar Khan is said to have seen her walking along the walls during the siege.[14] The extolling of such political and religious acts for the saving of Constantinople overlooks what were the real reasons for the successful defence of the imperial capital – the lack of experience and general ineffectiveness of the rudimentary siege technology and logistical capabilities amongst the Avars, the immense defensive structures of Constantinople, and the superiority of the Roman navy to whatever seaborne forces the Persians, Avars and Slavs were able to bring against them.[15] Without these factors, the Persian-Avar siege may well have succeeded.

Victory over the Avars was not the only major success achieved by the Romans in 626. Whilst the siege of Constantinople was playing out, Shahin made his move against Heraclius' force in northern Anatolia. His exact orders are unknown but they are likely to have been a combination of preventing Heraclius from relieving Constantinople and defeating this last Roman force. Shahin was successful in stopping Heraclius' army returning to the Bosphorus, although it could be argued that Heraclius had never intended to return to Constantinople for the Roman navy could have taken him to the capital had he so chosen. However, this leaves the question of why Heraclius handed over control of his army to Theodore around this time. It is possible that Heraclius felt that his brother was more capable in command of the army for the massed, static battle with Shahin that seemed inevitable, although it seems more likely that Heraclius did not plan to stay with the army but was forced to remain in its vicinity due to the risk of being captured or killed by Shahin or Shahrbaraz. It is also possible that Heraclius had positioned himself between the Anatolian front and the siege in order to keep in touch with both.

However, if Shahin had been successful in the first part of his orders, he seems to have miscalculated his attempts to implement the second part, with fatal consequences. Spotting an opportunity to destroy the Roman army, Shahin advanced against Theodore and the two armies met somewhere between Koloneia and Satala. It appears that, despite having a hardened core of veterans, this Persian army contained too many new recruits to be truly effective and Theodore was able to defeat it, a defeat that cost the Persian commander his life.[16] That the true extent of this Persian defeat is not recorded in the sources might suggest that it was not an overwhelming rout. However, this does not hide the fact that Theodore had won another victory for the Romans, which precipitated the death of a skilled enemy in Shahin.

The Final Campaign

The successful defence of Constantinople and the defeat of Shahin encouraged Heraclius not to return to the capital but to focus his efforts on taking the fight to the Persians. Realising that he had been somewhat fortunate in resisting the armies of Shahrbaraz, Shahin and Sarablangas during 624–625, Heraclius decided to take another approach, one that might bring him some much-needed manpower. To this end, he moved his army back to the Pontic coast and sent part of his staff and a small but experienced corps of men to Lazica by ship. The emperor himself joined them with 5,000 more men in early 627.[17] From the port of Phasis, near modern Poti in Georgia, the Romans struck out almost due east. This was because, while he had arrived in Caucasian territory, neither the Iberians nor the Laz were the aim of Heraclius' recruiting march; the real target lay to the north-east.

However, there is some confusion about the nature of the real target. They were almost certainly Turkic tribesmen but are frequently identified as Khazars, the tribe who would emerge as the rulers of the territory covering the northwest coast of the Caspian Sea before the seventh century was out. However, in the mid-620s the Khazars were still only one of a number of tribes under the sway of the West Turkic Khaganate so whether Heraclius was dealing with the Khaganate as a whole or a Caspian-based offshoot is not completely clear.[18]

What is clear is that this decision to make contact with the Turks had not been made on a whim. Heraclius aimed to use the pre-existing trading channels cultivated during the sixth century to induce the Turks to raid Persian territory while the forces of Khusro were fully committed to his newly conquered lands, hunting down Heraclius and attacking Constantinople. To this end, he sent an ambassador called Andrew to the Turks in 625, which bore fruit in mid-626 when a Turkic raiding party descended upon Persian territory from the Caucasus. Persian threats prevented an extended Turkic campaign but the captives and booty carried away seem to have whetted the appetite of the Turkic Khan.[19] Early in 627 the Turks returned and captured the newly constructed Sassanid fortress at Chora, modern Derbent in the Russian Republic of Dagestan, gaining control of the only route along the west coast of the Caspian Sea into Persian territory and allowing not only widespread raiding but also direct contact with the Roman army approaching from the west.

The meeting between the Turkic Khan and the Roman emperor took place at Tiflis, the modern-day capital of Georgia, Tblisi, and after much ceremonial exchanging of gifts, swearing of allegiance and proposing of marriage of Heraclius' daughter, Eudocia, to either the Khan himself or his son, the two leaders joined forces.[20] The Persian commander Prince Gayshan retreated in the face of this Romano-Turkic force as his army was ill-prepared, ill-equipped and too small to offer adequate resistance. However, when Heraclius and the Turkic Khan moved against Tiflis itself, the city refused to surrender. Even with the Romans pounding their walls with counter-weight trebuchets, the inhabitants continued to resist and, when word came that Sarablangas was approaching with a relief force of 1,000 cavalry, they were further emboldened to resist and even ridicule the besiegers.[21] So long did this siege continue without any headway being made that Heraclius decided to abandon it and strike directly at the Persians. The Turks were in no way prepared for such a campaign in the heat of Mesopotamia and with that the Turkic Khan withdrew with most of his army. It is reported that he gave 40,000 men to Heraclius but this is a massive exaggeration. While it would seem that the Romano-Turkic alliance was not a great success, given the failure at Tiflis and the returning home of the Khan before any invasion of Persia, even with the exaggeration of the men provided to Heraclius, the Roman army will likely have been bolstered with some high-quality cavalry and the Turkish raids of 626 and 627 had done significant damage to northern Persian lands.

This was not the only diplomatic coup achieved by Heraclius in late 626/ early 627. While Khusro had not removed any of the generals defeated during 624 and 625 from command, his patience had been sorely tested and detractors at his court will have preyed upon the wariness of the Persian king about a repeat of the revolt of Bahram Chobin. It is suggested that Khusro's disillusion-ment with Shahrbaraz came to a head following the siege of Constantinople. The failure of the siege had hardly been Shahrbaraz's fault. Persian naval strength in the Mediterranean was only in its infancy and if they had failed to capture Roman vessels in Syrian or Egyptian ports they would have been starting from scratch, and Shahrbaraz will have known that without parity in naval strength his presence at Chalcedon was essentially a futile gesture. How-ever, rather than as a general not willing to throw his army away in such futility, the Persian court may have seen Shahrbaraz's inactivity during the siege as the actions of a general who could no longer be trusted.

The story put about in succeeding years was that Khusro decided to remove Shahrbaraz and sent a letter to the second in command at Chalcedon, Kardarigan, ordering the death of Shahrbaraz. However, this letter was intercepted by the Romans and, during a meeting with the Persian general, Heraclius used it and the grisly rumours regarding Shahin's demise to con-vince Shahrbaraz that his best interests no longer lay in supporting Khusro. Shahrbaraz then falsified the letter to include the deaths of 400 Persian officers, a move that brought the entire leadership of the Persian force at Chalcedon firmly into Shahrbaraz's camp. The Persian general also seems to have pro-vided Heraclius with guides for his attack on Persia, perhaps in return for Roman backing for Shahrbaraz as a candidate to replace Khusro as the Persian king. A marriage alliance may also have been contracted at this time between Shahrbaraz's daughter, Nike, and Heraclius' son, Theodosius.[22] Of course, a Roman defeat or slow movement from Heraclius could easily end Shahrbaraz's neutrality and, in a strategically astute move, the Persian general moved his army back to Persian-held territory in northern Syria. From there, he could not only feed his men on the agriculturally rich lands but control communications between east and west, north and south and intervene in Persia or move against the Romans as circumstances dictated.

Whether this interaction can be completely believed or not, by the beginning of the campaigning season in 627 Shahrbaraz and his army had been neutralised as an immediate threat, marking a major turning point in the war. With his capital and lines of communication largely secure, Heraclius set out from Tiflis in mid-September 627 with the intent to invade Persia. The Turkic Khan either returned home north of the Caucasus or resumed the siege of Tiflis alongside a token Roman force, with the city eventually falling at an unknown date and suffering a devastating sack due to its insolence towards the Khan and the emperor.[23] Perhaps caught off guard by Heraclius' sudden move against him, as well as being comprehensively outnumbered, Sarablangas was forced to retreat without relieving Tiflis. Khusro himself is said to have expressed his surprise at Heraclius' decision to invade so late in the year. However, the suggestion that a large Persian force had been sent north to oppose the Romans could itself suggest that Khusro had planned a similarly late attack on Heraclius as he entered winter quarters.[24]

The presence of this Persian force under the command of an Armenian, Roch Vehan, may have become known to Heraclius as he pushed south past Dvin and across the Araxes.[25] The Armenian commander will likely have expected Heraclius to retreat west back to Anatolia along the north coast of Lake Van, much as he had done in 625. However, the Roman emperor surprised the Persians by driving almost due south from Dvin down the west coast of Lake Urmia, following a line similar to that of the modern border between Turkey and Iran. Too late did Roch Vehan realise that Heraclius was heading for Mesopotamia, leaving the Persian army playing catch-up with a force intent on striking at the governmental, population and trading centre of the Persian state.

Passing through Her and probably the Rawanduz Pass, Heraclius reached the Chamaetha region on 9 October, where he rested his army for the best part of a week. That Heraclius could afford to rest his army in one place for so long was a testament not only to how unawares he had caught the Persians with his autumn invasion but also how wary Roch Vehan was in his pursuit. Rather than following the Romans down the west coast of Lake Urmia and risk being caught in a trap or being left with a paucity of resources, Roch Vehan went down the east coast, following a similar route to one that Heraclius had taken in 624 from Nakhchawan to Ganzak. Even then, the Armenian commander still seems to have had trouble finding provisions;[26] however, from Ganzak, he moved along the south of the lake and picked up Heraclius' trail in Chamaetha.

It is perhaps during his week-long rest that Heraclius and his advisers began to plan for a confrontation with Roch Vehan. The emperor will no doubt have continued to make good use of scouts and local information, not only keeping tabs on the approaching Persian army but also in searching for a suitable battle-field. Perhaps in an attempt to lure Roch Vehan into battle, the Roman force began to move much more deliberately, taking up to six weeks to reach the Zab River on 1 December, whereas the far longer journey from Tiflis to Chamaetha had taken less than a month. Further proof of Heraclius' decision to force a battle may be seen with his immediate turn north-west after crossing the Zab. This demonstrated further strategic awareness from the emperor as it pre-vented the chasing Persian army from being able to blockade the Romans between the rivers of Mesopotamia. Such a move may also have suggested to Roch Vehan that the Roman army was attempting to flee; something that Heraclius further encouraged by removing most of his rearguard. Having already been outmanoeuvred by Heraclius and wary of the increasingly volatile Khusro, Roch Vehan seems to have allowed himself to be drawn into a pursuit across the plains of Nineveh.[27]

Marginal Victory Breeds Decisive Success – The Battle of Nineveh, 627

Once he realised that Roch Vehan was following him across the Zab, Heraclius sent the *magister militum per Orientem* Vahan to harass the Persian crossing. This attack proved vital, for amongst the prisoners Vahan took was a body-guard of the Persian commander who confirmed that the Armenian *spahbed* sought battle but was waiting for the arrival of 3,000 reinforcements from the west. Heraclius could not risk being surrounded and Roch Vehan did not want the Romans to escape Persian territory unscathed, making a confrontation all but inevitable. Therefore, on 12 December 627 Heraclius suddenly about-faced and squared up to the pursuing Persian forces. The exact location of the subsequent Battle of Nineveh is not clearly identifiable. An early attribution to the same plain that Alexander the Great defeated the Achaemenid Persian King Darius III at Gaugamela in 331 BCE may be based more on romantic notions than archaeological or geographical evidence but it is not beyond the realms of possibility that the battles took place rather close together. The village of Karamlays may be near the actual battlefield and the creek of the same name may have bisected it.

The precise movements of the battle are also unknown, but what seems clear is that, in accordance with the *Strategikon*, Heraclius had chosen a battlefield on open plains rather than the broken ground around the Zab river in order to deploy his soldiers in close order, which, even in the seventh century, was still the real strength of the Roman army. It is also suggested that the plains east of Nineveh were shrouded in fog and mist, preventing Roch Vehan from imme-diately recognising what Heraclius had planned immediately, allowing the Romans to begin their manoeuvres unseen and even hampering the accuracy of Persian archers. In the ensuing, mist-covered chaos, it appears that the Romans not only surprised the Persians with a sudden attack but also surrounded the

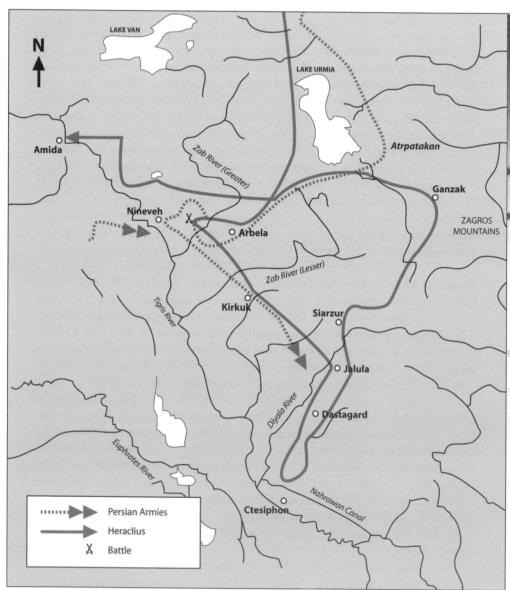

Heraclius' Campaign of 627–628.

Sassanid force, perhaps using the *Strategikon* tactic of attacking the Persian flanks.[28]

Whatever the exact events, Heraclius was victorious. However, it was far from the crushing rout that its place in history would suggest. Both armies remained in close proximity to each other after the battle, with the Roman cavalry being able to water their horses in full view of their Persian counterparts. As the day drew to a close it would seem that the Persians retired in reasonably good order to broken ground 'in the foothill of a steep mountain', possibly identifiable with Jabal 'Ayn al-Safra'.[29] They had certainly taken casualties, but whether they were as high as 6,000 of the 12,000 they supposedly brought to the battlefield is unlikely.[30] Roch Vehan himself did not survive the battle but the report that he died in single combat against Heraclius himself seems equally unlikely.[31] Further doubt about the veracity of the numbers recorded for this campaign and battle are highlighted in the suggestion that Heraclius had 70,000 men at Nineveh, bloated by the spurious numbers of Turkic cavalry. It is far more likely that Heraclius' army numbered between 25,000 and 30,000. Therefore, despite the Roman victory at Nineveh, the death of Roch Vehan and continued Roman numerical superiority, the Persian army continued to exist and, once it linked up with the reinforcements approaching from the west, it was still a viable threat to Heraclius.

Given that it was already well past the end of the campaigning season, the Persians will have expected the Romans to retreat following their victory, an expectation that may have encouraged their move to the northwest after the battle to meet up with reinforcements. However, in once again underestimating Heraclius' strategic boldness, they had presented the emperor with an opportunity to transform the minor success of Nineveh into a decisive political and military victory with one last aggressive move. By moving north-west, there was no longer an adequate Persian force between the Roman army and the agricultural heartland of the Iranian plateau. After resting for a week, Heraclius turned back east, recrossing the Zab somewhere near Altun Köprü on 21 December while a column of Roman cavalry under the *tourmarch*, George, was able to capture four bridges over the Lesser Zab, allowing Heraclius to cross safely on 23 December.[32] The emperor then spent Christmas in Kirkuk at the residence of Yazdin, Khusro's Nestorian Christian financial minister. Such contact with the Christian elite of the Sassanid state is unsurprising as it would provide Heraclius with valuable information and Yazdin himself would become a useful ally.

With the Romans showing no signs of returning west, Khusro's position looked increasingly precarious. His kingdom was tired of the protracted war and becoming greatly distressed by where the illusive Heraclius would strike next and, as his regime had been built on military success, the repeated failures since 624 against both Romans and Turks were greatly undermining its foundations. And now the Romans were on his doorstep. In a vain attempt to restore some of his lost prestige, Khusro ordered the Persian army defeated at Nineveh to place itself between Heraclius and the Iranian heartlands. The battered Persian army managed to ford both Zab rivers and place itself south of the Roman army but this was a largely futile gesture. At most only 10,000 strong, this force was no match for Heraclius' superior numbers and was relegated to shadowing the Romans as they drove deeper into Persian territory;

a mere bystander as the Romans captured and sacked the palace of Dezeridan and the city of Rousa. Even when the Persians found themselves in an advantageous position to contest the Roman crossing of the Diyala River, the mere approach of Heraclius was enough to persuade the Persians to flee, leaving the Romans to capture Jalula and its vast game reserve. They then celebrated the new year of 628 by feasting on the many animals it contained.

Whilst enjoying these benefits of conquest, deserters from Khusro's ranks informed the emperor that the Persian king was awaiting the Roman approach at Basaroth, about 40 miles south of Jalula. Heraclius jumped at this opportunity and, for a brief moment, it seemed that emperor and king were going to square off in a climactic battle to decide the final outcome of the war. However, the intelligence was either faulty or out of date for, by the time Heraclius arrived at Basaroth, Khusro had long since retreated. This is not surprising as the Persian king had been left with very few options with which to stop the Roman emperor. The capture of Jalula had given Heraclius control over the main arterial routes from Iran to Mesopotamia, cutting off any real avenue for reinforcements while Shahrbaraz was still unmoved in Syria. Realising the futility of an armed conflict in the early days of 628, the Persian king was left with no real option but continued retreat in the hope of concentrating his scattered forces elsewhere.

With no Persian force willing or able to stand against him, and with his army not being big enough to launch an extended invasion of the Iranian plateau, Heraclius was left with little option but to continue to undermine Persian morale and political stability by attacking and destroying palaces and religious buildings. This was hardly the glorious military task that he might have hoped for but the pragmatic need to end the war prevailed over any lingering Alexandrian dream. Therefore, Heraclius sent half of his army to claim Dastagard with its vast horde of booty while leading the other half to another palace at Bebdarch, which he destroyed, before himself journeying to Dastagard in time for Epiphany – 6 January 628.[33] He then wrote to Khusro claiming that it was not his wish to burn Persia to the ground and that it was time to end the fighting.[34] However, this appears to have been more a propaganda exercise than a direct plea for peace as it is likely that Heraclius distributed this letter to not only his army but to the populations of Persia as well. Rather cleverly, it portrays the Roman emperor as magnanimous in victory whilst highlighting Khusro's obstinacy in the face of certain defeat and the suffering of his people as the only real obstacle to peace, further undermining Khusro's already damaged reputation.

That this letter was merely for propaganda purposes would seem to be confirmed by Heraclius not waiting for a reply, as he left Dastagard on 7 January and set off in pursuit of Khusro once more. However, his advanced scout, George, found that the Nahrawan Canal that blocked the approaches to Ctesiphon was impassable due to the destruction of its main bridge. A probing force under Mezezios was sent to find another crossing but was unsuccessful and Heraclius abandoned any attempt to force his way to the Persian capital, returning north via Shahrazur, which he left on 24 February.[35] This was a prudent move as many of his imperial predecessors had found the lure of capturing the Persian capital irresistible only to come to grief over the logistical difficulties of campaigning so far into enemy territory. However, a week-long stay at Barza suggests that not being able to attack the Persian capital, to bring the Persian army to battle or invade the Iranian plateau had left Heraclius' campaign somewhat directionless. However, while he was there a delegation from Shahrbaraz, led by the *chilarch* Gourdanaspa Razei, arrived with the news that the Romans hoped for.

End Game
It turns out that Heraclius need not have worried about not striking at Ctesiphon. The damage he had dealt to the regime of Khusro II was already terminal and its final death throes were particularly bloody. When Khusro had fled Dastagard in late 627 not only did he have to face the military and political pressure exerted by Heraclius, he had also been stricken by dysentery, which further affected his ability to rule and added in the volatile element of the succession. Not constrained by primogeniture, Khusro further inflamed an already combustible situation by choosing his son Merdasan over his firstborn son, Siroes. This rebuke, together with the disaffection over how the war was going, led Siroes to rebel against his father in collaboration with a large number of the Sassanid hierarchy. Siroes approached Gourdanaspa and promised that he would raise army pay and make peace with Heraclius if Gourdanaspa would persuade sections of the army to support him against Khusro.

The presence of two of his sons in the coup could suggest that Shahrbaraz and even Heraclius himself played some role in this subterfuge.[36] The coup may also have spread to the Christian clergy for, mere days before his martyrdom at Bethsaloe on 22 January, St Anastasius the Persian predicted 'in a few days you will be freed and the impious and bad king will be killed'.[37] This was taken as a miraculous prophecy from a holy man worthy of canonisation but it could easily have been from insider knowledge. Indeed, the presence of both military and religious leaders in the conspiracy against Khusro, two factions that had for centuries vied for influence over the running of the Sassanid state, suggests just how far Khusro had alienated them both.

Whatever the origins of the coup, it swung into action in late February, securing the arrest of Khusro on 23 February 628 as Siroes assumed the throne with the Sassanid name of Kavad II.[38] After five days of mockery and torture, the former Sassanid king was executed by archers along with his chosen successor, Merdasan. For a man who had presided over the expansion of the Sassanid state to its greatest extent and reduced the mighty Roman Empire to the brink of extinction, the death of Khusro II seems rather ignominious and undeserved, albeit somewhat typical of Persian kings. However, despite his conquests in Syria, Palestine, Egypt, Armenia and Anatolia, he was a far from popular ruler and it was as much his own arrogance and greed that caused his undoing as it was Heraclius' invasions or Shahrbaraz's neutrality.[39] Another reporting of Khusro's final demise has him imprisoned in a room in one of his many palaces, where he starved to death having been given no food but vast amounts of gold, silver and precious stones, highlighting his love of material wealth over the welfare of his people.[40]

Staying true to his word, Kavad II immediately contacted Heraclius, who had arrived at Ganzak by 11 March, seeking to come to terms and speaking of restoring the good relations fostered between Mauricius and Khusro II. From such a position of dominance astride the main communication junctures of the Sassanid state, having outmanoeuvred every Persian force sent against him for the past three years and watching the Sassanid collapse into infighting, Heraclius may have been forgiven for extracting a very heavy toll from Kavad for peace. However, as had been proven over the past two decades, Heraclius recognised the perils of his own strategic position as well as the state of his own empire and its lack of stomach for further fighting. With his 'last Roman army' still deep in enemy territory, large swathes of Roman territory in enemy hands, the Avars liable to attack again at a moment's notice, and Shahrbaraz still in the field with a sizeable force, Heraclius was more than willing to accept a peace treaty based on the *status quo ante bellum* of 602.

Therefore, after receiving Kavad's peace overture on 24 March, Heraclius presented his terms to have all prisoners freed, reparations, evacuating of Roman territory and a broad peace agreement with his Turkic, Caucasian and Arab allies. He also expressed regret that events had gone so far as to make Khusro's passing almost inevitable as divine punishment for bringing such suffering to the Roman and Persian peoples.[41] When word of Kavad's acceptance of these terms came on 3 April, Heraclius could finally begin the long journey home. Leaving Eustathius behind to conduct further negotiations regarding the paying of reparations and the repatriation of religious relics, Heraclius and his army left Ganzak on 8 April and returned to Roman territory through southern Armenia and northern Mesopotamia. The precise movements of the emperor after the cessation of hostilities are not known for certain but it would seem that he wintered near Amida before making a symbolic return to Constantinople. The exact date is unknown but he would seem to be present in the capital on 21 March 629 for the issuing of a new law. Whatever the date, having finally brought the long and destructive war to an end, Heraclius and his people will have celebrated, perhaps for nine days and nine nights.[42]

However, despite the war being over, Heraclius' concerns were not at an end. Even with a peace treaty between the two powers being formalised, large numbers of occupying Persian forces remained in Roman territory and either did not immediately accept Kavad's decree to return home or, like Shahrbaraz, did not recognise Kavad's authority as *šahan šah*. It took letters from both Kavad and Shahrbaraz, delivered by Heraclius' brother Theodore at the head of a large Roman army, to convince many of the Persian garrisons to return home. Even then Theodore had to attack the recalcitrant Persian garrison at Edessa with catapults in order to persuade it to leave. It is also reported that many Jews, wary of potential punishment for their collaboration, encouraged Persian forces not to leave and after the stand-off at Edessa many Jews were attacked, forcing Heraclius to issue a direct imperial order forgiving the Jews of their transgressions and for Christians to desist from taking further retribution.

Once these occupying forces had been repatriated to Persia, the Sassanid military situation will have improved greatly and was perhaps in a healthier state than that of the Romans. Military defeat across the entire eastern Mediterranean and the depredations of foreign occupation had left the Roman army and its recruiting infrastructure in a desperate state; a state that would take years to put right. That Heraclius had been able to cobble together a coherent force capable of invading and defeating the Persians from such limited resources was little short of miraculous. However, politically, it was a different story. Heraclius may have endured civil war and years of campaigning that will have tired him out and had been faced with the deaths of four children – two boys and two girls[43] – but his twenty years of good wartime rule and eventual victory saw to it that the dynasty that he established was on a secure basis.

In Persia, it was completely different. The excising of Khusro II from power had been particularly bloody with the 'executions of prisoners and Zoroastrian apostates [heightening] an atmosphere of crisis and doom in the final moments'.[44] The most high profile killings came from Kavad himself as he is thought to have killed up to eighteen of his own brothers to ensure the security of his accession. Such a massacre of siblings was not that uncommon amongst the Sassanid hierarchy, given the propensity for the Persian king to keep a sizeable harem, and would not cause problems so long as the new king had either an extended reign or a firmly established succession. However, Kavad II had neither. In autumn 628, after a reign of only eight months, he died and was succeeded by his son, Ardashir III, who was a boy of only seven years. The political turbulence caused by this rapid succession of rulers was exacerbated by the traditional feud between the military and the clergy flaring up once again as soon as war had been replaced with negotiations and the object of their mutual disdain had been replaced with a new king who they hoped to influence.

There remained one other large obstacle to a lasting peace – Shahrbaraz. With the war now over, the general whose neutrality had proven so vital remained in a strong if slightly awkward and ill-defined position. He still had a large army under his direct control stationed in Syria but he had come to an accord with the emperor separate from the rest of the Sassanid hierarchy and Heraclius had now forged a peace with a Persian king that Shahrbaraz did not recognise and refused to follow orders to return home from.[45] Therefore, with Persian forces still occupying some of his territory and feeling honour-bound due to past promises, Heraclius was dragged back into the increasing maelstrom of Sassanid politics to break this impasse. He met with Shahrbaraz near Arabissos in July 629 and together they hammered out an arrangement that would see the evacuation of the remaining Persian forces from Roman territory, the return of the True Cross and other relics, and the marriage of Shahrbaraz's daughter, Nike, and Heraclius' son Theodosius.

In essence, this summit at Arabissos marked not just the start of Shahrbaraz's campaign to take the Persian throne from the Sassanids, but also its culmination. The support and legitimacy offered by the emperor, tacit or otherwise, allowed Shahrbaraz to rapidly return home through Roman Mesopotamia and use his military strength to quickly sweep aside the disorganised resistance of the Sassanid court. With the murder of Ardashir on 27 April 630 Shahrbaraz assumed the Persian throne. Therefore, as Heraclius celebrated the transmission of the Holy Sponge and the Holy Lance by Shahrbaraz's son, Niketas,[46] and the lavish ceremony that accompanied the True Cross in its return to Jerusalem on 21 March 630, the proposed marriage alliances between his family and those of the new Persian king and the Turkic Khan would seem to have brought stability to a region that had been ravaged by warfare for the best part of three decades thanks to the building of personal bridges between the three main powers. The future seemed bright.

However, these rulers were in for a rude awakening. They were correct that the end of what was to be the last Romano-Persian war of 602–628 signified a new dawn for the Middle East but this new era was to be unlike anything that Heraclius or Shahrbaraz could have expected and came from an even more unexpected source.

Chapter 5

A New Challenger Approaches

Once the Arabs were a wretched race, whom you could tread under foot with impunity. We were reduced to eating dogs and lizards. But, for our glory, God has raised up a prophet among us . . .

Brown (2006), 193

'Ignorant of Divine Guidance' – Pre-Islamic Arabia[1]

That the wild card that was to trump Romano-Sassanid dominance of the Middle East was nomadic in nature would not have been all that surprising. Migratory raids and invasions from steppe peoples had been common occurrences in both the east and west for centuries and would continue to be so for centuries to come. Two such nomadic tribes, the Avars and Turks, had just played major roles in the war between Heraclius and Khusro. However, while both of these tribal groupings would continue to cause trouble for the Romans and the Sassanids respectively, neither of them were to upset the balance of power as dramatically as another group of quasi-nomadic merchants. While the Romans and Persians had been playing out their destructive and ultimately fruitless conflict, Arabia was undergoing a revolution that in less than a generation was to transform it from a patchwork of tribal regions into a homogeneous state united behind a new religion – Islam.

Knowledge of pre-Islamic Arabia is somewhat scant.[2] However, enough is known to say that, despite the arid, rocky geography that predominates the region, its inhabitants were far from the primitive nomads that might be expected. Nomadic Bedouin were present throughout the Peninsula with their tribal society valuing 'courage, hospitality, loyalty to family and pride of ancestry' but lacking more developed concepts of political or judicial law beyond the authority exercised by the tribal leader.[3] However, agriculture was possible near the desert oases, allowing towns like Medina to flourish. These oases often served as flashpoints between nomadic and sedentary Arabs as both required the water they provided for their herds, flocks and irrigation.

Pastoral nomadism and sedentary agriculture were not the only ways of life in Arabia. With its geographic proximity to the territories of the African continent beyond the reach of the Nile and its tributaries, and the seaborne trade routes with the Indian subcontinent through the Persian Gulf and the Gulf of Aden, Arabia was a conduit for many of the wares of these locations for the eastern markets of the Roman Empire. This led to towns like Mecca growing

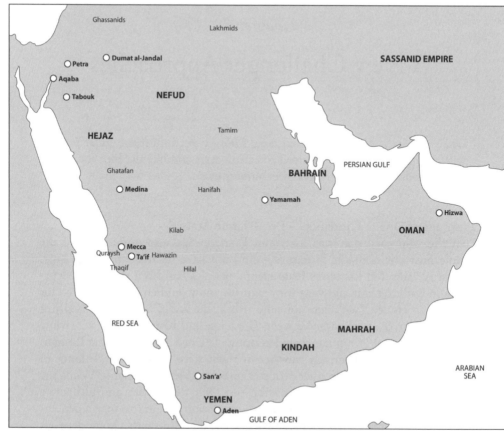

The Arabian Peninsula.

rapidly as major points along these trade routes, which had become increasingly important during the protracted Romano-Persian conflicts of the sixth and seventh centuries.

The expansion of such agricultural and mercantile settlements saw the wealthy traders and large land owners grow in power, essentially constituting a ruling aristocracy. However, despite this socio-political development, their long history of civilisation, the growth of agriculture and trade, and the expansion of town settlement, the peoples of the Arabian Peninsula had not escaped the constraints of tribal life. This was due to the difficult geography promoting the need for the support and security of communal life and the bond of kinships offered by such familial links. This continued importance of tribal culture is expressed in the prevalence of poetic verse in Arabian society. The Arabs did have a written language and Arabic inscriptions are recorded but poetry seems to have been an oral tradition. This singing of the deeds of their great ancestors helped develop a 'common poetic language out of the dialects of Arabic.'[4]

This tribal way of life was most prominent amongst the Bedouin tribes of the Arabian and Syrian deserts and it was through their tendency towards raiding that most contact with Rome and Persia was made. Despite its relative remoteness in the grand scheme of political and military machinations between the imperial powers, Arabia had a long interaction with both.[5] Outside of traders, the Romans made their first contact with Arab tribesmen when Pompeius Magnus annexed Syria and Palestine in 63 BCE. This introduced the Romans to the combination of trading and raiding that characterised the northern Arab tribes. Seeking further glory and perhaps to root out these raids, the emperor Augustus sent a military expedition down the east coast of the Red Sea under Aelius Gallus in 26 BCE, which seems to have made contact with the long-lived Kingdom of Saba in southern Arabia. Aside from proving to the Romans how inhospitable parts of Arabia were, this expedition failed to achieve anything of significance.

Despite not subduing them, the Romans treated the Arabs as they did every other neighbour: they made it worthwhile for the Arabs to trade with and even serve in the Roman army in order to exploit their 'familiarity with the local terrain, climate, and military methods of the empire's potential enemies'.[6] This led to some cultural interchange between the Romans and Arabs, particularly in the frontier regions. Arab tribes such as the Ghassanids adopted Christianity and became extremely useful Roman allies, in terms of military manpower, providing a buffer against the raiding Arab tribes and as a counter-weight to Persian influence. However, perhaps the best example of Romano-Arab interaction is that a certain Marcus Julius Philippus born in Trachonitis in what was the Roman province of Arabia reigned as *Augustus* between 244 and 249.

Aware of this Roman interaction and spurred on by potential military glory and commercial benefits, the Sassanids looked to extend their influence in Arabia as soon as they overthrew the Parthians in the 220s. Ardashir claimed the regions of Ahraz and Meshan along the western coast of the Persian Gulf and may even have reached Bahrain, while Shapur I extended Persian control to Oman. Early in the reign of Shapur II an Arab incursion from Bahrain into the heartland of Persia saw the Sassanid army launch an extensive and brutal revenge campaign into Arabia which culminated in the deportation of many Arabs to Persian territory. In northern Arabia, much like the Romans with the Ghassanids, the Sassanids established a close relationship with the Arab Lakhmid dynasty of Hira to provide a buffer and a counter-weight. These two Arab confederations, Ghassanid and Lakhmid, regularly fought what amounted to proxy wars for their imperial overlords. The Sassanids were also not above promoting an Arab chieftain to high office with one of the Lakhmids, al-Mundhir III b. al-Nu'man, being appointed ruler over a large part of eastern Arabia.

However, despite the presence of Arab cavalry in both the Roman and Persian armies, relations between the Great Powers and their Arab allies were far from smooth and by the seventh century had taken a significant turn for the worse. The collapse of the Roman alliance with the Ghassanids seems to have stemmed from a religious disagreement. Despite being Christian, the Ghassanids adhered to the Monophysite doctrine, contrary to the offical Roman stance. Undermined by such religious entanglements, the final straw came with the arrest of the Ghassanid leader al-Mundhir III b. al-Harith by the future emperor Mauricius whilst he was serving as *magister militum per Orientem*. Despite having served together successfully, the failure of a Roman-Arab army to take Ctesiphon or prevent the sack of Edessa re-opened old religious wounds and, perhaps in an attempt to divert any blame away from himself or through plain jealousy, Mauricius accused al-Mundhir of collusion with the Persians. Despite the baselessness of the accusation, Tiberius II chose to believe his general and ordered the arrest of al-Mundhir. After a period of house arrest in Constantinople, on the accession of Mauricius, al-Mundhir was exiled to Sicily. This provoked a revolt by al-Mundhir's son, Nu'man, who successfully raided Roman territory for two years. The arrest of Nu'man whilst he was travelling to Constantinople in the hope of reconciliation only served to heighten tensions further, while the Roman army sent to put down the revolt destroyed the pre-eminent position the Ghassanids had enjoyed amongst the northern Arab tribes.

The crumbling of the Romano-Ghassanid alliance should have put the Persians in a prime position to extend their influence in Arabia. However, as already seen, Khusro II squandered this potential advantage by inciting a revolt amongst the Lakhmids with his murder of al-Nu'man III. Even with the pro-nouncing of a great Arab victory at Dhu Qar in 609, intermittent Sassanid-Lakhmid fighting continued virtually unabated right up until the Muslims defeated the Lakhmids in 633. Whatever the reason behind these events, it is clear that neither the Ghassanids nor the Lakhmids were in a fit state to play a major role in the unification wars of Muhammad or to slow the advance of the burgeoning caliphate in the 630s.

These existing relationships with the Roman and Persian empires are also reflected in the religion of pre-Islamic Arabia. As a trading crossroads for all points of the compass, Arabian religion was a patchwork of different beliefs. The majority of Arabians followed some form of paganism with innumerable gods and goddesses being worshipped and associated with all manner of inanimate objects or life-giving phenomena. However, even before the advent of Islam and despite the presence of so many deities, Arabian society believed in the existence of one supreme deity, Allah. He was seen as being so far above the day-to-day concerns of man that He was rarely involved in religious ceremonies. There were also Christian and Jewish communities present in Arabia, further strengthening the monotheistic beliefs of other Arabs.

While it would be assumed that these monotheistic beliefs spread south from Roman and Persian lands, in the seventh century the most recent wave of religious influence was actually arriving from the south and west. Through their extensive cultural and trading links with the African continent across the Red Sea, the tribes of the Yemen had imported Coptic Christianity from the Ethiopians. These ideas leeched north along the trade routes, meeting similar ideas advancing south from the Roman Empire and the Ghassanid and Lakhmid tribes; the halfway point between these two advancing ideas was in an area of Arabia that was already a cultural melting pot of pastoral nomadism, sedentary agriculture and merchant trading – Mecca.

Muhammad

By the early-seventh century, religious, social and political conflict was taking its toll on Arabian society, with mercantile and agricultural wealth and power becoming increasingly incompatible with the communal existence of the tribal systems. This was particularly true in and around prospering towns like Mecca and Medina where the *nouveau riche* merchants and landowning farmers could challenge the military dominance of the nomads. The protracted wars between the Romans and Persians exacerbated this situation by disrupting the normal flow of trade and goods, leaving the more settled traders and nomadic tribesmen to fight over what little remained.

It was in this cauldron of divergent ideas, clashing cultures and varying beliefs that a new religion appeared. In around 610, a down-on-his-luck, middle-aged merchant found himself so despairing of his lot in life that he took to 'wandering disconsolately among the grim hill-tops' outside Mecca to find some meaning or purpose.[7] He found it in a series of divinely inspired visions and messages regarding the end of the world and man's judgement by Allah. The merchant, Muhammad b. Abd Allah b. Abd al-Muttalib, began to preach that only through Islam, the submission to the will of Allah, and in showing gratitude through regular prayer, benevolence and restraint could a man gain entry to Heaven. If he did not, the pain and torture of Hell awaited. Muhammad's preaching took the form of reciting his visions in the poetic verse that had long dominated Arabian culture; however, more importantly for the future of his new faith, he also compiled these verses into what became known as the 'Recitations' or the Qur'an. Despite it probably taking some time to assume its definitive form, the Qur'an is not just a text of sacred and spiritual significance. Due to other surviving Arabic sources on the origins of Islam and the life of Muhammad being written at least a century removed, the Qur'an also represents a contemporary historical account of the events in early-seventh century Arabia.

Through his teachings, Muhammad quickly gathered a small but vehemently loyal community from amongst his family and tribal relations, known as 'Umma' or 'people of God', who were willing to follow him as the Prophet of Islam. However, as with virtually any new idea that opposes the established way of things, Muhammad and his 'Umma quickly came into conflict with the tribal elements of Arabian society, particularly Muhammad's own tribe, the Quraysh. Not only did its leaders not accept that Muhammad was a messenger from God, they viewed him as someone determined to undermine their way of life and their position within it, which was one of prominence given their trading connections with Syria and southern Arabia, their alliance with the pastoral tribes around Mecca and their stewardship of the shrine of the Kaaba and its Black Stone, reportedly placed there by Abraham and Ishmael.[8]

Their worry about being undermined was not unjustified for 'seldom has a religion made so explicit the sanctions by which a man should rule his life as did Islam.'[9] A Muslim was to spend his entire life preparing for his Judgement by God. This conflicted with tribal society in that it taught an individual to fear God's Judgement rather than fear bringing shame upon his tribe. A man was to be an individual with his reputation not sullied or enhanced by which tribe he belonged to or the deeds and accomplishments of his forefathers. It is even suggested that Islam's distaste for alcohol was less to do with avoiding drunkenness than it was about removing a motivation for an Arab to emulate his ancestors, something which it was thought to be alcohol-inspired.[10] This god-fearing basis and the presence of a sacred text put Islam squarely in the same Abrahamic, monotheistic bracket as Judaism and Christianity. This is unsurprising given the presence of Jews and Christians in Arabia, the pre-existing presence of Abraham in Arabian culture, the shared Semitic ethnicity and geographic proximity of the Arab tribes and the peoples surrounding the Fertile Crescent and the Syrian and Arabian deserts. Indeed, by spreading Islam across the Arabian Peninsula, Muhammad and his successors distanced Arabian society from its tribal and nomadic roots and brought it more into line with the civilisations of Rome and Persia.

Muhammad's uncle, Abu Talib, managed to shield him from reprisals despite the other Qurayshi leaders claiming that they would oppose Muhammad 'until one side perishes'.[11] However, this opposition intensified as Muhammad began to attack pagan gods and ceremonies and by 622, with the deaths of Abu Talib and the Prophet's wife, Khadija, Muhammad's position at Mecca had become untenable and, along with his 'Umma, Muhammad moved to the neighbouring city of Yathrib, later renamed Medina. So important was this *Hijra* that the date on which it began, 9 September 622, was soon established as the first year of the Muslim calendar. The importance of the *Hijra* stems from the fact that it essentially marks the advent of Muslim political power for Muhammad quickly found the tribes in Medina more accepting of his teachings. Through their newly revealed philosophy and willingness to arbitrate disputes, the Muslims cut through the conflicting strands of mercantile wealth, agricultural land-owning and communal tribalism to bring several Medinan tribes into an alliance that was able to project power on a regional level.

This growth in power of Medina brought it directly into conflict with Mecca as Muhammad and his allies looked to take advantage of their position close to the trade routes that led north to Syria. To that end, and taking Bedouin tactics as their model, the Muslims began raiding Meccan caravans, justifying these raids as a way of recompense for the belongings they had had to leave behind in Mecca. Of course, the Meccans viewed these raiders as nothing short of bandits and thieves. This increasing emnity led to a growing number of skirmishes between the forces of Medina and Mecca throughout late 623 and early 624 but the first clash worthy of being classed as a battle came at Badr on 13 March 624/ 17 Ramadan, 2 AH. Intelligence reports and his need to gain a victory of note led Muhammad to commit over 300 men to a raid on one of the richest and, therefore, most well-protected Meccan caravans. Following a Muslim victory in a 3-on-3 duel, a barrage of arrows and a disciplined charge ordered by Muhammad broke the Meccan line, signalling the first real victory for Islam and providing proof to its allies and perhaps even to the Muslims themselves that a new power was rising.

However, defeat at Badr did not break the Meccans and, after just over a year of continued raiding, the two forces met again at the foot of Mount Uhud on 19 March 625/3 Shawwal, 3 AH. Despite good strategic planning in the choice of the battlefield to forestall the superior Meccan cavalry and again forcing back the Meccan infantry, the Muslims squandered their hard-won advantage by over-committing at an inopportune moment in an attempt to capture the Meccan camp. This allowed the Meccan cavalry commander, Khalid b. al-Walid, of whom greater things were to come in the next decade, to lead his cavalry around the line of battle and attack the Muslim rear and flank. Muhammad was able to affect a retreat up the slopes of Mount Uhud but Khalid had turned the course of the battle dramatically from an almost certain Muslim victory to a stalemate.

Despite the lack of a clear-cut winner at Uhud, using the increasing power of Muhammad as a rallying point, the Quraysh were able to build a coalition of Jews, Bedouin nomads and their own men to challenge Muslim control of Medina. By late March 627, perhaps 10,000 Quraysh and their allies were marching on Muhammad's position. Knowing that they could not overcome such a force in open battle, the Muslims resorted to blocking the northern approaches to Medina with a network of trenches to be defended by the 3,000 inhabitants of Medina eligible for military service. The subsequent confrontation, known as the Battle of the Trench, was in reality a siege of Medina that lasted from 31 March 627 until late April. Unprepared for such fighting, the Quraysh and their allies proved ineffective against the Muslim defences, particularly as the trench and the prudent harvesting of crops before the siege by the Muslims left the Meccan cavalry something of a bystander.

With military action at an impasse, the siege now became a battle of wits as Muhammad and his spies began to spread dissension amongst the Quraysh

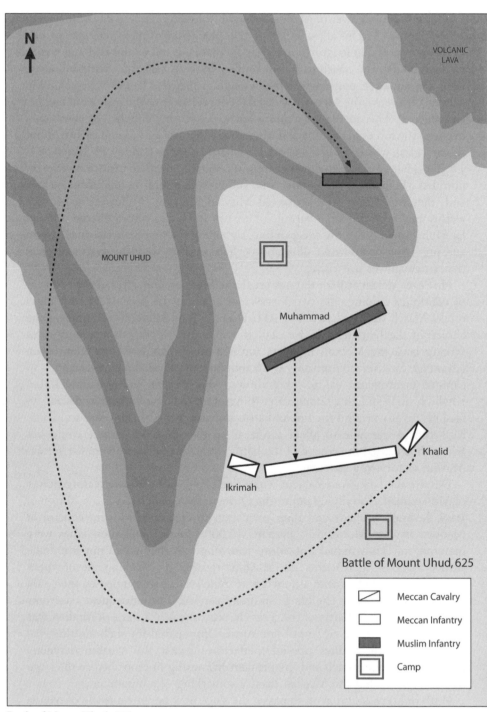

Battle of Mount Uhud, 625.

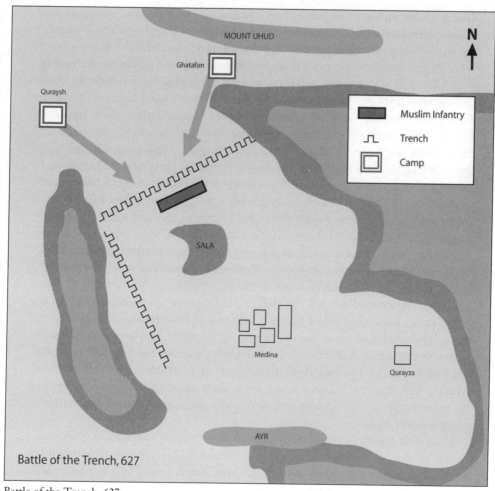

Battle of the Trench, 627.

coalition. The main target for their espionage was the burgeoning agreement between the Quraysh and a hitherto neutral Jewish tribe living in the high-lands south of Medina – the Qurayza. Due to a pre-existing pact, Muhammad had neglected to construct any defences opposite the Qurayza but, now that they seemed about to throw their lot in with the Quraysh, they held a position that could completely undermine Medina's defences. However, through skilful exploitation of the hesitation of the Qurayza, Muhammad was able to fore-stall any joint attack on Medina. In turn, such a delay saw many of the con-stituents of the Quraysh coalition fall out over the lack of progress of the siege and, after some poor weather further worsened the conditions in their camp, the coalition broke up. While again not a great victory, the successful defence of Medina further enhanced the reputation and stature of Muhammad and

Islam. These military campaigns had a profound effect on the 'Umma as well. These shared experiences transformed an alliance of people gathered together by shared religious ideas into a true community; one whose religious ideals were forged into fervent convictions by the heat of battle and in the knowledge that Allah had not only granted them victory but had actively fought for them.

It is also through these battles that Muhammad's teachings reached their final form. Rituals such as praying towards Mecca rather than Jerusalem became fully defined and rules regarding morality, property, marriage and inheritance were put in place. This solidifying of Muslim ritual and belief separated Islam from the other Abrahamic religions, particularly Muhammad's position as a genuine messenger from God. Such a divorce could have greatly undermined Muhammad's cause as Jewish and Christian tribes had played a major role in his successes since the *Hijra*. However, this was not the disaster it might have been, for Muhammad no longer had to rely on their military support as the growing number of converts to Islam, in particular within Mecca itself, and the increasing control the Muslims had over the trade routes to the north, forced the Quraysh to come to the negotiating table in March 628. For his part, Muhammad needed the skills and manpower of Mecca as well as the boost to his cause that access to the Kaaba would have provided. Negotiations eventually produced a ten-year truce and, while many Muslims were not satisfied with the terms of this treaty of Hudaybiyyah, it saw the Quraysh recognise Muhammad and his people as political equals. It also highlighted to many non-Muslim Meccans that Islam was not some alien belief system but one that had its roots firmly in Arabian culture and with which they shared many rituals, practices and ideas.

With this treaty in place, Muhammad then turned against other enemies, including the Nadir, the Qurayza and, most audaciously, the Arabian provinces of the Roman Empire. Even though his army was defeated by a Romano-Arab force perhaps under Heraclius' brother, Theodore, at the Battle of Mu'ta in September 629, such audacity highlights how Muhammad's following had expanded greatly since the Battle of the Trench, as Muslim armies were now measuring in the thousands rather than the hundreds. However, perhaps the most important event for the future spread of Islam came on 31 May 629 when Khalid b. al-Walid converted to Islam. Perhaps no one man aside from Muhammad himself would do more to spread the faith than Khalid. The Prophet himself recognised Khalid's skills early on, declaring him *Saifullah* – 'the sword of Allah' – after he successfully extricated the bulk of the Muslim army from Mu'ta, staving off a potential slaughter. However, perhaps even the Prophet could not have foreseen how fully Khalid would live up to the title bestowed upon him over the course of the next decade. Having said that, Muhammad clearly had long-term plans as he sent messengers to the Roman and Persian emperors, asking them to accept Islam. The ignoring of these invitations could have been used by Muhammad as a means of justifying the wars of conquest he and his successors were to initiate.

However, before such foreign adventures could be planned, unity at home had to be ensured. The ten-year truce agreed with Mecca had lasted a mere two before a squabble between their allies brought the Muslims and the Quraysh back to the point of war. An ultimatum from Muhammad went unheeded and, by the last days of 629, perhaps 10,000 Muslims and their allies were camped outside Mecca. The Quraysh recognised the futility of continued resistance in the face of such forces and, although there was no formal surrender when Muhammad moved his army to take control of Mecca on 11 January 630/ 20 Ramadan, 8 AH, there was very little resistance. Declaring a general amnesty, Muhammad visited the Kaaba where he and his followers cast down the statues of the old gods, persuading many Meccans that their pagan gods had failed them and to accept Islam.

The Death of Muhammad, Establishing of the Caliphate and the Ridda Wars

However, soon after the conquest of Mecca, Muhammad came to realise that bringing Islam to his neighbours was not going to be so bloodless. Perhaps only a fortnight after capturing Mecca, the Muslim army was on the move again to face an alliance of the tribes of Hawazin and Thaqif. These Bedouin were reported to have planned an attack on Medina before Muhammad had moved against Mecca but when the forces met at the Battle of Hunayn in early February, despite being ambushed in a valley, the Muslims scored a decisive victory. A follow-up victory at Autas left the remains of the alliance to retreat to the city of Ta'if. Despite the failure of the subsequent Muslim siege, the threat of a second siege led the inhabitants to surrender and accept Islam. A further expedition north towards Tabouk with a force of perhaps 30,000 men, sup- posedly in response to rumours of an impending Roman invasion, seems to have brought many of the restless tribes in the north into line. Indeed, the increasing military strength of Muhammad and his followers seems to have been enough to coerce large parts of Arabia to accept the political and military predominance of Medina.

However, despite this continued success, it was clear that age was catching up with the Prophet and his next pilgrimage to Mecca in early 632 was to be his last. The address he gave during this visit is perhaps one of the most poignant as he urged Muslims not to fight amongst themselves or seek revenge for past arguments. He also professed that he would fight until all men should confess that 'there is no god but God', which would be incorporated as one of the two major tents of the Islamic creed – the *shahadah*. To be recognised as a Muslim, an individual must accept the unique, indivisible nature of God and that Muhammad was God's Prophet through an honest profession of the *shahadah*.

There is no god but God, and Muhammad is the messenger of God.

In the early days of June 632 Muhammad fell ill with a fever and died in the house of his wife Aisha at Medina on 8 June. As his strength failed, it is reported that the Prophet wished to dictate a letter, expressing his wishes for the future of the Muslim community. However, Umar b. al-Khattab is said to have told Muhammad that his writings in the Qur'an were enough for Islam. While there is some controversy regarding Umar's motives for dissuading Muhammad from dictating what may have essentially been a last will and testament, there is no less truth in his pronouncement. The Qur'an and the message it transmits encapsulates the real legacy of Muhammad's mission. He may have borrowed doctrines, practices and beliefs from Judaism, Christianity, Manichaeanism and the indigenous traditions of Arabia but this was and is no cause for concern amongst Muslims, for Muhammad never claimed to be revealing a new truth; merely that he was the last in a long line of divinely inspired prophets that included Adam, Abraham, Noah, Moses, David, Elijah, John the Baptist and Jesus, who all preached the same monotheistic religion. Part of Islam's mass appeal was that it incorporated 'words and images already known and understood';[12] however, such familiarity did not lessen the impact of Muhammad's teachings. In the cultural hotpot of seventh-century Arabia, Islam was something new; something that was able to cut through the many different and at times conflicting belief systems and establish itself as the predominant force. This was Muhammad's greatest achievement.

However, Muhammad's legacy did not involve the inception of a new religion alone. In spreading his revelations, he had become an increasingly powerful temporal leader as well. Therefore, due to his combined civilian, military and religious authority, the death of the Prophet brought not only great sadness but also great confusion. Who was to succeed him as leader of the burgeoning Muslim state? There were three distinct groupings amongst the followers of Muhammad – those recently converted from amongst the leading families of Mecca; those of Medina who had embraced Muhammad and his 'Umma; and those who had made the *Hijra* with him. A conclave of these leading members of the community chose Abu Bakr, one of Muhammad's earliest followers, to be the first caliph. While there was no thought that Muhammad could be succeeded as the revealer of divine wisdom, the early caliphs maintained an aura of religious authority as well as a growing political power that saw them as something of a mixture between Pope and emperor.

However, the choice of Abu Bakr was not universally accepted as some thought that Muhammad had designated his cousin and son-in-law, Ali b. Abi Talib, as his successor. This dispute between the supporters of Ali and the majority who accepted Abu Bakr would bubble under the surface and emerge again at the deaths of each of the first four successors of Muhammad – Abu Bakr, Umar, Uthman and Ali himself. This dispute gradually evolved into something more divisive than who would lead the Muslim community as a dogmatic schism emerged between those who believed that the caliph should be chosen or elected by the 'Umma and those who believed that the descendants of Ali were the rightful heirs to the Prophet; a schism that still remains today between Sunni and Shia Muslims.

However, for the time being, Ali seems to have given tacit acceptance of Abu Bakr's election for the good of the Muslim community. It is possible that such Alid pragmatism was encouraged by the growing unrest across Arabia. It seems that many Arab tribes felt that the alliances they had struck with Muhammad ended with his demise. This forced Abu Bakr into immediate military action. A second expedition to the outer reaches of the Roman Empire deployed by Muhammad under the command of Usama b. Zayd seems to have forced several apostate tribes to re-embrace Islam rather than face a Roman force. However, in the absence of this army, many other apostate tribes took the opportunity to advance on Medina but Abu Bakr managed to raise a scratch force that thwarted these rebels long enough for Usama to return.

Abu Bakr and his generals now embarked upon a calculated series of campaigns to force religious and political unity across Arabia, which were to become known as the Ridda Wars or the Wars of Apostasy. These campaigns were to be the first real attempt of the Muslim 'Umma to extend its direct influence beyond the west coast of the Arabian Peninsula and they were to prove spectacularly successful. Khalid b. al-Walid led the main Muslim army into the heart of central Arabia, where two self-proclaimed prophets, Musaylima and Tulayha, were gathering support. By the end of September 632, after two successive victories at Buzakha and Ghamrah, Tulayha had been subdued and a further month of campaigning saw the remainder of central Arabia brought under control. Khalid then marched further east to confront Musaylima, who had already defeated the two Muslim corps already sent against him. The remains of these defeated corps, along with further reinforcements from Medina, joined Khalid in early December, who then moved to Yamamah. The resultant battle was a bloody exchange but ended in another decisive victory for Khalid and the death of Musaylima.

Khalid was not the only Muslim general to wage a successful campaign against the apostate. The Battle of Dibba in late November saw the rebelling Azd tribe defeated in Oman by Ikrimah. The same forces then intervened in Mahrah, encouraging one apostate group to re-embrace Islam before using the added manpower to defeat a larger group. A night attack on the apostate forces gathered at Hajr and a secondary victory on the coast of the Persian Gulf brought Bahrain to heel by the end of January 633. Forces loyal to the caliph in Yemen under Fairoz the Persian, a companion of Muhammad who had already dealt with one rebellion during the Prophet's final months, were able to defeat a second round of apostate rebels late in 632. The last region to revolt was Hadhramaut, not doing so until January 633, and the military power of the

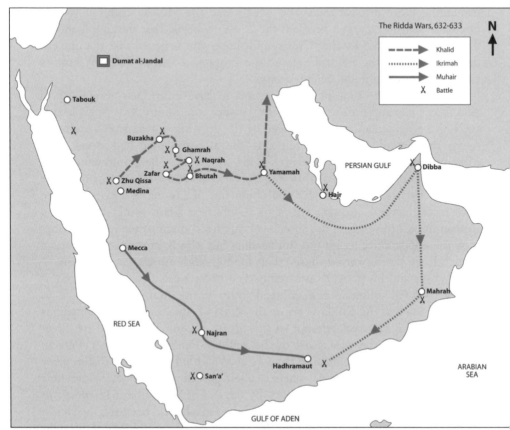

The Ridda Wars, 632–633.

rebel Kindah tribe was enough to force a stalemate with local Muslim loyalists. However, the timing of the revolt proved its undoing for the Kindah were quickly surrounded by the arrival of the corps of Muhair and Ikrimah operating in the Yemen and Mahrah respectively. Their swift capture of the rebel strong-holds of Zafar and Nujair brought an end to the Ridda Wars barely six months after they began.

This unification of Arabia under the leadership of the Caliphate at Medina was a great political and military success for Abu Bakr. However, perhaps more importantly, it demonstrated to those who still doubted the power of Islam that the followers of the Prophet were not only extremely devout but had also stumbled across a series of gifted political and military leaders. It might be expected that after such a military undertaking Abu Bakr would have stood down his forces and spent time consolidating Muslim control of Arabia. However, the thought never seems to have entered his mind for, before the blood spilt at Yamamah had time to run cold, Khalid and his army had been earmarked for a much grander expedition. To the north, there were still Arabs who had yet to submit to the Will of Allah and, beyond them, the princes, kings and emperors who had so readily dismissed Muhammad's offer of salvation through Islam were about to receive an up-close display of the power of that message.

The Muslim Army

Due to the largely accepted idea that 'the Arab conquests were made possible by the opponents' weaknesses rather than by the power of the nascent Muslim armies', pre-conquest Arab forces have received very limited attention.[13] How such forces were brought together, organised and led have yet to be studied in any real detail. The main reason for this is the state of the source material. Unsurprisingly, aside from their deployments as scouts within their own armies, the Romans and Persians are silent about the military organisation of the Muslims, while the Arab accounts present their own problems.[14] Their religious nature often attributes victory to the convictions of those involved and their submission to the Will of God rather than military organisation, skill and bravery. Events can be distorted to further an agenda or by the employing of literary *topoi* to bolster an otherwise unknown part of the narrative. Later Islamic sources also tended to portray their predecessors in anachronistic terms, projecting the social, political and military organisation of their periods back onto that of early Islam, imposing 'a false sense of organisation and method on military manoeuvres, which were, in reality, much more chaotic'.[15] Such an abundance of potential problems makes any attempt to reconstruct any aspect of the early Muslim military fraught with danger and undermines any chances of firm conclusions.

The earliest Muslim military actions would have been a combination of caravan looting and raids against neighbouring Bedouin tribes to bolster resources, seek vengeance, discourage potential enemies, claim strategic points or enforce religious conversion. Such raids reflected the enemies that the fledgling Muslim army faced and how rare true pitched battle was in Arab warfare. They also 'contributed a great deal to the Muslim community in terms of wealth, experience and the achievement of political and strategic goals.'[16] However, as the enemies of Islam grew in size and stature such an unstructured army would not have been successful, forcing Muhammad and his advisers to improvise and incorporate a more structured approach to administration and organisation.

Perhaps the most immediate change brought about by the rise of Islam came in the realm of army leadership. Aside from tribal leaders, who owed their status to their ancestry and personal success, pre-Muslim Arab war parties had little in the way of a command structure. Under Islam, ultimate military authority, itself something of a novelty across much of the Arabian Peninsula, lay with Muhammad and his caliphal successors; however, as campaigns became further removed from Medina, it became necessary to appoint individuals to military command. In choosing men of certain tribes for certain commands, the Prophet and his caliphal successors demonstrated an understanding of tribal politics while the appointments of men like Khalid and Amr, later converts to Islam, showed that Muhammad was willing to promote military talent ahead of standing within the Muslim community. It should also be pointed out that the repeated instances of rapid communication and dictation of military movements attributed to the caliphs in Medina should be treated with scepticism.[17] Some major redeployments may have been ordered by the caliphs but the majority of decisions will have been taken on the ground by those men the caliph had entrusted to achieve the strategic objectives of the campaign.

The leadership of skilled individuals such as Khalid may have encouraged the emergence of a more structured military beyond its tribal make-up. The Muslim army does seem to have used similar formations to late antique Roman and Persian armies with right and left wings and a centre. Advance guards, vanguards and rearguards are also mentioned. An even more organised structure is recorded at the Battle of Qadisiyyah, where the Muslim commander, Sa'd b. Abi Waqqas, had divided his force into sub-groups of ten. However, it is likely that such subdivisions were superimposed on the past by later writers for, even with this interposing of a religio-political hierarchy and the appearance of numerous independent corps during the Ridda Wars, there was little sign of what would be described as a regular, even semi-permanent army.

As with other antique forces, the early Islamic army was largely divided into cavalry and infantry. However, a tentative warning must be sounded regarding the blurring of the two as cavalrymen would often fight dismounted and infantry could be transported on horse or camel.[18] The vast majority of Arab horse of the early period was light cavalry used as raiders and skirmishers or as lancers, rather than horse archers or heavy cavalry such as the cataphracts of the Roman and Persian armies. It is also worth noting that horses were not abundant in Arabia; a fact that might explain why Arab cavalry relied more on mobility and skirmishing to avoid costly casualties both in terms of men and horses.[19] It might also partly explain why it was infantry that bore the brunt of the fighting in Arab warfare. The core of the Muslim infantry was made up of swordsmen who carried a straight, hilted blade – the *sayf* – that was used for thrusting and slashing. They also made use of iron-tipped spears and javelins. Another sizeable part of the Muslim infantry used the archery skills that hunting with a bow honed. The Arab bow seems to have been a smaller variant than its Persian counterpart but it is possible that the more rapid fire offered by the smaller bow allowed Muslim archers to more effectively shield their infantry and cavalry.

Little physical material remains of early Muslim defensive equipment, and that which does survive is difficult to date or source. Muslim sources rarely speak of military equipment unless the articles themselves were famous, such as the swords, shields, bows and lances of Muhammad, and it is likely that most Muslim soldiers will have fought without the full military panoply. Instances of Arab chain-mail armour do survive, although how widespread its use was in the Muslim army before the conquests is difficult to gauge. Mail was expensive to buy or make, meaning that perhaps only the richest Arab soldiers or those who had served in the Roman or Persian armies will have had such armour. Helmets may have been less prevalent before the conquests with a hood of mail called a coif being used instead to protect the head. Shields were carried by both cavalry and infantry and, while they are not well described in the sources, the few surviving descriptions suggest that the normal Arab shield was wooden or leather made into a 'small disk, certainly less than a metre in diameter'.[20]

A less significant section of the Muslim army was that given over to siege engines. Most Arab settlements had some kind of fortifications but few were prepared for a prolonged siege so the Muslims will have had little experience of siege warfare. Siege equipment such as the swing-beam *manjaniq*, similar to the trebuchet of Europe, is seen in later Muslim armies; however, the extent to which such machines were used by the Arabs of the 630s is difficult to say. A *manjaniq* was deployed during the siege of Ta'if in 630, although its lack of success against modest defences is telling, which may explain why such machines were more likely to be used as anti-personnel weapons rather than against fortifications.[21] There is also no evidence for the torsion-based pre-decessors of such machines, which further suggests that Arab siegecraft was largely basic. However, while it is easy to downplay the siege abilities of tribal societies such as the Arabs and the Avars, they proved themselves to be quick learners and highly adaptive to such situations. The Arabs in particular seem to have quickly realised that 'victory often depended on preliminary political success rather than sheer military power'.[22] With this realisation, Muhammad, his successors and their commanders proved themselves adept at separating a settlement from its allies through negotiation or blockade and then offering 'protection and toleration in return for a fixed tribute'.[23] Through such a combination, even the most major of cities – Damascus, Ctesiphon, Jerusalem, Antioch and Alexandria – would prove to be within the grasp of Muslim forces.

With the advent of Islam's temporal power, a vague outline of a recruiting process begins to emerge. Volunteers or prescribed tribes gathered at Medina or at a predetermined site, were formed into an army and then sent into the field. Most of the *muqatila* – 'fighting men' – who served in the Arab armies were of Bedouin origin, which is unsurprising given that raiding, fighting and familiarity with riding, spears, swords and archery were integral parts of their daily lives.[24] However, the rapid expansion of the Muslim community brought with it a wider spectrum of potential soldier. There is some evidence that the Muslims equipped some of their more settled or poorer members to fight.[25] Alliances with Jewish, Christian and other non-Muslim tribes played major roles in the military survival and successes of Muhammad and his 'Umma in its earliest years. Clients and slaves were also present in Muslim armies with the likelihood being that not all of them were Arabic in origin. Defection also added to the military strength of the Muslim armies while at the same time undermining its opponents.

The recorded sizes of Muslim armies are often hard to accept due to their seemingly formulaic nature. They are usually portrayed as being particularly small in number throughout their earliest history, such as raiding parties featuring forces numbering less than 100. However, the rapidity with which Muhammad was able to field armies of up to and beyond 10,000 might be cause for some suspicion – 300 at Badr; 700 at Uhud; 3,000 at Mu'ta, 10,000 at Mecca and 12,000 at Hunayn. During the attacks on Roman and Persian territory, the Muslim armies are also regarded as being on the small side with perhaps as few as 6,000 fighting at Qadisiyyah and the garrisons in southern Mesopotamia perhaps only numbering up to 4,000.

This seeming paucity of Arab soldiers must also be tempered by the exaggerated reporting of the armies of their Roman and Persian foes. The Great Powers probably maintained a numerical superiority over the Muslims but it was almost certainly not as overwhelming as the suggestions of the Muslim sources, which at times attempt to put armies in the order of hundreds of thousands in the field. Many of the proposed numbers for Muslim armies need to be viewed from a contemporary perspective. The previous two centuries or more had seen a marked decline in the size of armies deployed by the Romans and Persians;[26] so much so that Mauricius considered an army of 5,000–15,000 to be well proportioned and 15,000–20,000 to be large.[27] The fact that the Muslims may have been able to field a force of anything between 20,000 and 40,000 at Yarmuk suggests that the numerical gradient they faced was not as severe as is usually thought.

However, in spite of some advances compared to the pre-Islamic period, the early Muslim military remained simplistic. Aside from perhaps the greater desert mobility that camels provided, they were at a technological disadvantage to their Roman and Persian adversaries and, while perhaps not overly serious, they were at a numerical disadvantage too. Organisationally, even after the successes of the Ridda Wars, the Muslim army was still closer to a tribal war party than it was to the professional forces that the Romans could field. They were not paid nor provided any benefits and their enrolling in the army was not recorded in any way. However, these men were fuelled by the prospect of booty, encouraged by the martial bonds of their tribe and buoyed by the morale offered to them by their religion, and, once they were brought together under the Muslim banner and led in battle by a cadre of skilful practitioners of war, they were to prove an increasingly irresistible force. And in the 630s, the Great Powers were about to find out how devastating such a force could be.

Chapter 6

The Islamic Eruption

What could be more lamentable and more terrible to those upon whom they fell? To see how a people, coming from the desert and barbaric, run through land that is not theirs, as if it were their own; how they, who seem only to have simple human features, lay waste our sweet and organised country with their wild untamed beasts.

St Maximos the Confessor (Laga (1990), 186)

Eye of the Storm – the Roman and Persian Empires between the Wars
After returning to Roman territory in 628, Heraclius could congratulate himself on a job well done. The integrity of the Roman Empire had been restored; an ally now sat on the throne of the Sassanids, the potency of Roman arms had again been proven and, perhaps most importantly, with the imminent restoration of the True Cross and other relics, the pre-eminence of Christianity has been demonstrated. He may have expected that after almost twenty years of unbroken warfare he would be able to get some rest. However, those years of war had caused such devastation and displacement that the work of the newly styled Πιστὸς εν Χριϭω Βαϭιλευϛ – 'Faithful in Christ Basileus' – was far from finished. The end of the Romano-Persian War of 602–628 might have seen the restoration of a similar accord to that of Mauricius and Khusro II in the last years of the sixth century but both empires had spent a vast amount of energy and resources to return to what was essentially a *status quo ante*. While Heraclius' reputation and military victories will have gone some way to restoring Roman authority over the territories recovered from Persia, there was still a lot of physical and psychological damage to deal with; damage that could not be fixed with the stroke of a pen or an agreement between allies. The infrastructures, economies and way of life in those regions directly affected by the conflict will have been greatly disrupted and the end of hostilities 'did not instantly restore the old high stream of revenues to Constantinople.'[1]

Militarily, Heraclius favoured demobilisation to relieve some of the financial pressure on the imperial treasury, especially as 'it was hard to justify paying large sums for the army when no great enemy was in sight.'[2] There is little evidence for the size of Heraclius' army at any stage during his reign or for the extent of these post-war demobilisations. However, it is unlikely that Heraclius reduced the numbers of what would be considered the regular army so most of his cuts would have come from discharging non-Roman contingents. Even if such a move was provable, the service of such forces was always poorly recorded compared to the regular forces so it would not provide much help for estimating the Roman army of about 630. It is suggested that the army was smaller than that of Justinian, perhaps being somewhere between 98,000 and 130,000.[3] However, the increasing political crisis in Persia may have made Heraclius think twice about demobilisation. The threat of an enterprising Persian general or king deciding to make a grab for the prestige of an attack on Roman territory meant that the Roman emperor was obliged to maintain a sizeable force along the eastern frontier. These fears will have been somewhat allayed as Persian began to fight Persian, but the presence of Roman forces in Persian Mesopotamia when the Muslims attacked in 633 may suggest that Heraclius was still exercising caution or was even attempting to further strengthen the Roman position between the rivers.

Heraclius' continued preoccupation with Persia and with reducing the budget may be best demonstrated in the lack of military action taken to reestablish the Roman position in the Balkans, which had been almost irrevocably smashed by the Avars and the Slavs. The extent of the campaigning that Mauricius had needed to cow the Avars in the 590s and the risk of another Phocan-like mutiny from the mass transfer of troops will have further discouraged Heraclius from redeploying to the Balkans. That Heraclius would refuse to reclaim the environs of his own capital meant that any attempts to retake control of Spain from the Visigoths or to reassert the waning imperial authority in Italy in the face of an increasingly confident Papacy and the continually unchecked Lombards would have been even further from his mind.

In the realm of religion, the military victories achieved by Heraclius offered no solution to the controversies surrounding the nature of Christ. Along with his marriage to Martina, Heraclius' promotion of Christian worship, cults and the veneration of relics to galvanise the Empire during the war may well have exacerbated the religious disputes; disputes that were already centuries old, with no solution in sight even when Heraclius himself got directly involved.[4] Perhaps most importantly for the future of the Empire, the losses in military and civilian manpower through combat, disease and other medical issues would have ranked in the thousands, perhaps higher, and would take years to recover.[5] Some of these shortages could have been alleviated by the influx of refugees from Persian territory. However, they would have provided a combination of potential benefits with their 'multifaceted talents and knowledge and a potential security issue being extra mouths to feed and bodies to settle or house'.[6] Such a flood of people may also have played a role in encouraging Heraclius to maintain a military presence along the Romano-Persian frontier.

Despite his attempts to reduce the military budget, Heraclius seems to have immediately instituted a sizeable rebuilding programme, throwing large amounts of public funds into restoring the ruined sites around Constantinople and other large cities. In hindsight, these resources may have been better diverted elsewhere as the Empire would face continuous financial trouble throughout the remainder of the seventh century, but in the early 630s the boost to public morale will have seemed more immediately important. The marriage of the future Constantine III to Gregoria, the daughter of Nicetas, sometime before February 630 was not only a further cementing of the Heraclian dynasty but also another opportunity for morale-boosting celebration and pageantry.

The most prominent celebration of 630 was the imperial pilgrimage to see the restoration of the True Cross to Jerusalem. However, it may have had an unforeseen consequence. Heraclius' presence in Jerusalem, along with some limited attempts perhaps to re-establish the Ghassanids buffer system, may have given rise to the Muslim belief that the Roman emperor was planning a campaign against them; a belief that may have encouraged them to take advantage of the political vacuum in northern Arabia. The termination of monetary payments to the remaining Arab clients as a cost-cutting measure seems to have 'increased tensions, resentments, and violence, and disrespect for imperial authority in some areas on the margins of settled regions in Palestine and Syria'.[7] This was demonstrated by the reported widespread raids of 632. It is not recorded who these raiders were but it is likely that they were Arabs, Muslims or otherwise.

It is not known what the Romans and Persians really knew about Muhammad's consolidation and expansion of power in Arabia. Rumours must have perforated the frontiers to some extent but it is unlikely that local authorities will have paid all that much attention. Petty kingdoms of the Arabian sands had risen and fallen at regular intervals in the preceding centuries, and if word reached Heraclius and Shahrbaraz they will have seen this 'Umma as no threat and its new Islamic 'superstition' as nothing but a passing fad.

The Romans were not only distracted from the unification of Arabia by their own internal healings but also by the catastrophic political collapse of Sassanid authority that took place in mid-630. Shahrbaraz's removal of Ardashir III may have seemed like the advent of a new political stability based on military power and the alliance with Heraclius but it quickly descended into chaos. His military usurpation backed by the Roman emperor meant that Shahrbaraz was unpopular with much of the Sassanid hierarchy from the outset and, once he demonstrated the slightest military weakness, he was vulnerable. As it was, Shahrbaraz failed his first military test, ultimately sparking the unravelling of his regime.

The nature of this military test was not unfamiliar to the Persians. Despite the failure of the Romano-Turkic alliance to capture Tiflis in 627, the success of Heraclius' invasion and the subsequent Persian disarray had encouraged the Turkic Khan to try again. After a two-month siege, the Turks were finally able to storm the walls of Tiflis and 'a dark shadow of dread came upon the pitiful inhabitants of the city [that did not lift until] the wailing and groaning ended and no one was left alive.'[8] This success further emboldened the Turks to invade Armenia, perhaps in an attempt to subjugate it. Shahrbaraz, who was seemingly only just on his way to Ctesiphon from Syria, sent 10,000 men under Honah to deal with this invasion. However, by chasing after a retreating Turkic contingent, Honah and his army fell into a trap and in the subsequent slaughter the Turks 'did not spare a single one of them.'[9] The loss of such a large number of men proved fatal to Shahrbaraz as he was assassinated barely six weeks after he had removed Ardashir.

Normally, such Persian dynastic in-fighting would not have been much cause for concern for the Roman emperor but this was an abnormal situation. Not only had Heraclius lost an ally in Shahrbaraz, he was now faced with a potential return to conflict as the Sassanid state fell into increasing political disarray. The deaths of Khusro II, Kavad II, Ardashir III and now Shahrbaraz in rapid succession, along with the circumstances, had significantly weakened Sassanid authority. The situation was exacerbated by Kavad's 'killing of almost every eligible or capable male heir in the Sasanian family'.[10] The extent of this fratricide was not fully realised until it came to finding a suitable Sassanid candidate to replace the usurper Shahrbaraz. That the choice eventually fell on a daughter of Khusro II, Buran, demonstrates the dire state to which the Sassanid family had been reduced.

Throughout her fifteen-month reign Buran had some success in reorganising the war-torn Persian state by rebuilding infrastructure and lowering taxes, as well as maintaining good relations with Heraclius. However, she could do little about the increasing destabilisation of imperial authority. Rival claimants and increasingly powerful and disloyal generals and officials undermined any successes she achieved and when she was deposed by one such general in October 631 Sassanid central authority fell into complete chaos; so chaotic that the chronology of the early 630s is far from clear. Later historians and numismatic evidence suggest that in the year following Buran's deposition at least seven different people claimed the Sassanid throne. Her immediate successor in Ctesiphon was Buran's own sister, Azarmigduxt, but she too seems to have fallen foul of the military after only a few months. Across the Empire other distant Sassanid relatives and military leaders emerged as contenders, with the regnal names of Hormizd VI, Khusro III, Peroz II, Khusro IV and Khusro V all mentioned in the record.[11] The accession of Yazdgerd III in mid-632 seemed like just another name to be added to the confusion but, through strong leadership and some good fortune, Yazdgerd would achieve some semblance of order and through the support of the military would reign for nearly two decades. Normally, such an extended reign would be beneficial to restoring a regime's standing but, as already mentioned, these were far from normal times and Yazdgerd's twenty years were the most turbulent in Sassanid history and would ultimately prove fatal.

While the forces available to Heraclius can be somewhat estimated, the state of the Sassanid military in the early 630s is a complete mystery. The defeats suffered during Khusro's war with the Romans will have undermined the less than professional military structure of the Sassanid state and this will have been further destabilised by Shahrbaraz's rebellion, Honah's defeat by the Turks, and the civil wars. Therefore, despite the lack of information, it would not be going too far to suggest that the Persian military was not in its best shape to deal with what was about to emerge from the desert.

It is easy to criticise the post-war strategies of the Romans and Persians: Heraclius for being more concerned with the economic, infrastructural and spiritual well-being of his empire than its military strength and battle readiness; the Persians for so readily descending into resource-sapping internecine conflict. However, such criticism is heavily tainted by the benefits of hindsight and the over-expectation that the Great Powers should have been able to predict the Arabic storm that was about to erupt. After having been at war with each other for the last twenty-six years, expending vast amounts of resources in an ultimately fruitless conflict, it cannot be surprising that the Romans and Persians would become more insular in their outlook in the immediate aftermath. However, even if it is understandable, this insularity was to have far-reaching consequences for Rome, Persia and virtually the entire ancient world.

Khalid and the Muslim Conquest of the Euphrates

Given the rapidity of the transferring of his attention from the successful conclusion to the Ridda Wars and the unification of most of Arabia to looking to spread the teachings of Muhammad beyond the Peninsula, it would seem that Abu Bakr was well aware of the state of both the Roman and Persian empires. Whether this is true or not, the poor state of his opponents greatly aided the progress of the Muslims. For their initial impact, the destruction of the Ghassanid and the Lakhmid buffer states seems to have been vital. It certainly appears to have been the lack of a strong Lakhmid state along the southern bank of the Euphrates that allowed a local Arab tribal leader, al-Muthanna b. Harith, to launch several successful raids into Mesopotamia. Despite there being no links between him and the Islamic regime in Medina, the success of al-Muthanna, including a possible visit to Medina, may have encouraged Abu Bakr to attempt more adventurous military expansion. However, it is likely that Abu Bakr's motives for expansion lay more in national unification than they did in imperialism, as there was a considerable Arab presence, both sedentary and nomadic, along the banks of the Euphrates and had been for centuries. Therefore, 'the first phase of the conquest of Iraq was, in short, merely a continuation of the Ridda Wars – the subjection by the Islamic state of the Arab tribes.'[12]

Abu Bakr's initial move was to send Iyad b. Ghanm against Dumat al-Jandal, an oasis town on the very edge of the desert connected to Hira by a long-

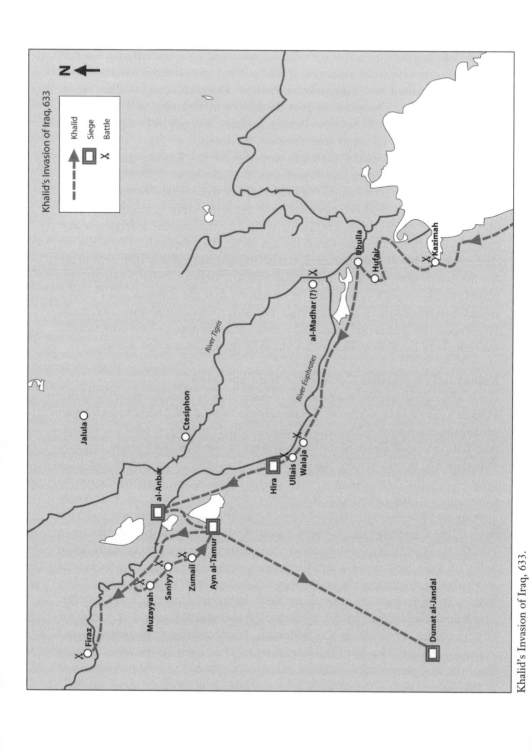

Khalid's Invasion of Iraq, 633.

established caravan route. The caliph also sent Khalid, fresh from his victories in the Najd and at Yamamah, north along the coast of the Persian Gulf with orders to continue upriver to Hira. The plan appears to have been for Iyad to take Dumat al-Jandal, probably as a supply station between Islamic territory and the Euphrates, before meeting up with al-Muthanna and Khalid arriving from downriver to attack Hira in a pincer movement. However, Iyad was unable to reduce his target quickly and was forced into a lengthy siege. This left the subjugation of the Euphrates to the others.

The recording of the opening phases of the Muslim attacks on Persian territory must be treated with caution. The sheer number of 'battles' fought in the period from late spring 633 to April 634 gives the suggestion that even the most minor of skirmishes was promoted to the stature of a 'battle' and that the number of enemies faced was heavily exaggerated for propaganda purposes. The formulaic nature of some of the battles may also encourage scepticism regarding their historicity. When Khalid departed from Yamamah is much debated, as is much of the timeline of his campaign, but it was likely somewhere around late-spring/early-summer 633.[13] The composition and size of his force is also not fully understood. Despite suggestions of a sizeable army of 18,000 comprised of Bedouin, Medinese and other tribesmen, it is likely that Khalid's force was quite small, perhaps 2,000 strong with a core of men from Medina and the Quraysh surrounded by other tribal contingents. Khalid may have gathered more men on his march to Hira, as much of the basis for the higher estimates for his force come from the suggestion that four separate contingents of 2,000 men joined him before he reached the Euphrates.

The first recorded battle of Khalid's campaign took place at Dhat al-Salasil, probably in late-April 633, and is better known as the Battle of Chains. The confrontation is marked by Khalid's ability to manipulate his opponent, a Persian governor called Hormuz, into chasing after the highly mobile Muslim column back and forward across the deserts of eastern Kuwait. Only when the Persian force, which was likely a force of Arab auxiliaries rather than a Persian army and not anywhere close to the 40,000 that is recorded in the sources, was thoroughly exhausted did Khalid square up to it near the town of Kazimah. The Muslim dispositions are unknown although they were likely somewhat similar to those of the Persian force, which was arrayed in its traditional three divisions of a centre and a left and right wing. The reason this encounter at Dhat al-Salasil got its name is from the suggestion that parts of the Persian line were chained together, in an attempt to either force unity on unwilling troops or to present the enemy with a sign that they were ready to fight to the death. However, whatever the reasoning for it, after Khalid supposedly killed Hormuz in single combat, a general attack by the entire Muslim line was enough to break the Persian force.

With this victory, Khalid forged further north towards Ubulla, where another Persian force, consisting of the survivors of the Battle of Chains and units supposedly sent under Qarin in response to a letter sent to Yazdgerd III by

Hormuz, seems to have been gathering. Perhaps wrong-footed by the rapidity of the Muslim advance or even unnerved by the sudden appearance of a Muslim detachment under al-Muthanna, Qarin retreated from the Nahr al-Mar'a canal outside Ubulla up the banks of the Tigris. Having reconnoitred the Persian position at a place called al-Madhar, Khalid seems to have wasted little time in taking advantage of what he will have perceived as a negative approach by Qarin and, before April 633 was through, he had squared up to the Persian force. This Battle of the River followed a suspiciously similar course to that of the Battle of Chains with the Persian commander slain in single combat and a general Muslim attack being enough to break the Persians. The victorious Muslim army was now able to turn northwest and follow the Euphrates upriver towards Hira.

In response to this advance, the Persians seem to have decided to intercept Khalid before he reached Hira. In doing so, the Persians may have removed garrisons from along the route of Khalid's march, allowing him to cover the large stretch of territory between Ubulla and Hira in a short period of time and without facing any concerted effort to stop him. The plan was for one force under Andarzaghar, reportedly the governor of Khurasan, to march from Ctesiphon and establish itself at the place chosen for the interception of Khalid – Walaja, a site not positively identified[14] – where it was to await the arrival of a second force under Bahman. Together, they would crush Khalid with their superior numbers. The question could be asked as to why these forces did not march together as one. However, whatever the reason for Bahman's tardiness, whether it was that his force was not ready or that it took a different route to the battlefield to relieve logistical pressure on the countryside, or because it was coming from a different location, the division was to prove vital.

Once again, Khalid had moved quicker than the Persian authorities anticipated. Arriving at Walaja sometime in May 633, days before Bahman, and perhaps learning of the imminent arrival of another Persian army, Khalid forced battle on Andarzaghar before he could be reinforced. What followed is described as Khalid's tactical masterpiece – a double envelopment of the Persian force, on a par with what Hannibal the Carthaginian had achieved against the Romans at Cannae over 800 years previously in 216 BCE. Using the surrounding geography to his advantage, the night before the battle Khalid was able to secretly position two cavalry contingents behind a ridge to the rear of the Persian lines. Andarzaghar may have deployed his men with their back to this ridge due to the Muslim superiority in cavalry and therefore hoped the ridge would give added protection to his rear and flanks. However, his position may also have been dictated by that of Khalid opposite.

The battle began with a general attack by the Muslim infantry, although the Persians quickly gained the upper hand in driving the Muslims back. Depending on the source, this was either because Andarzaghar made his superiority in infantry count with a careful use of his reserve or because Khalid ordered his centre to execute a fighting retreat. As the Muslim centre gave ground, it drew

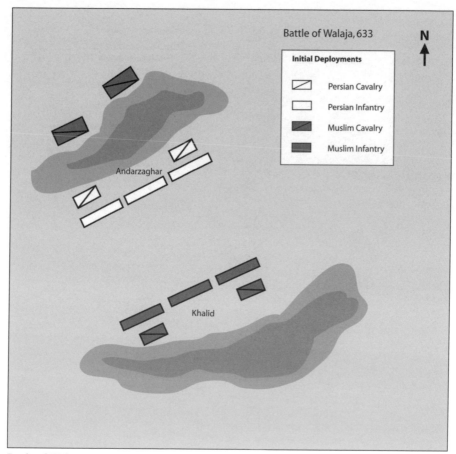

Battle of Walaja, 633: Deployments.

the Persian force away from the ridge and into the crescent-shaped formation of the Muslim line. Khalid then threw his cavalry against the exposed Persian flanks and Andarzaghar's own horse, forcing the Persian lines to buckle inwards, further exacerbating the crescent shape of the battle lines. With the entire Persian force now fully engaged, Khalid signalled his cavalry hidden behind the ridge to attack the rear of the Persian force. Assailed from all sides, the crush of humanity within the crescent saw to it that the Persian soldiers were unable to wield their swords and spears to any effect and many were slaughtered where they stood. As if the tactical genius of the victory was not enough, Khalid is also said to have won a duel against a Persian known as *Hazar Mard* – 'A Thousand Men' – due to his immense size.

Khalid's victory at Walaja is usually hailed as that of an outnumbered force being victorious over a vastly superior foe through a general's use of tactics, speed and the geographical layout of the battlefield. However, while Andar-

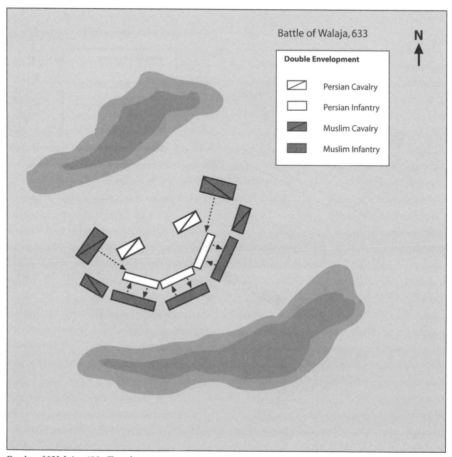

Battle of Walaja, 633: Envelopment.

zaghar's force is recorded as being anything up to 50,000 strong, it was probably no larger than that of Khalid, which was at most 15,000 and probably less, being made up of survivors of Dhat al-Salasil and al-Madhar plus some reinforcements from Persian-allied Arab tribesmen and local Persian garrisons rather than being a true Sassanid imperial army. It is also reported that, despite the success of the Muslim envelopment, several thousand Sassanid soldiers were able to escape, including Andarzaghar; although he is supposed to have later died of thirst by fleeing into the desert rather than towards the Euphrates. However, even if the scale of his victory at Walaja was exaggerated, there can be little doubt that before he had reached his objective at Hira the opening months of his campaign along the frontiers of the Persian Empire had demonstrated that Khalid was a skilled practitioner of war.

Despite the defeat at Walaja, Yazdgerd remained keen to intercept Khalid before he reached Hira. Therefore, Bahman was ordered to march to Ullais and join up with the remnant of Andarzaghar's army and the massing Christian Arabs. Bahman himself seems to have returned to Ctesiphon to confer with Yazdgerd, leaving his subordinate, Jaban, to lead the army to Ullais with orders not to engage the Muslims until Bahman rejoined them. However, for whatever reason – the emperor being ill is reported – Bahman did not return to the army.

Informed of Jaban's movements, Khalid attempted to reach Ullais before him in order to defeat the Christian Arab forces and prevent having to face a numerically superior combination. However, Khalid's advance was not quick enough and when he arrived on the battlefield he found perhaps 30,000 enemies. Undeterred, Khalid refused to give the Perso-Arab force time to organise and attacked almost immediately. Little is known of the exact course of the resultant Battle of Ullais but it seems to have descended into a bloody infantry contest, something that Jaban may have planned with his choice of having the Euphrates and Khaseef guarding his flanks from a cavalry attack. However, any further Sassanid battle plans were thrown into disorder by Khalid's unexpected attack. After several hours of hard fighting that may have cost Khalid upwards of 2,000 men, the Perso-Arab force attempted to disengage and retreat back towards Hira. At this point, and demonstrating the ruthlessness that would characterise many of their pursuits, the Muslims launched a vicious cavalry assault on the retreating Sassanid ranks and inflicted such heavy casualties that the River Khaseef ran red.

This victory at Ullais seems to have induced some of the local Arab tribes into surrender to Khalid, accepting the Muslim *jizya* tax, but it was not enough to prevent the Muslim commander from having to invest Hira. However, the defeats of Persian garrisons and Arab tribes at Walaja and Ullais, coupled with the likelihood that Khalid offered reasonable terms, meant that the inhabitants of Hira did not resist for an extended period of time, surrendering before the end of May 633. The capitulation of Hira meant that Khalid had completed the mammoth task of bringing the Lower and Middle Euphrates under control in just a few short months.

Yet not all resistance had been broken and, whether he had permission or not, Khalid was on the march again within a month. The exact timeframe and sequence of the next events is unclear, as they have been tangled with Khalid's later march to Syria and perhaps embellished. Most of the scepticism that surrounds Khalid's advances after capturing Hira surrounds the feats attributed to him despite his very limited manpower resources. It would appear that he took only the core of men that he brought from Yamamah, 2,000 at most and perhaps even fewer, with the rest of his force remaining at Hira or returning to their tribal lands. Due to this paucity of troops, Khalid's initial strike northwest from Hira was more a raid to discourage other Arab tribes than a concerted effort to subdue them.[15]

From Hira, Khalid again continued to follow the Euphrates, eventually coming to al-Anbar, where a Sassanid garrison under Shirazad attempted to resist but surrendered after a hailstorm of Muslim arrows, and favourable terms were offered in July 633. Khalid then headed south down the western shore of what is now Lake Milh in Iraq to assail Ayn al-Tamur, where a Christian Arab force, perhaps also with a limited number of Sassanid frontier troops, was defeated in late-July 633. The record is muddled enough that the sieges of al-Anbar and Ayn al-Tamur may have taken place in reverse order. While at Ayn al-Tamur, Khalid is said to have received a letter from Iyad, asking for aid against Dumat al-Jandal. The letter detailed how, despite being reinforced by Abu Bakr, Iyad had been unable to reduce the desert town due to the size of its garrison and the reinforcements it had received from the remnant of the Ghassanid coalition. With both sides unable to force victory, the siege had quickly descended into a stalemate of missile exchange and occasional, half-hearted sallies from the garrison.

Knowing the importance of the trading town to communication with Medina, Khalid raced south to the desert's edge. Arriving at the siege, Khalid recognised that Iyad had been correct regarding the strength of the garrison and that any attempted storming of its walls would be extremely costly. Therefore, taking command of Iyad's force, Khalid redeployed them in a full blockade – although the question could be asked why Iyad had not done this already – but camped far enough from the walls to entice the defenders into another sally. The garrison commander, a Christian Arab called Judi b. Rabi'a, growing increasingly frustrated by inactivity, duly obliged. Iyad repulsed an attempt to break out to the south while Khalid's main force broke the main thrust of Judi's charge. It is possible that, instead of a sally, a pitched battle was fought between the garrison and Khalid's army but the result was the same.[16] Hundreds were killed or captured by the besiegers and, while it did not immediately lead to the surrender of the town, the defeat and casualties severely undermined its ability and resolve to continue resisting. How the siege ended is unknown but it appears that at some stage during late-August 633 the Muslims broke in and put the remaining garrison forces to the sword.

With communications to Medina secure, Khalid then returned north to Hira with Iyad, where in late-September 633 he heard troubling news of a large force being gathered together near al-Anbar by Bahman, consisting of what remained of his army from Ullais, local Sassanid garrison forces and large numbers of Christian Arabs. Hearing of this and deciding to defeat these forces before they could congregate, Khalid reacted with typically decisive alacrity. Leaving a small garrison under Iyad at Hira, Khalid was re-established at Ayn al-Tamur with a force of up to 15,000 men within days. Dividing this force into three, Khalid then sent two of the divisions against the separate Sassanid forces congregating at Husaid and Khanafis while keeping the third in reserve under his command in order to deal with any counter-attack by the Christian Arab forces coming together in the desert. However, this daring move failed to prevent the Sassanid forces coming together for, while the attack on Husaid was successful, it was not properly coordinated with that on Khanafis. This allowed these Sassanid forces to meet up with the Arab tribesmen at Muzayyah.

With this failure at Khanafis, it was even more imperative that Khalid prevent the enemy forces at Muzayyah, Saniyy and Zumail coming together. To that end, he now took his biggest risk yet – a night attack. With extraordinary skill and no lack of good fortune, Khalid's three corps managed to converge a few miles from Muzayyah from three different directions – Husaid, Khanafis and Ayn al-Tamur – completely undetected. What followed is classed as the Battle of Muzayyah but was little short of a massacre as the Perso-Arab camp was surrounded and stormed. The survivors fled towards Saniyy but Khalid seems to have kept pace with them and was able to fall upon this second camp in a similar surprise fashion in mid-November 633. That a third such night attack was successful at Zumail soon after may provoke some wariness regarding the similarity between these three 'battles' but, even if there is some embellishment, it does appear that Bahman's proposed Perso-Arab counter-attack was thwarted by the end of 633.

Perhaps the least reliable of Khalid's recorded moves came in the aftermath of this defeat of Bahman's congregating force. Moving further up the Euphrates, he struck at what was considered the last remaining Sassanid garrison along the Euphrates at Firaz in late-December 633/early-January 634. This was right at the very fringe of Persian Mesopotamia with the Roman frontier directly opposite; so close in fact that it is reported that a Roman force joined the Sassanids in squaring up to Khalid. The presence of Romans at the Battle of Firaz does correlate with its proximity to the Romano-Persian border and Heraclius' stationing of troops in Persian territory after the defeat of Khusro; however, their presence would not have taken the forces opposing Khalid up to the preposterous levels they are recorded at – ten times bigger than the Muslim force – and the question must be asked as to why would the Romans get involved in a pitched battle against what they would still have seen as Arab raiding of Persian land? Because of that, the suspicion of the Roman presence at Firaz being a complete fabrication is difficult to shake, but, without sufficient evidence to the contrary, a suspicion is all that it remains. The crux of the battle seems to have been the need for the coalition to cross the Euphrates to engage the Muslim host. Khalid challenged their crossing, pinning them against its banks with his infantry and then struck around their flanks with his cavalry. The decisive moment came when the Muslims captured the bridge the Romano-Persian force had just crossed. Assailed from virtually all sides, the coalition forces broke and, finding their main escape route blocked, many plunged into the river in a vain attempt to escape death.

There is a suggestion that when the outcome of the Battle of Firaz was in the balance Khalid promised to perform the Hajj – a pilgrimage to Mecca – should Allah grant him victory. Therefore, victorious once again, Khalid garrisoned Firaz and then sent his army back to Hira before, not wanting to attract attention, sneaking south to Mecca with a small retinue to fulfil his oath. While Khalid did make it back to the Euphrates safely, despite his care not to be discovered word did reach the caliph, who rebuked Khalid's recklessness in a letter. However, when he was organising an attack on Qadisiyyah, one of the last Persian positions south of the Euphrates, a second letter reached Khalid from Abu Bakr. His campaign to impose Islamic rule, direct or indirect, over the Arab tribes south of the Euphrates had been an unmitigated success, a triumph of speed of movement and decisive action; but now he was being transferred. However, this was not a demotion. While Khalid had been campaigning along the Euphrates, other Muslim forces had been simultaneously establishing themselves against the other great imperial power of the Middle East. Khalid was heading to Syria.

The Muslim Invasion of Syria

With Muhammad's plan to unite all Arabs under the banner of Islam, the presence of Semitic peoples within them made parts of Syria and Palestine targets for Muslim armies from an early stage. However, there were other incentives for advances into the Levant aside from ethnic nationalism. It held great religious and cultural significance as the source of the Abrahamic roots of Islam and Arabic society as a whole. Jerusalem itself, already the centre of Judaism and Christianity and therefore revered for its connections to other Prophets of Islam such as Abraham, Solomon and Jesus, would become recognised as the site of the *mi'raj*, the Prophet's 'miraculous nocturnal ascent to heaven'.[17] Syria and Palestine also had long-standing trade connections with the Arab world, with Muhammad himself recognising the potential benefits to his burgeoning empire, having visited Syria several times. As with the Euphrates, there had probably never been a more favourable time to make advances into Syria and Palestine, given the destruction wrought by the Persian invasion, the war weariness of the Romans, and the destruction of the Ghassanid tribal alliance. That there was some evidence that Heraclius was attempting to resurrect this alliance will have worried Muhammad, for a strong, Roman-backed tribal system will have posed a great threat to the Muslim state. Rapid expansion into Syria was therefore viewed as something of a strategic necessity, as well as providing religious, cultural and financial benefits.

Recognising this opportunity, the Prophet had sent raids into Syrian territory since even before his conquest of Mecca in 630, including Khalid's saving of the Muslim force from destruction at Mu'ta in September 629. He was planning another expedition under Usama b. Zayd at the time of his death on 8 June 632; an expedition that Abu Bakr dispatched upon his accession. The exact aims of Usama's expedition are unknown but there is a possibility that the northern reaches of Muhammad's system of alliances had begun to unravel in the face of Roman attempts to re-establish the Ghassanid alliance. As with his decision to move against southern Iraq, buoyed by the successes of the Ridda

Wars and wary of Roman attempts at reconstruction, Abu Bakr launched a more adventurous expedition against the frontiers of the Roman Empire.

As with most other events in early Muslim history, the invasion of Syria and Palestine is illuminated by numerous accounts that pose many irreconcilable chronological problems. However, a general overview of the major occurrences can be extracted, dividing operations into three separate phases: the initial invasion in 633 until the arrival of Khalid at some time around Easter 634; the decisive engagements between the increasingly confident Muslim forces and the imperial armies sent against them, culminating at Yarmuk in August 636; and finally the decade-long consolidation of the territories won in the wake of the total collapse of Roman military resistance in Syria and the eventual establishing of the Romano-Muslim frontier.

To carry out this expedition, Abu Bakr ordered the bringing together of four separate forces under Amr b. al-As, Shurahbil b. Hasana, Abu Ubayda b. al-Jarrah and Khalid b. Said. However, there seems to have been some disagreement or at least second thoughts regarding the appointment of Khalid b. Said. He seems to have been sent north to bring more of the Arab tribes back into line, but a defeat forced him to withdraw. It may have been due to this that Khalid b. Said was replaced in his command by Yazid b. Abi Sufyan. These four commanders and their corps were largely independent of one another but there is some suggestion of a supreme commander, who had overall authority of joint operations. However, there is no consensus from the sources as to who it was – Amr, Yazid or Abu Ubayda.

Where these commanders were sent is more widely agreed upon. Amr was directed to drive into Palestine, an area he had personal experience of from his pre-Islamic commercial travels. It was also the region of the Roman Levant that was the most lightly defended. With the eastern field army deployed in northern Syria and Mesopotamia, it is likely that any troops in Palestine were irregular Arab tribesmen and semi-professional *limitanei*. Furthermore, these men were not kept as one large group ready for battle. Instead, they were divided across the provinces in small groups of 100–200 men and were 'best suited for passive, low-intensity stationary guard duty, or for defending well-fortified fixed positions'.[18] To face these defences, it is recorded that Abu Ubayda, Shurahbil and Yazid each set off with 7,000 men, while Amr had just 3,000, which correlates with other reports that the total size of Muslim forces after reinforcements arrived was 24,000.[19]

Leaving Medina in late-autumn 633, Amr followed the caravan route up the coast of the Red Sea before crossing the modern border of Saudi Arabia into Jordan near the head of the Gulf of Aqaba. From here, he drove across the Negev Desert towards Gaza, perhaps following a similar line to the modern frontier between Israel and Egypt. Upon emerging from the sands, Amr approached the villages of Dathin and Badan and conducted some negotiations with a local Roman leader, probably the garrison commander of Gaza. What exactly Amr would have hoped to gain from such negotiations can only be guessed at but the Roman commander will have had no reason to treat Amr as anything more than just another Arab raider. Unsurprisingly, these negotiations proved fruitless and a skirmish broke out between Amr's column and local Roman forces, sometime in February 634, known as the Battle of Dathin.[20] The resultant Muslim victory was a warning to the Romans of the potential potency of these 'raiders' but it was far from decisive and Amr seems to have focused more on establishing a base of operations somewhere between the Dead Sea and the Gulf of Aqaba.

The other Muslim commanders operated to the east of the Sea of Galilee, the River Jordan and the Dead Sea. While closer to the larger Roman troop concentrations in northern Syria and Mesopotamia, Abu Ubayda, Shurahbil and Yazid will have faced similar opposition to Amr – small, scattered garrisons used to defending fixed positions rather than chasing after highly mobile raiders.[21] Abu Ubayda was active in the Golan region south of Damascus and may have threatened the Ghassanid capital at al-Jabiya. He is also reported to have been responsible for the capture of the first Roman city by a Muslim force – Areopolis, also known as Ma'ab.[22] Yazid seems to have campaigned in the Balqa region to the east and north-east of the Dead Sea. From there he sent a detachment under Abu Umama across the Jordan to disperse a Roman force of perhaps 5,000 men under a certain Sergius, first at Araba and then again at al-Dabiya.[23] However, this entire episode is obscure and, as neither of these locations has been identified, it should be significantly downgraded in terms of importance. Having fought at Yamamah and only recently been sent to aide Usama b. Zayd, it is possible that Shurahbil and his forces were sent merely as backup to Abu Ubayda and Yazid and to keep an eye on those Arab tribes only just returned to their allegiance to Medina. However, as Shurahbil and his men disappear from the sources after his arrival in the region to the east of the Dead Sea, it is dangerous to rely on an argument of silence to determine his role in the early stages of the invasion of Syria.

While specifics and chronology is lacking for these early campaigns, and despite Abu Ubayda's attack on Areopolis, it seems that none of the four armies were directed at the large towns, cities or agricultural areas, sticking instead to the desert fringe where 'Arabic-speaking nomadic and semi-nomadic tribes would have been the dominant elements in the population'.[24] If the Muslims were not targeting major locations in Roman territory, it would explain why the Roman sources are almost completely silent about the presence of 24,000-man foreign armies operating in their lands, or why the field armies of Mesopotamia and northern Syria did not move against them sooner. With the success of these initial movements in establishing four armies at strategic points in and around the Roman frontier without attracting much in the way of an imperial response, Abu Bakr saw an opportunity to make sizeable gains. However, before sending these armies against the urban centres of Syria and Palestine, the caliph decided that they needed some reinforcement. Whether this was due to a need for more men or perhaps for the want of a seasoned and successful military commander to lead the attack on the Romans is not known for certain. But, whatever his reasons, in early 634 Abu Bakr sent for Khalid b. al-Walid.

Chronological Problems and Khalid's Arrival in Syria

Upon receiving his orders from Abu Bakr to travel to Syria, Khalid took little time in setting off with about half of the men he had originally brought from Yamamah to Iraq – between 500 and 800. However, how he got there and where he set off from is not agreed upon. Some interpretations suggest that Khalid left Iraq only a month after the armies of Amr, Shurahbil, Abu Ubayda and Yazid left Medina. It could be that Abu Bakr had planned to send Khalid to Syria all along, but the more likely explanation is that some of the Arab sources have placed the events in Syria several months too late. Some sources have Khalid going straight to Syria through the desert emporium of Palmyra just after the Battle of Firaz. Others have him crossing the desert from Dumat al-Jandal via Sab Biyar and its well. Perhaps the most suitable is that of Khalid receiving his orders in Hira and then moving back to Ayn al-Tamur before driving north-west through the desert to the environs of Palmyra, eventually arriving north-east of Damascus.

To save further time, Khalid seems to have chosen a dangerous route through a particularly waterless stretch of the Syrian Desert, identified sometimes as between Quraqir and Suwa, rather than follow the Euphrates north or the caravan route through Dumat al-Jandal to the south. However, Khalid's column could not carry enough water for all the men and horses for this six-day trek. The solution to this conundrum, taken from a Tayyi tribesman called Rafi b. Amr, is one of Khalid's more famous exploits. Some twenty camels were forced to drink large amounts of water and then had their mouths bound shut to prevent them from eating or chewing their cud, which would have spoiled the water. These camels were then slaughtered and the water in their stomachs harvested as it was needed during the desert crossing.[25]

However, again, this cannot be stated with certainty and with the arrival of Khalid in the Syrian theatre the chronology becomes almost irreparably muddled. Even the attempts of later Arabic historians to make sense of it failed to produce a coherent stream of events of the Muslim assault on the towns and cities of Syria, the Roman response and the Muslim breaking of Roman resistance. Now that there was direct contact between the Romans and the Muslims it might be expected that Roman sources would have paid closer attention to the military situation in Palestine and Syria and so help provide a more coherent account. However, the surviving accounts of Theophanes, Elias of Nisibis and Michael the Syrian do not provide the type of insight that might be hoped for. The vagueness of their work might have been a symptom of the general decline in Roman historiography over the preceding centuries or the

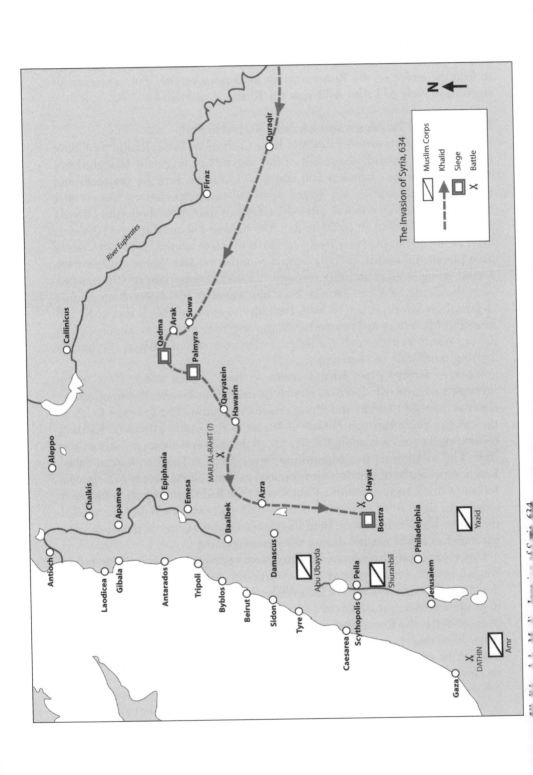

The Invasion of Syria, 634

Legend:
- Muslim Corps
- Khalid
- Siege
- Battle

result of the upheaval caused by decades of war and hence their dependence on the same contradictory Arab sources. However, the most frequently agreed upon chronology sees the major events begin with the siege of Bostra, followed by the Battle of Ajnadayn, the captures of Pella, Damascus, Baalbek, Emesa and finally the Battle of Yarmuk and its aftermath.[26]

Regardless of the route he took, Khalid seems to have emerged from the desert at Suwa, and after passing through Palmyra he managed to inflict a defeat on the Ghassanids, possibly at Marj al-Rahit, while they were celebrating a festival, perhaps Easter, which in 634 fell on 24 April. His sudden appearance to the north-east of Damascus seems to have subverted whatever pre-existing or improvised defences the Romans had in place to deal with the other Arabian forces; although such hyperbole might be misleading as the Roman military situation in the Levant seems to have been almost of an ad hoc nature rather than the kind of organised military effort that might be expected from them. Following his dispersal of the Ghassanids Khalid then marched south to Bostra to join up with the forces of Abu Ubayda, Shurahbil and Yazid.

Wanting to gain the plaudits of capturing Bostra before Khalid's arrival, Abu Ubayda and Shurahbil are thought to have attacked the city only to find themselves outmatched by the garrison. It took the arrival of Khalid and perhaps Yazid to restore the situation. A second engagement the following day saw the combined Muslim forces drive the garrison back behind the walls of Bostra and by the middle of July 634 the city had capitulated and agreed to pay the *jizya* tax.

There is an alternative and more colourful version of the capture of Bostra. Before the Muslim attack on the city, the Roman commander called Romanus challenged Khalid to single combat. With the growing reputation of his prowess in such confrontations, Khalid willingly accepted. However, as the two were preparing to engage, a religious debate broke out and, after asking some questions about Islam, Romanus pronounced the *shahadah*, accepting Allah as the one true god and Muhammad as the Prophet. The Roman commander then led an Arab contingent under Abdur-Rahman, the son of Abu Bakr, through an underground tunnel that bypassed the city defences. These infiltrators opened the gates to the besieging Muslim forces, leaving the city to be quickly overrun. The credence such an episode should be given is probably negligible as the name of the Roman commander conjures up ideas of storytelling symbolism – Romanus succumbs to the Muslim faith.

The Battle of Ajnadayn

Despite the capture of Bostra by mid-July 634, the Muslims did not have long to celebrate this success as reports came in from spies deployed by Shurahbil that the Romans were marshalling a large force near Ajnadayn, about 40km south-east of Jerusalem. Heraclius himself seems to have been in Emesa, modern-day Homs in Syria, and, whilst his presence might have originally been for administrative and religious reasons, it quickly developed into that of a strategic overseer to 'devise military responses [and]. . . to engage in diplomatic negotiations'.[27] However, despite the presence of the emperor and the possibility that the Roman force was commanded by his brother, Theodore, the numbers recorded for the Roman force at Ajnadayn are spectacularly exaggerated.[28] Modern attempts to reconstruct the size of this Roman army suggest that it was not more than 10,000, with a core of Armenians under their own general, Wardan.[29] Conversely, the combination of the armies of Khalid, Abu Ubayda, Shurahbil, Yazid and Amr perhaps reached 15,000.

That the Romans might have found themselves outnumbered at Ajnadayn suggests the state to which their resources had fallen and that they had underestimated the threat posed by the Muslims, viewing them as just another example of the chronic raids of previous generations. However, that the Muslim commanders struck before Theodore could gather a more substantial force should not be underestimated.

It appears that this first major engagement between Roman and Muslim forces was a bitterly contested one. While there are numerous stories of subterfuge and personal bravery, it would appear that it was Muslim numerical superiority and the ability of the Muslim supreme commander – separately identified as Khalid or Amr – to take advantage of it. To that end, the Muslim force seems to have been divided into three main corps with three smaller supporting groups, one held in reserve under Yazid and the others deployed as flank guards. Theodore probably arrayed his men in a similar formation. The opening moves of the battle saw the longer-range Roman archers attempting to reduce the numbers of their opponents or get them to break formation. This was then followed by several duels before the Muslim army launched a general attack that saw some ferocious fighting but no clear winner by nightfall. A second day of similarly ferocious fighting saw Wardan killed and the Muslim flank guards committed, but the Romans still did not break. It was only when Yazid's reserve entered the fray that the weight of numbers finally told and Theodore's army began to crumble. Splitting into three separate groups, the surviving Romans made for Gaza, Jaffa and Jerusalem respectively but many were cut down by a ruthlessly pressed Arab pursuit.

Despite their army not being of the highest quality, the importance of the Roman defeat at Ajnadayn should not be underestimated. Khalid's march across the desert from the banks of the Euphrates and the subsequent fall of Bostra had greatly undermined whatever defences the Romans had been able to throw up along the frontiers, but this defeat of Theodore's army was a major blow to the defence of the entire Roman east. As Theodore and Heraclius withdrew from Emesa and retreated back to northern Syria, the Muslim army was left free to attack wherever it wanted. In the face of this abandonment, the Romans, both military and civilian, fled 'to the apparent security of walled towns in Palestine and Syria'.[30] It is understandable why the Romans would

1. Justinian I: gold solidus, issued between 527–538 from Constantinople mint. Obverse: helmet, cuirass, spear and shield, DN IVSTINIANVS PP AVC. Reverse: angel holding long cross and cross on globe, VICTORIA AVCCCA CONOB.

2. Justin II: gold solidus, issued between 565–578 from Constantinople mint. Obverse: diadem, cuirass and globe of Victory, DN IVSTINVS PP AVI . Reverse: Constantinople seated with helmet, tunic, mantle, aegis, spear, cross on globe, VICTORIA AVGGG **D* CONOB.

3. Tiberius II Constantine: gold solidus, issued between 579–582 from Constantinople mint. Obverse: crown, cuirass, shield and crossed globe, Dm TIb CONSTANT PP AVI. Reverse: cross on steps, VICTORIA AVCCE CONOB.

4. Mauricius: gold solidus, issued between 583–601 from Constantinople mint. Obverse: crown, cuirass, helmet, cross on globe, DN MAVRC TIb PP AV. Reverse: angel with long cross with P and cross on globe, VICTORIA AVCCI CONOB

(All coin images courtesy of Noble Numismatics – www.noble.com.au)

5. Phocas: gold solidus, issued between 602–603 from Constantinople mint. Obverse: cuirass and crown with cross, holding cross on globe, ON FOCAS PERP AVI. Reverse: angel with long cross with P and cross on globe VICTOR[I]A AVGG B.

6. Heraclius: light weight gold solidus, issued 611–613 from Constantinople mint. Obverse: crown, cuirass with cross, ** HERACLIVS PP AVI. Reverse: cross on steps and star, VICTORIA AVG **.

7. Heraclius, Constantine III and Heraklonas: gold solidus, issued between 635–636 from Constantinople mint. Obverse: Heraclius centre, Constantine III left, and Heraklonas right, cross above. Reverse: cross on steps, monogram of Heraclius left, VICTORIA AVGUE CONOB.

8. Constans II and Constantine IV: gold solidus, issued between 654–659 from Constantinople mint. Obverse: crowned Constans left, Constantine right, DN CONSTATINUS C CONSTI. Reverse: cross on steps, VICTORIA AVGUE CONOB+.

(All coin images courtesy of Noble Numismatics – www.noble.com.au)

9. Khusro I: silver drachm, issued in c.570 from Ctesiphon mint. Obverse: crown, name in inner margin, crescent moons on outer margin. Reverse: fire altar with attendants.

10. Hormizd IV: silver drachm, issued c.582 from Ahwaz mint. Obverse: winged crown, name in inner margin, crescent moons and stars in outer. Reverse: fire altar with attendants.

11. Khusro II: silver drachm, issued c.627 from Balkh mint. Obverse: winged crown, name in inner margin, crescent moons and stars in outer. Reverse: fire altar with attendants.

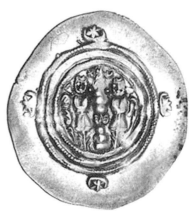

12. Yazdgerd III: silver drachm, issued from Gundeshapur mint. Obverse: beard, winged crown, name in inner margin, crescent moons and stars in outer. Reverse: fire altar with attendants, crescent moons and stars in outer.

13. Band-e Kaisar,
Shushtar, Iran.
(*Courtesy of Ali Aghah*)

14. Battle Between
Heraclius and Khosrau
(*The Legend of the True
Cross* by Piero della
Francesca, Basilica of S
Francesco, Arezzo, Ital

15. Church of the Holy Sepulchre, Jerusalem. (© *Anton Croos, 2008*)

16. Column of Phoc
Rome.

Ctesiphon. (*Courtesy of the Library of Congress, USA*)

Greek Fire – 'the fleet of the Romans setting ablaze the fleet of the enemies'. (*Codex Skylites tritensis, Bibliteca Nacional de Madrid*)

19. Hagia Sophia. (© *Osvaldo Gago, 2008*)

20. Hagia Sophia Interior. (© *Christophe Meneboeuf, 2011*)

21. St. Helena and Heraclius taking the True Cross to Jerusalem (Miguel Jiménez y Martín Bernat, 1481).

Justinian's Court. (*San Vitale,*
Ravenna, courtesy of the Yorck Project)

23. Justinian. (*San Vitale, Ravenna,*
courtesy of the Yorck Project)

24. Walls of Constantinople: a restored section of the walls near the Pege Gate. (© *Bigdaddy1204*)

25. Constantinople: the Pege Gate. (*Courtesy of CrniBombarder!!!*)

have thought in such a defensive manner, as it had worked in the past and there was little reason to assume that the well-established fortifications of such cities, towns and strongholds, sufficiently manned, would not survive any assault that the Arabs could conjure up. Once the raiders had had their fill of the Roman countryside and unprotected minor settlements, they would return home.

In the past, this would have been a sound strategy. However, in the 630s, it was to prove disastrous. In identifying these Muslim forces with the endemic Arab raiders of the past the Romans had failed to appreciate the cohesion, determination and perseverance that Islam had instilled in them. This meant that by hiding behind walls the Romans were diluting their own military potential as these garrisons became isolated and their offensive options limited and predictable, and, once the Muslims proved able to capture such strongholds through diplomacy or blockade, the Roman defensive position unravelled.

Ajnadayn also brought into sharper focus the political, religious and personal problems at the centre of the Empire. While he did survive Ajnadayn, the battle marked the beginning of the end of Theodore's career. Returning to the emperor at Emesa, the brothers seem to have fallen out over the defeat and Theodore's criticism of Heraclius' marriage to their niece, Martina – Theodore is recorded as saying of his imperial brother that 'his sin is continually before him'.[31] An angry Heraclius replaced his brother with Vahan and Theodore Trithurios and sent his brother to Constantinople. The dating of Theodore's despatch to the capital is uncertain as there is some evidence that he took part in the Roman counteroffensive in 636, reoccupying Emesa and Damascus, but at some stage he was removed to Constantinople, where he was imprisoned and humiliated by Martina.

This public humiliation of Theodore encouraged the military hierarchy present at Constantinople to plot to remove Heraclius, Martina, Heraclius Constantine and Heraklonas from power. The most prominent members of the conspiracy were leading Armenian commanders such as David Saharuni and Varaztirochs, and the *magister officiorum* Theodore, son of the humiliated Theodore and, therefore, the emperor's nephew. Their plan was to force Heraclius from the throne either through political pressure or, more realistically, bloodshed, and replace him with his illegitimate son, John Athalarichos, who had evidently returned from being a hostage with the Avars. However, before the plotters could execute their plan they were betrayed by an unnamed palace official and all were subsequently arrested.

Varaztirochs, who seems to have been reticent to kill Heraclius and his family and may have only been privy to the plot, was treated with some leniency, being exiled to Africa.[32] Athalarichos and Theodore were also allowed to live in exile but, due to their membership of the imperial family and therefore potential future threats, not before enduring the horrendous ordeal of political mutilation. It is perhaps with Heraclius and his religiously infused reign that such disfigurement was first used to remove an individual from the succession. As the emperor became increasingly identified as the temporal representative of God, it became almost paramount that he be unencumbered by any physical defect. To this end, both Athalarichos and Theodore had their hands and nose removed. Athalarichos was then exiled to Prinkipo Island in the Marmara Sea while Theodore was sent to Gaudomelete, probably a late Roman name for the islands of Malta, with his captors given specific orders by Heraclius to cut off one of his legs upon arrival.[33]

Despite the failure of this attempted coup, the fact that there had been one at all will have shaken morale. The accusation that Heraclius had become tainted by the incestuous nature of his marriage to Martina will have struck particularly hard at the increasingly religious heart of the seventh-century Roman Empire. The plot of Athalarichos and its accompanying betrayal of family members, something else that Heraclius had relied heavily upon, and the deepening military crisis on the eastern frontier were increasingly seen as the divine consequences of the sin the emperor had committed in the choice of his second wife. The plot also highlighted the weakness of Heraclius' military position, for when David Saharuni escaped his prison and made his way back to his Armenian brethren, the emperor did not have the military strength to bring him to justice. It had been just six years since Heraclius had returned triumphant from the war with the Persians but now, as 634 came to an end, the Roman Empire seemed in little better military or political state than the Sassanids. And it was about to get much worse.

Chapter 7

636 – The Year of the Muslim Beast

God helping him, [Heraclius] discovered, that his empire would be laid waste by circumcised races.

Fredegarius, Chron. 65

The Death of Abu Bakr, the Succession of Umar and the Fall of Damascus

In the aftermath of Ajnadayn, it is suggested that the Romans attempted to disrupt Muslim movements by destroying river crossings and even the river banks, flooding much of the Jordan valley. However, while the Muslims do seem to have moved back east of the Jordan, ostensibly giving chase to Roman forces that survived the battle but perhaps also to prevent an overextension of their lines of communication, it did little to prevent Muslim advances continuing apace. The next targets were the twin cities of Pella and Scythopolis, also known as Fahl and Baysan, which sat almost directly opposite each other across the Jordan. Another Khalid victory before the walls of Pella saw the city invested in perhaps a four-month blockade before capitulating, while Scythopolis seems to have fallen to Amr and Shurahbil without a fight. The exact dates of Ajnadayn and these subsequent manoeuvrings around the Jordan are disputed with some placing Ajnadayn as late as January 635 but the more likely dating is in late-July 634. This earlier date is usually preferred as 'it is generally supposed to have occurred during the last months of Abu Bakr's caliphate, and the news of the Muslim's victory is supposed to have reached him on his deathbed.'[1]

Abu Bakr fell ill in early-August 634 after catching a chill; although there is some suggestion that it was the lingering effects of being poisoned a year previously. Realising he was dying and wary of the potential for a repeat of the infighting that had marred the death of the Prophet, Abu Bakr, after much consultation with his advisers and colleagues, decided to appoint his own successor. The choice eventually fell on Umar b. al-Khattab. Having pronounced his choice and composed his will, Abu Bakr died on Monday 23 August 634 and was buried beside Muhammad. Despite having his detractors as someone who usurped the caliphate from Ali, Abu Bakr had been an invaluable early supporter of and adviser to Muhammad. Once he assumed power, by whatever means, it is difficult to deny his territorial successes. By building on the religious, social and political foundations established by the Prophet, in a little

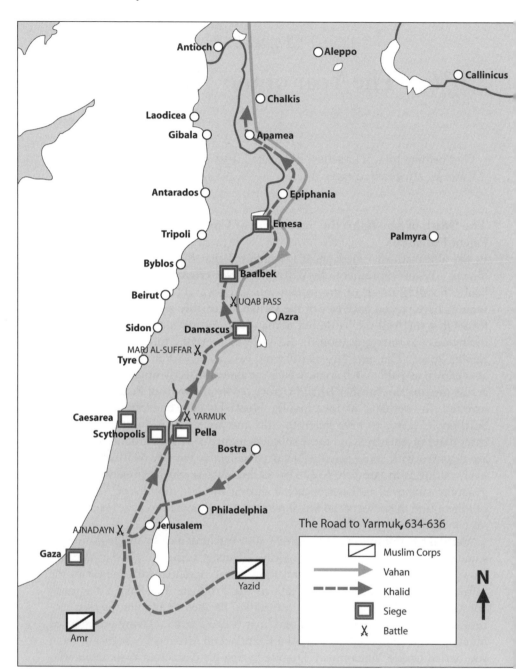

The Road to Yarmuk, 634–636.

over two years as caliph Abu Bakr had taken the Arab caliphate from part of a network of alliances across the Arabian Peninsula to a burgeoning pan-Arabic state capable of squaring up to and defeating two of the most powerful empires of the ancient world.

Umar was not a popular choice. He was feared rather than loved and, like Abu Bakr, was faced with dissension from those who thought that Ali should have ascended to the caliphate. However, the new caliph quickly proved himself to be a gifted orator and a shrewd politician, garnering large-scale support from the poor and the Bedouin through his emancipation of many slaves taken during the Ridda Wars. He also attempted to bridge the divide with Ali by delivering disputed lands to him. Militarily, it is usually stated that Umar's accession marked a turn towards consolidation of conquered territories rather than further expansion. However, this may only be due to his accession coinciding with the lull following the Battle of Ajnadayn, for Umar's reign would not only see a continuation of the conquests but their acceleration in almost every direction. However, perhaps the most important task performed by Umar was in addressing the growing administrative demands of the increasing size of the caliphate, bringing a political and administrative structure to the Arab territories that by the time of his death in 644 would stretch from modern Libya in the west to the Indus Valley in the east and from the Gulf of Aden in the south to the Oxus River and the Caucasus Mountains in the north.

However, despite Umar's long-term positives for the organisation of the Arab caliphate, one of his initial decisions was a peculiar one. As the combined Muslim forces now moved towards Damascus, word arrived that Khalid was to be removed from supreme command of the army, if he truly held such a position, and replaced by Abu Ubayda. Whether there was some familial animosity between them – they were cousins – or Umar feared Khalid's prowess was detracting from the power of Islam is not known for certain. There is also some suggestion that Abu Ubayda hid this transfer of authority from Khalid until after the assault on Damascus was completed, perhaps because he wanted to take credit for any victory or because he recognised the skills of Khalid. Whatever the reasoning, Khalid was removed from any position of command superiority he might have held over Abu Ubayda, Amr, Yazid and Shurahbil.

However, it did not disrupt the Muslim juggernaut, and as the remnants of the Roman forces fell back on Damascus the Muslims were in hot pursuit. There may have been a bloody battle on the plains south of Damascus at Marj al-Suffar, with Khalid winning another victory at great cost, losing as many as 4,000 men. However, due to the great differences in the chronological placement of this encounter and suggestions that it may even be a confused retelling of Ajnadayn, Marj al-Suffar may not have taken place in the preamble to Damascus or even at all. When the Damascene garrison did not sally forth to offer battle, the city was tightly invested in a blockade, with each of the Muslim corps – Khalid, Shurahbil, Yazid and Abu Ubayda – taking up positions opposite the city's gates. The Muslims also sent a separate detachment under Abu al-Darda to garrison the nearby village of Barzeh. The importance of this small satellite garrison may be demonstrated by their ability to provide advanced warning to the besieging forces at Damascus of a Roman relief force approaching from Emesa. This allowed the Muslim commanders to send a detachment of their forces to intercept and eventually defeat this relief force in the Uqab Pass, north of Damascus.

This siege seems to have lasted at least four months, perhaps more, only ending in late-August/early-September 635 when, exhausted by their exertions and demoralised by the lack of aid from Heraclius, the Damascenes opened their gates to one of the Muslim commanders. However, once again, the sources do not agree on which commander – Khalid, Abu Ubayda or Yazid – was involved in this negotiation and the waters are further muddied by the simultaneous breaking into the city by another of the commanders. Whoever they were, the two commanders met in the middle of the city and agreed to treat Damascus as a city that had surrendered peaceably.

The Roman Calamity at Yarmuk
With Yazid left in command of Damascus, Khalid, Abu Ubayda and Shurahbil spent the last months of 635 driving north, capturing Baalbek and then Emesa, from where Heraclius had only recently retreated. The rapidity of the collapse of the urban backbone of Syria will have startled Heraclius and perhaps finally awakened the emperor to the fact that the Arabs they were facing posed a far greater threat than the more traditional raiders. The defeat at Dathin could have easily been written off as a skirmish, whilst Ajnadayn could be explained by the suddenness and superiority in numbers of the Muslim attack. However, the losses of Damascus, Baalbek and Emesa could not be so easily explained.

In response to this revelation, Heraclius and his generals began to gather together as many men as they could find in the hope of delivering a decisive knockout blow to the Muslims. As is to be expected, the estimates for the force placed under the command of Vahan and Theodore Trithurios are truly staggering in their exaggeration, ranging anywhere up to 250,000 and even beyond.[2] It would have been difficult enough for the Romans to have recreated their usual military establishment of the East – a 20,000-strong field army – in the interlude between the end of the Persian War and the Arab invasion, let alone raise hundreds of thousands of men in just a few short months.

What remained of the eastern field army, attested contingents from Antioch, Chalkis, Aleppo, Mesopotamia and Emesa, as well as any remaining forces from the defeats at Ajnadayn, Pella and Damascus and any further allied contingents from the Armenians, Ghassanids and even some Slavs might have produced a force approaching 40,000 men. However, even this may have been beyond Heraclius' military capabilities in the 630s. If the emperor had not been able to raise an army of such a size to fight the Persians, how would he be able to do so against the Muslims in a period when he had overseen some demilitarisation? It may therefore be more correct to envisage a Roman force at the lower end of the range of 15,000–40,000.[3]

The sources for the size of the combined Muslim force at Yarmuk are far less extravagant than those for the Roman army, with many of the primary and secondary sources settling at around the 24,000 mark.[4] There is also some suggestion of a steady stream of reinforcements, perhaps totalling as many as 6,000, reaching the Muslim camp throughout the battle.[5] Even taking into account a margin for error for both armies, this would suggest that, while the likelihood remains that the Romans did enjoy something of a numerical superiority, the opposing forces at Yarmuk were far more comparable in size than is usually supposed.

As Vahan and Theodore Trithurios marched south, the Muslims decided to not attempt to face them until they had reunited their own forces and chosen a more advantageous battlefield. Therefore, they relinquished many of their territorial gains, allowing the Romans to reoccupy Emesa, Baalbek and Damascus without a fight. Retreating south, the Muslims found themselves in the potentially dangerous situation of being surrounded by the advancing Roman army and the still sizeable garrison forces in cities such as Caesarea. However, it is possible that the Romans were also wary of committing to battle until their preparations were complete and may even have harboured some hopes of resolving this confrontation through diplomacy and subterfuge. Therefore, what followed was something of a game of cat and mouse, which has led some historians to refer to the eventual showdown as the Jabiya-Yarmuk campaign rather than an isolated Battle of Yarmuk, with several weeks of manoeuvres and preliminary engagements before a final confrontation in mid-August 636.

The decisive strategic move came when Khalid advised Abu Ubayda to fall back towards what is now modern Daraa in the southwest of Syria, near the border with Jordan. This move not only protected the Muslim communications with Arabia by putting the river Yarmuk in the way of any Roman flanking attack, it also provided them with a 'topographically and strategically strong position' should a battle take place.[6] This was because by taking up a position along the eastern side of the plain of Yarmuk, Khalid and Abu Ubayda were forcing the Romans to approach them from the broken ground of the hills to the north and so place themselves between the Muslim force and the ravines and valleys that surrounded the Yarmuk river and its Raqqad and Allan tributaries. Most importantly was that the Raqqad and its gorge, which was to be directly behind the Roman lines, only had one crossing point – a bridge at Ayn Dhakar.

Recognising the strength of their position, the Muslims seem to have launched a skirmishing attack on the approaching Roman column around Jabiya to the north of the eventual battlefield. The Romans beat off this attack

but it is possible that the Muslim commanders meant for this minor engagement to further encourage their Roman counterparts into fighting on the
Yarmuk plain. This choice of battlefield was also a good one in terms of
logistics because the plain of Yarmuk not only provided space to make full use
of the Muslim cavalry, it provided enough pasture and water to sustain both the
Arab army and the Roman forces, further encouraging the Romans to take up
the gauntlet that had been thrown down to them.

While the Romans may have been slow to force an encounter in the hope of
encouraging the Muslim army to break up, instead the repeated delays only
served to reveal and deepen the cracks in their own hierarchy. There were
clashes between Roman soldiers and the Syrian population over requisitions,
and the restored administrator of Damascus, Mansur, refused to provide Vahan
with supplies as he passed through. However, the most important dissension
was to be found amongst the ranks of the Roman generals. Vahan had been
appointed as the supreme commander of the force by Heraclius but the poly-
glot nature of the army seems to have caused tension. Vahan and Trithurios
mistrusted each other, with the latter perhaps upset at being overlooked for the
supreme command. Two of the Roman generals, George and a man identified
as Buccinator, also seem to have had a dispute over which of them was superior
in rank.[7] While these four high-ranking generals played out their personal disputes, the Ghassanids and their commander Jabalah seem to have been relegated from the decision making and even much of the fighting, despite the
insight they could have provided on their Muslim opponents.[8]

Such internal squabbles could have not only affected Roman performance on
the battlefield but may also have clouded the strategic thinking of Vahan and
his subordinates in the weeks leading to battle. Despite the strategically dis-
advantageous position amongst the gorges of the Yarmuk and Raqqad rivers,
Vahan may have been almost forced into making a decisive move to the Yarmuk
plain to assert his authority and keep his army together. Of course, the danger
of such a position would only come into play should the Romans lose the
tactical exchanges and, despite the losses at Dathin, Ajnadayn, Pella and
Damascus, this was not something that the Romans would have legislated for.
As for the Muslim leadership, there was one major decision taken. On the eve of
battle, a meeting of the Muslim commanders saw Abu Ubayda cede supreme
command to Khalid. Whether Abu Ubayda capitulated to the majority opinion
of his subordinates or genuinely thought that Khalid was the better choice for
the upcoming contest is unknown.

When the two forces finally squared up to each other on 15 August 636
across the Yarmuk plain their initial deployments were similar, with their main
infantry forces divided into four separate battle groups – left flank, left centre,
right centre and right flank, supported by units of cavalry. The Roman right,
commanded by George, was probably deployed a mile to the north of the
Yarmuk gorge. The two sections of the Roman centre were likely comprised of

the armies of Vahan and Theodore Trithurios while the left wing, which would seem to be dangerously exposed in the middle of the wide open plain, was commanded by Buccinator. In an attempt to take advantage of their numerical superiority in infantry the Roman line seems to have stretched up to 13km from north to south. Each of these four Roman divisions had an accompanying cavalry force, while Vahan also seems to have retained a sizeable cavalry reserve under his command in the rear, perhaps to protect the Roman camp and the all-important bridge over the Raqqad at Ayn Dhakar. Ghassanid cavalry also seems to have been deployed to protect the Roman rear and this bridge, as well as a skirmishing force.

In order to prevent being outflanked by the sheer length of the Roman line, the Muslims deployed their forces in a similar manner. Yazid and his corps were deployed on the Muslim left opposite George; Abu Ubayda commanded the left centre and Shurahbil the right centre, while their right flank opposite Buccinator was given to Amr, who had marched north from Palestine to join the Muslim army retreating from Damascus. The Muslim flanks were each supported by a cavalry detachment, while a single detachment supported Abu Ubayda and Shurahbil in the centre. Similar to Vahan, Khalid retained command of the majority of the Muslim cavalry, held in the rear as a reserve. It is

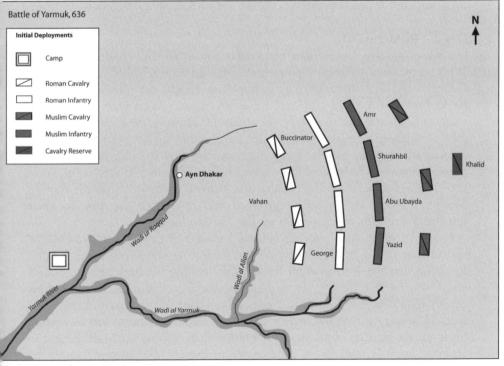

Battle of Yarmuk, 636: Deployments.

worth noting that, despite the seemingly structured outlook that these initial deployments give, the Battle of Yarmuk better resembled a series of almost separate engagements thanks to the distance between many of the corps, with the commanders given an independence of movement within an overall strategic plan.[9]

Day 1 – 15 August 636

At dawn, with the armies arrayed a mile apart, a series of duels took place. This had become a regular Muslim tactic in an attempt to not only buoy the morale of their own men and damage that of their opponent but to also kill as many enemy officers as possible before the battle commenced. As they had a group of soldiers, the *mubarizun*, trained especially for this kind of one-on-one fighting, it is not surprising that the Muslims won the majority of these duels. By midday, tired of these preliminaries and wary of losing anymore officers, Vahan ordered a probing attack along the entirety of his front line to gauge the strength of the Muslim infantry. Such a broad frontal offensive would have quickly exposed any weakness in the Muslim line but it seems that Vahan only committed a third of his infantry to this attack and the Muslim veterans were able to cope with it. This relatively low-intensity combat lasted throughout much of the day and, despite some minor flashpoints, neither side were able to make any sort of headway before contact was broken off as the sun went down.

Day 2 – 16 August 636

On the second day, Vahan launched a more concerted effort to destroy his foe. With his two centre divisions pinning the Muslim centre, Vahan launched both George's and Buccinator's wings in ferocious attacks that drove the Muslim flanks back. Both Yazid and Amr were forced to commit their cavalry contingents in an attempt to restore the situation. However, even with this reinforcement, both Muslim wings began to crumble under the weight of the Roman attack. One popular story suggests that only the intervention of the Muslim women, who berated those men who had retreated back to camp, saved the Muslim flanks from total collapse for, shamed by their taunts, the routing Muslim infantry and cavalry regrouped and re-entered the fray on their respective flanks in time to shore up the Muslim lines.

However, once again proving himself a master of cavalry deployment, the real saviour of the Muslim army on the second day of Yarmuk was Khalid. Realising that the Roman right flank, while making headway against Yazid's corps, was moving slowly due to their interlocking of shields, Khalid led his cavalry reserve to the more embattled northern flank of the Muslim army. Here it could be argued that Buccinator's offensive had been almost too successful. Such was the ferocity of his attack that rather than causing the Muslim right to crumble inwards towards its own centre to initiate the surrounding of the Muslim army, it had retreated backwards towards its camp. This may not seem

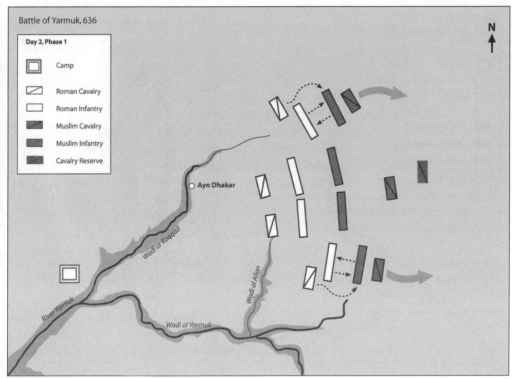

Battle of Yarmuk, 636: Day 2, Phase 1.

negative for Buccinator and the Romans as a whole but in the grand scheme of the battle, and with someone as astute and fast-acting as Khalid in the field, it quickly became so. In his haste to press the retreating Muslim right, Buccinator lost contact with the divisions of the Roman left centre that were providing protection for his own right flank, leaving his corps exposed.

Recognising this vulnerability, Khalid rallied the Muslim infantry and sent Amr's cavalry around the Muslim northern flank to attack Buccinator's left. At the same time, Khalid led his cavalry reserve into the gap opening between the Roman left and left centre. The combination of attack from three sides first stalled Buccinator's advance before forcing him back. Buoyed by this success, the Muslim centre under Abu Ubayda and Shurahbil then launched a counter-attack that pushed back the Roman centre, opening a similar gap between the Roman right centre and George's advancing right wing, into which Khalid again launched his cavalry reserve. With Yazid's cavalry attacking his right, George faced a similar three-sided attack to Buccinator and was obliged to retreat back to his original position. Therefore, in spite of a hard day's fighting and Roman breakthroughs on the flanks, Khalid's restorative attacks saw the battle lines reform along a similar line as they had started the day. This failure

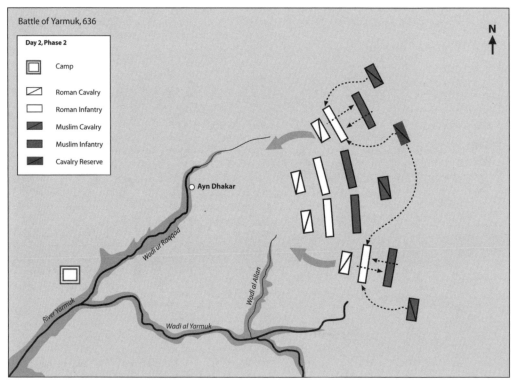

Battle of Yarmuk, 636: Day 2, Phase 2.

of Vahan's grand attack plan seems to have greatly disheartened the Romans, while the Muslims were emboldened by their successful repelling of such an attack and the daring of their commander.

Day 3 – 17 August 636

The successful counter-attacks of Khalid's cavalry seem to have shaken Vahan enough for him and his generals to overlook the fact that initially his plan had been a success. The Muslim flanks had crumbled under the onslaught of George and particularly Buccinator, and a similar attack orchestrated with more coordination between the flanks and the centre so as not to present Khalid with gaps to exploit may well have carried the day for the Romans. However, on the third day, Vahan chose instead to focus solely on the Muslim right flank, with little or no fighting taking place on the southern end of the battle between George and Yazid. While the Roman right centre fought a holding engagement with Abu Ubayda's corps, a more concerted attack was launched by the Roman left centre and Buccinator's left wing. However, in something of a repeat of the previous day, once Buccinator and the Roman left centre began to drive back the forces of Amr and Shurahbil, gaps opened between the Roman divisions

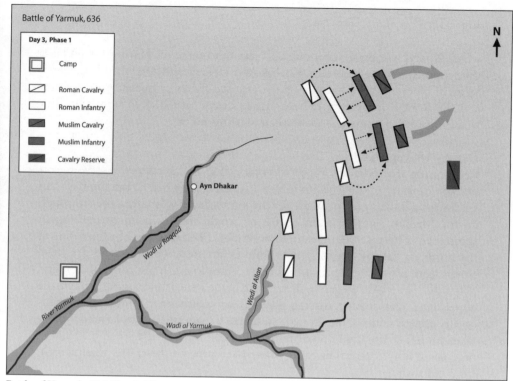

Battle of Yarmuk, 636: Day 3, Phase 1.

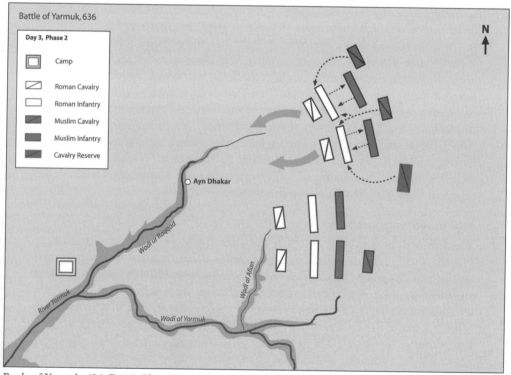

Battle of Yarmuk, 636: Day 3, Phase 2.

which Khalid was once again quick to take advantage of. Having forced back the supporting Roman cavalry, Khalid, Abu Ubayda and Amr then launched a series of bloody cavalry assaults on the exposed flanks of Buccinator's division and the Roman left centre. These caused heavy casualties to both sides but again forced the Romans back to their starting point.

Day 4 – 18 August 636

Recognising that Khalid's repeated committing of his cavalry reserve meant that the capacity of the Muslim forces was being stretched to the limit, Vahan stuck with a similar plan of attack for the fourth day. By forcing a breakthrough on the Muslim right or right centre he would force Khalid to once again commit all of his reserves in restorative attacks. Then with the Muslim forces of the northern half of the battlefield fully committed, Vahan would use fresh troops from his own right flank and right centre to crush the corps of Amr and Shurahbil. The plan began well as Buccinator's men once again gained the upper hand against Amr, forcing the Muslim commander to deploy all of his cavalry just to contain the Roman advance. Vahan must have scented victory when his left centre then drove Shurahbil's right centre back, forcing Khalid to once again fully commit his cavalry reserve to prevent the entire Muslim right from collapsing.

However, before Vahan could order the attack from his right centre and George's right wing, Khalid launched the corps of Abu Ubayda and Yazid in a spoiling attack against their opposites, which prevented the Roman right from delivering what might have been the *coup de grâce*. In an attempt to free themselves from these attacks, the Roman right and right centre threw all of their archers, both mounted and foot, against Abu Ubayda and Yazid. This action gives the fourth day of the Battle of Yarmuk the name with which it is remembered in many Muslim chronicles – 'the Day of Lost Eyes' – as large numbers of Muslim soldiers were left at least partially blinded by the superior range of the Roman archery. However, these mutilations were not endured in vain as Abu Ubayda and Yazid were successful in preventing the Roman right from having any major impact on the fighting to the north. Without these reinforcements, the Roman left and left centre were once again forced back by the repeated flank attacks of the Muslim cavalry.

Day 5 – 19 August 636

The failure of his second grand plan was a decisive blow to Vahan's confidence, as well as to his manpower. The extent of this disconsolation was highlighted on the fifth day when the Romans failed to array for battle. Instead, Vahan sent an emissary to the Muslims to ask for a brief truce. Recognising that the morale and fighting strength of the Romans were hanging by a thread, in declining this offer of a truce, Khalid showed his determination to take full advantage of their predicament. In order to do so, instead of attempting to force battle, he spent most of the day covertly gathering together virtually all of his available cavalry – perhaps upward of 8,000 men – into one vast strike force hidden behind his lines. However, it is important to note that not all of the Muslim cavalry were used for this force. A small detachment of about 500 men under Dharar b. al-Azwar was sent under cover of night to capture the bridge over the Raqqad gorge at Ayn Dhakar. The success of this nocturnal venture and the ability of Dharar to hold the bridge against Roman and Ghassanid counter-attacks would have drastic consequences for Vahan's army on the sixth and final day of the battle.

Day 6 – 20 August 636

The determination of Khalid, the success of Dharar and the growing disillusionment in the Roman camp meant that in the hours since the disengagement at the end of the fourth day there had been a complete role reversal in who directed affairs. Since the beginning of the Roman counter-attack earlier in 636, the Muslims had been on the defensive, retreating in the face of Roman advances and reacting to Vahan's manoeuvres on the plain of Yarmuk. However, now, it was Khalid's turn to dictate battle. When both forces arrayed to continue the fighting on the sixth day it was the Muslim infantry who launched a general attack along the length of their line. With the Roman infantry committed to battle, Khalid then struck with his cavalry force at the Roman left. Due to the overwhelming size of this cavalry corps, Buccinator's cavalry was quickly swept aside, leaving his infantry dangerously exposed. Vahan seems to have recognised the huge flank attack that was unfolding and ordered his three surviving cavalry squadrons to converge on his cavalry reserve at the rear of the Roman formation for a counter-attack. However, whether through poor coordination, communication, or the sheer rapidity of Khalid's attack, the Roman cavalry were unable to respond in time to save Buccinator. Under the combined weight of Amr's frontal assault and Khalid's flank attack, the Roman left, which had on several occasions come close to winning the battle for Vahan, completely disintegrated.

Despite large numbers of Roman soldiers still fighting, the collapse of Buccinator's left wing completely undermined the position of the Roman army, particularly as the remnant of Buccinator's men were driven into the rest of the Romans. The disruption this caused was compounded by Amr's corps now wheeling around to assault the exposed flank of the Roman left centre. Vahan had one last card to play in a counter-attack from his congregating cavalry force. However, true to his growing reputation, Khalid refused to allow the Roman cavalry time to organise and, as soon as Buccinator's flank collapsed, he threw his cavalry strike force in a lightning attack. Demoralised, disorganised and taken by surprise, the Roman cavalry was swept aside, fleeing into the hills to the north and leaving what remained of the Roman infantry to their annihilation.

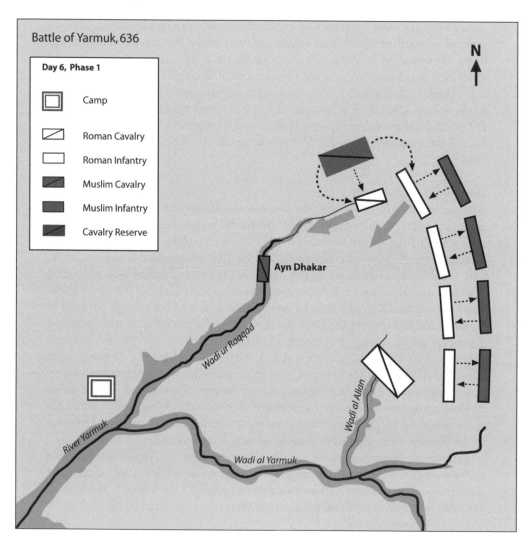

Battle of Yarmuk, 636: Day 6, Phase 1.

Despite being abandoned by its allies and assailed from the front, flank and rear, the Roman infantry fought bravely and may even have saved itself by disengaging from the Muslim forces and the mounting of a fighting retreat. However, with no Roman cavalry on the field, it was now that the true extent of the weakness of the strategic position that Vahan had been drawn into was fully realised. Most important of all was the Ayn Dhakar bridge, firmly in the hands of Dharar's cavalry. With Khalid's cavalry and the Muslim infantry blocking any escape routes to the north and east and Dharar controlling the only escape rout to the west, the Roman infantry found themselves trapped between the Muslim forces and the gorges of the Yarmuk and its Raqqad tributary. As a

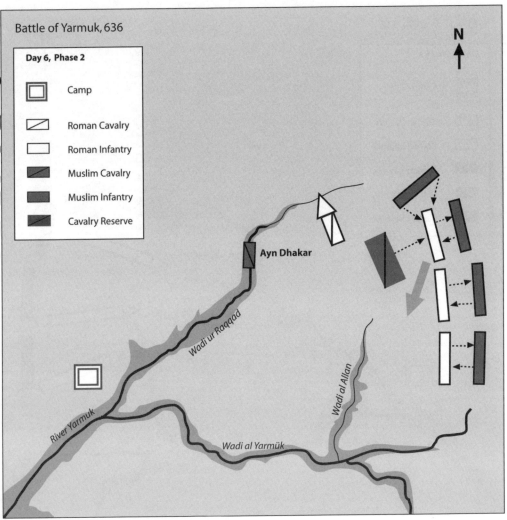

Battle of Yarmuk, 636: Day 6, Phase 2.

result, many more Romans were killed attempting to descend the ravines or trusting themselves to the waters below.

However, from this 'position of no escape' a number of Romans were able to escape the battlefield at Yarmuk. The majority of these survivors had likely fled north before Khalid's cavalry strike or had been guarding the Roman camp on the western side of the Raqqad, but some did manage to escape across the gorges as well. Unfortunately for these men, their ordeal was not over. This was because the true extent of the Roman calamity at Yarmuk was not solely down to events on the battlefield itself but also 'the rapidity, thoroughness, ruthlessness, relentlessness, and determination with which the Muslims exploited

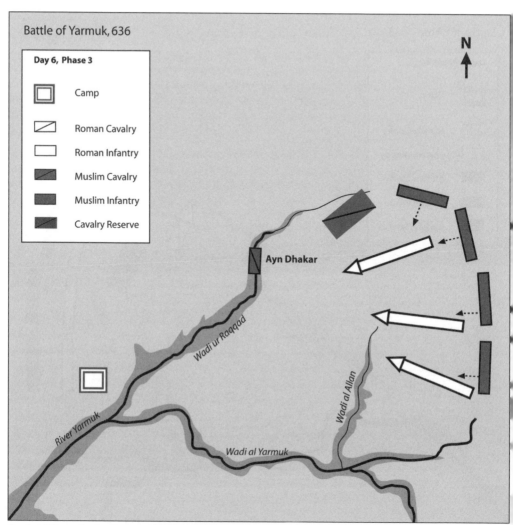

Battle of Yarmuk, 636: Day 6, Phase 3.

their victory'.[10] Rather than rest and celebrate, cavalry contingents spread out in every direction to hunt down survivors and it is with this chase that the Roman army that had retaken the cities of Syria in the early months of 636 ceased to exist.

A large toll was also exacted on the leadership of the Roman army. Theodore Trithurios, George and Buccinator all perished in the fighting or aftermath while Vahan was either killed in combat or survived to retire in disgrace to a monastery in Sinai.[11] The Ghassanid commander, Jabalah, who was largely ignored and underused during the Jabiya-Yarmuk campaign, defected to the Muslim camp in order to escape death, only to later return to the Roman side.

Another commander whose presence in the Roman army at Yarmuk is recorded but not understood is Niketas, the son of Shahrbaraz. He may have had some kind of leading position, further adding to the confusion of leadership already in existence between Vahan and Trithurios. He survived the battle, making it as far as Emesa before being overtaken by Muslim riders. Upon his capture, Niketas immediately attempted to save his skin by defecting. Instead, he was slain.[12] The loss of these leaders, along with the disgracing of Theodore, will have undermined any Roman attempts to build another army to challenge the Muslim presence in Syria, for not only was their prominence and experience impossible to replace in the short term, their deaths may have made national groupings such as the Armenians less willing to provide such large numbers of troops and leaders. This left Heraclius in an increasingly desperate military situation, for without a field army of any size in operation his Syrian, Mesopotamian and Armenian provinces lay virtually undefended, with only a few isolated garrisons left to face the rampant Arabs.

Between the Rivers – The Battle of the Bridge, 634

636 was not just a pivotal year for the future of Roman Syria. It also saw the decisive Muslim breakthrough in Persian Mesopotamia. By the time he left for Syria in late-633/early-634, Khalid had conquered virtually all Sassanid territory south of the Euphrates and safeguarded these conquests by establishing a series of garrisons. Ostensibly, these new Muslim territories were left under the command of Amr b. Haram, an early supporter of Muhammad, but, in reality, al-Muthanna, who had played such a large role in Khalid's campaign, was the real authority around Hira. However, the constant threat of military reprisal from the Sassanids still remained and the Qadisiyyah garrison that had been Khalid's next target was still unsubdued. Due to this threat, al-Muthanna sent repeated messages to Medina asking for reinforcements, perhaps going as far as to visit the Muslim capital to ask Abu Bakr in person once more.

Yet it was not until after the accession of Umar in August 634 that this request was fulfilled with the dispatch of a force under Abu Ubayd b. Ma'ud. With a core of about 1,000 volunteers from his Thaqif tribe gathered at Medina, and picking up contingents from local tribesmen as he marched north, Abu Ubayd may have had about 4,000 men by the time he arrived at Hira. Joining forces with al-Muthanna and about 1,000 of his kin, these two began raiding across the Euphrates. A series of encounters between this Muslim column and Perso-Arab forces are recorded but the sequence and exact location, beyond being in the alluvial plains between Hira and Ctesiphon, of many of these raids cannot be established.[13] What is known is that these raids proved enough of an irritant and close enough to Ctesiphon to provoke a sizeable Persian response, with Bahman marching from the Persian capital to the Euphrates.

Despite the claims of some sources and his success along the Euphrates, it is probable that Khalid had not faced a true imperial Sassanid army. Much like the Romans in Syria, Yazdgerd and his generals were slow to react to what they would have perceived as just another instance of Arabic raiding. The Persians will have been further encouraged to downplay the Muslim attack by their continued dealing with the aftermath of not just the invasion of their territory by the Romans and Turks but also the destructive period of civil war that had followed Shahrbaraz's assassination. Therefore, it would be somewhat unrealistic to expect Yazdgerd to be able to recognise and react immediately to the emergent threat from Islam. Perhaps only the defeat at Walaja and the fall of Hira saw to it that Yazdgerd and his generals 'began to take the business of the Arabs more seriously.'[14] Furthermore, after the defeats of Bahman's congregating forces at Muzayyah, Saniyy and Zumail in late 633, it may have taken a year before Yazdgerd could field another army.

Whatever the circumstances, with Abu Ubayd's force campaigning along the Euphrates and Bahman advancing south from Ctesiphon, a confrontation was inevitable. It appears to have occurred sometime in November 634 at a river crossing near the present day site of Kufa, variously recorded as Mirwaha or al-Qarqas.[15] Situated on the eastern bank of the Euphrates, Bahman reputedly had up to 30,000 men to intercept the raiding Muslims, although the likelihood is that this is an exaggeration. As for the Muslim army, it is possible that the success of their raiding into Mesopotamia both in terms of prestige and material wealth may have bolstered the force of Abu Ubayd and al-Muthanna to as many 9,000. However, it is more likely that it remained closer to the 5,000 recorded at the time of Abu Ubayd's arrival at Hira.[16]

With the Euphrates dominating the battlefield, the focus of the subsequent fighting was the bridge that separated the two armies. Buoyed by previous successes and perhaps in search of personal renown, Abu Ubayd took an overly aggressive stance against Bahman and attempted to force a crossing of the river. However, while this crossing was successful, Abu Ubayd's aggression was to prove disastrous. Bahman may have allowed the Muslims to cross the river before attacking to maximise casualties; however, accounts of the battle suggest that it was the presence of elephants in the Persian army that decided the outcome. The smell and clamour they exuded disrupted the Muslim cavalry and, when Abu Ubayd led an attack against them, he himself was trampled by a rampant white elephant. With their commander killed, a large part of the Muslim bridgehead collapsed. It was then that this Battle of the Bridge turned from a defeat into a disaster as the retreating Muslims were driven into the river itself, leaving 1,000 Muslims dead from combat and perhaps a further 3,000 carried away by the Euphrates. There is some suggestion that the bridge was in fact destroyed by a Muslim Arab to force his comrades to continue fighting rather than fleeing. The forces of al-Muthanna, who was wounded, do seem to have survived the battle largely intact, which could suggest that perhaps they formed the Muslim rearguard or were able to find another way across the river.

The Muslim army seems to have disintegrated in the aftermath of this defeat with al-Muthanna returning to his homelands at Ullais and Abu Ubayd's Thaqif kinsmen returning to Medina. However, despite the totality of their tactical victory at the Battle of the Bridge, the lack of a Persian follow-up would appear to be something of a strategic blunder. Again, much like the Romans, the Persian hierarchy was demonstrating a lack of understanding about what the words, deeds and writings of the Prophet had done for the Arabs. In the past, such a devastating defeat would have broken any pretensions that Arab raiders might have had regarding Mesopotamia. They probably expected those settlements conquered by Khalid to simply return to their original Sassanid allegiance without having to intervene any further militarily, perhaps with al-Muthanna serving as a successor to the Lakhmid buffer state. Whatever the reasons, the failure of the Persians to press their victory over Abu Ubayd in November 634 was not the military anomaly that it would appear to be; the anomaly was the failure of the Muslims to capitulate in the face of such a defeat.

The Battle of Qadisiyyah

Despite the lack of a Muslim capitulation following the Battle of the Bridge, there was a definite lull in the fighting along the Euphrates, stretching out to perhaps a year. With so many of his forces deployed in Syria against the Romans, Umar seems to have had some trouble in finding volunteers for a proposed reinforcement of the Muslim outposts along the Euphrates. So low were volunteer numbers that the caliph turned to a thus far untapped section of Arabia – those tribes that had rebelled during the Ridda Wars. Abu Bakr had refused to use these tribes due to their apostasy but Umar, combining outward leniency with military pragmatism, was only too happy to allow them to enlist. However, even with these new resources, Umar was still unable to bring together a force of any substantial size. Several different tribes did contribute contingents but it was the Tamin and the Bajila who provided the most, around 1,000 men each. Such was Umar's need for men that the Bajila leader, Jarir b. Abdullah, had a strong enough bargaining position to see himself not just appointed commander of this new force but also permitted the quarter share of the spoils that would normally be due to the caliph. This lofty position accorded to Jarir, along with the size of the force under his command, seems to have led to confrontation with al-Muthanna, who retained some semblance of overall authority.

Despite his wound, al-Muthanna wasted little time in reinitiating the type of raiding that had been so profitable in the run-up to the Battle of the Bridge. Some accounts suggest that he also won a pitched battle against the Persian army at Buwayb. However, it would appear that this 'Battle of Buwayb' was the exaggeration of a minor engagement 'designed to enhance the reputation of al-Muthanna and his tribe among later generations and to counter the disgrace of his humiliating defeat at the Battle of the Bridge.'[17] Even when the reinforcements of Jarir arrived at Hira, the casualties suffered in the reverse at the Bridge and the fear of a repeat performance saw to it that Muslims were careful to avoid any large-scale confrontation with the Persian army, sticking to hit-and-run raids.

This somewhat precarious position of not being able or lacking the confidence to fight a pitched battle, along with the squabble over superiority between Jarir and al-Muthanna, led Umar to launch an even more comprehensive recruitment drive. To diffuse the tension between Jarir and al-Muthanna, these new recruits were to be led by a man who was clearly superior to both. Umar originally meant for that person to be himself, with some preparations being made for his journey to Hira. However, he was talked out of this gambit, agreeing instead to appoint a companion of Muhammad to the overall command of the Iraqi front. The choice fell upon Sa'd b. Abi Waqqas, a veteran of the Battle of Badr, who arrived at Medina at the head of 1,000 Hawazin. Sending out calls for further recruits as he travelled north along the Medina-Hira road, by the time Sa'd arrived along the Euphrates he must have commanded an army comparable to any Muslim force that had yet been sent against the Sassanids. The Jarir/al-Muthanna squabble had been settled with the latter's succumbing to his wound and Sa'd also quickly diffused any potential trouble from the Shayban by marrying al-Muthanna's widow and appointing al-Muthanna's brother, al-Mu'anna, to council.

The arrival of Sa'd proved to be well timed, for, having finally established full control over his realm and buoyed by Bahman's victory at the Battle of the Bridge, Yazdgerd was now giving his full attention to his southern border. For the task of crushing this Muslim menace, the Persian king appointed Rustam Farrokhzad to command the large force of infantry, cavalry and elephants that he was bringing together. However, there is little agreement over just how big this Persian force was, with anything from 30,000 to 210,000 being recorded.[18] However, despite the absurdity of the latter, it is likely that even the smallest recorded size of Rustam's force held a significant manpower advantage over the combined forces of Sa'd.

Despite some sources claiming that the Muslims were able to field a force of enormous proportions,[19] it is far more likely that Sa'd commanded a force of between 6,000 and 12,000.[20] Attempts have been made to back this up by establishing the tribal composition of the Muslim force, with six distinct contingents being identified: Sa'd's 1,000 Hamazin; 2,300 Yemeni; 700 from al-Sarat; anything from 2,800 to 7,000 tribal recruits from central Arabia; the pre-existing forces of Jarir and al-Muthanna, which probably numbered around 3,000; further reinforcements sent by Umar of up to 2,000; a contingent of 400–1,500 under al-Mughira b. Shu'ba from south-eastern Iraq; and two separate armies sent from Syria under Sa'd's relative, Hashim b. Utba, and Iyad

b. Ghanm of 300–2,000 and 1,000–5,000 respectively.[21] Sa'd is also accredited by some of the sources with bringing a greater level of organisation to this army, dividing his men into units, each with their own commander and based on a subdivision of ten men. While it is likely that there is some anachronistic reporting from the sources, it is possible that lessons were learned from the defeat of Abu Ubayd on the Bridge and that Sa'd's army was far more organised as a military force than the previous Arab hordes of tribal warriors.

Marching from Ctesiphon, Rustam took up a position opposite the Muslim force about thirty miles to the east of Hira. Neither Rustam nor Sa'd seems to have been overly hurried in forcing battle on their opponent, as it is suggested that, while both forces took up their respective positions in July 636, the Battle of Qadisiyyah does not seem to have occurred until mid-November. It would be easy to suggest that Sa'd's failure to force a confrontation was due to a wariness of another sizeable defeat; however, he did not attempt to extricate his men from battle at any stage. His sending out of reconnaissance scouts and raiding parties into Mesopotamia, along with his arrogant demand that Rustam accept Islam, also suggest that he was not shirking away from a fight. However, it does seem that he was in repeated contact with Umar and will therefore have known that there was a steady drip of reinforcements from Arabia, Syria and southern Iraq on the way to bolster his ranks. For his part, Rustam may have been hoping for a repeat of the Muslim debacle at the Battle of the Bridge. However, Sa'd did not allow himself to be goaded into the same kind of reckless attack that had cost Abu Ubayd so dearly. It is also possible that Rustam, much like Heraclius and his generals in Syria, may have thought that the Muslims might crumble in the face of the large host he had brought to Qadisiyyah.

Day 1 – 16 November 636

The course of the Battle of Qadisiyyah is muddled by the lack of 'an overall picture of the evolving tactical situations' and relies heavily on oral traditions, which tend to embellish the actions of individuals and tribes.[22] However, it appears that by mid-November Rustam had decided that, as the Muslims gave little inkling of retreating and had actually increased in strength through rein-forcements, he would have to initiate battle. With that, early on 16 November 636 he ordered a canal of the Ateeq that separated the armies to be filled in to allow his forces easy passage. With the Persians safely across the canal, both forces now deployed for battle in a similar formation of four separate divisions of infantry, each supported by a division of cavalry. Aside from size, the only real difference in the tactical layout of the armies was that the Sassanids had a corps of eight elephants deployed in front of each of their four infantry divisions.

The Persian right was commanded by Hormuzan, the right centre by Jalinus, the left centre by Beerzan and the left by Mihran. Rustam took up a position behind his right centre near the Ateeq to provide him with a good view of the

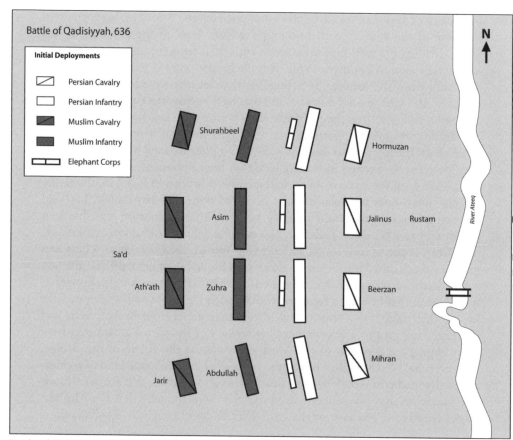

Battle of Qadisiyyah, 636: Deployments.

battlefield. The Muslim right was commanded by Abdullah b. al-Mutim, the right centre by Zuhra b. al-Hawiyya, the left centre by Asim b. Amr and the left wing by Shurahbeel b. al-Samt. The cavalry contingents of the right centre and right wing were commanded by Ath'ath b. Qais and Jarir respectively. Sa'd seems to have been taken unwell in the run-up to the battle and was therefore not active on the battlefield, choosing instead to take up a position in the town of Qadisiyyah from where he could direct operations through his deputy, Khalid b. Arfatah.

With the two armies arrayed less than a kilometre apart, the increasingly traditional duels took place, with the Muslim *mubarizun* once again proving their superiority. By the middle of the day, having lost several of his champions and not wanting to risk more of them or the morale of his men, Rustam ordered Mihran to launch an attack against the Muslim right. Preceded by a hail of arrows, the Persian elephants charged Abdullah's infantry forcing them backwards. An attempt by Jarir to stabilise the situation by leading a flank attack with his right wing cavalry was intercepted and routed by Mihran's heavy horse. Recognising that his right flank was in danger, Sa'd reacted quickly to restore it. From the Muslim right centre, regiments of Ath'ath's cavalry and Zuhra's infantry launched a flank attack on Mihran's infantry while Jarir's cavalry reformed and checked the Sassanid cavalry advance. These counter-attacks undid Mihran's early advances and restored the Muslim line.

With his left wing attack stalling, Rustam ordered similar attacks on the Muslim left and left centre. Once again, in the face of a barrage of arrows, flank attacks by Hormuzan and Jalinus' cavalry, and the trampling power of the elephants, the Muslims began to give ground. However, Asim was able to blunt the Persian charge. His light infantry and archers disrupted the elephants to such good effect that Jalinus had to remove them from battle. Building on this success, Asim launched a counter-attack with his entire right centre that forced Jalinus' corps back to its starting point. Buoyed by this, Shurahbeel's left was able to affect a similarly successful counter-attack, first taking out the elephants

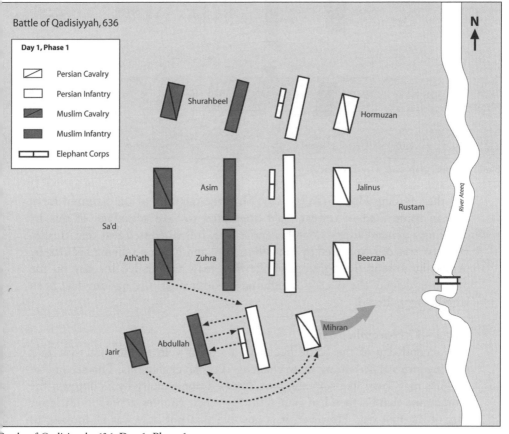

Battle of Qadisiyyah, 636: Day 1, Phase 1.

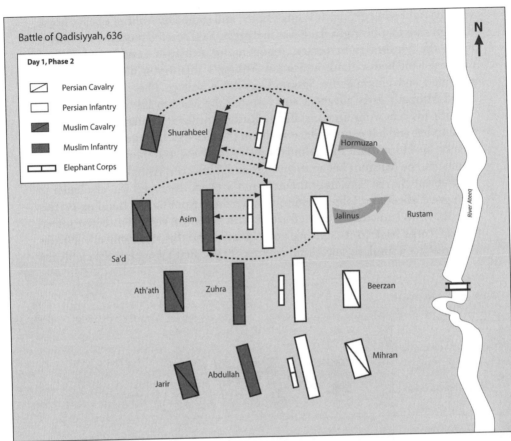

Battle of Qadisiyyah, 636: Day 1, Phase 2.

and then forcing Hormuzan back. With three-quarters of the Sassanid force now in some kind of retreat, Sa'd attempted to take advantage of this by ordering a general attack along his entire line. It is suggested that this Muslim offensive was only rebuffed by the failing light and Rustam rallying his men by personally joining the fighting. While Sa'd may have ended the day on the offensive, despite the casualties endured by both sides, the fighting had been largely inconclusive.

Day 2 – 17 November 636
The second day of the battle began in a similar vein to the first with Sa'd sending forward his *mubarizun* to challenge Persian champions. This second set of duels may seem like something of a missed opportunity by Sa'd, given the momentum that his men had gained through their counter-attacks in the latter part of the first day. However, it is possible that not only was he looking to further undermine Persian morale, Sa'd may also have known of the imminent

approach of reinforcements from Syria, which began to arrive while the duels were still taking place. These reinforcements under Hashim b. Utba were divided into several groups in order to give the Sassanids the impression of a steady stream of men arriving in the enemy camp. With the continued success of the *mubarizun* and the arrival of Hashim, Sa'd decided to launch a similar general attack along the length of the battle line. However, perhaps again with Rustam risking his own life in the fighting, the Sassanid lines remained firm throughout the day and at dusk both armies retreated back to their camps.

The arrival of this first batch of Muslims reinforcements from Syria brought with it an individual who would achieve particular prominence throughout the remainder of the Battle of Qadisiyyah and the Muslim advances in the years to come – the commander of Hashim's advanced guard, Qaqa b. Amr. Even before he arrived on the battlefield, Qaqa was receiving praise for being at least partially responsible for dividing his advanced guard into numerous groups to give the impression of larger numbers. Once he reached Qadisiyyah, Qaqa is credited with plunging straight into the ongoing duels and personally killed not only Beerzan, commander of the Persian left centre, but also Bahman, the victor at the Battle of the Bridge. During the subsequent general attack ordered by Sa'd, Qaqa is recorded as deploying a ruse to disrupt the dangerous Sassanid cavalry, disguising camels as monsters. He is also said to have led a group of the *mubarizun* through the Persian lines in an unsuccessful attempt to kill Rustam. Such inventiveness and initiative would appear to have impressed Sa'd as it is reported that Qaqa was promoted to battlefield command for the remainder of the fighting. However, without taking too much away from his potential ingenuity and skill, many of these episodes attributed to Qaqa seem suspect and were probably the invention of later Muslim written and oral sources.

Day 3 – 18 November 636

The threat of further reinforcement of the Muslim army encouraged Rustam to seek a decisive breakthrough on the third day of battle. Therefore, the Persian commander launched a full-scale general attack. Its ferocity, particularly the elephants, pushed the Muslim corps back and opened sizeable gaps between them. Rustam took advantage of this by sending his cavalry into these breaches. One Sassanid cavalry regiment is thought to have penetrated as far as the old palace at Qadisiyyah that Sa'd was resident in.

With his line in trouble, Sa'd had to react quickly and his immediate aim was to neutralise the Persian elephants wreaking havoc amongst the Muslim infantry. To that end, he ordered his skirmishers, archers and spearmen to concentrate on the great beasts and by the middle of the day the Muslims had succeeded in driving them back into the Sassanid ranks. Taking advantage of the confusion the retreating elephants caused, Sa'd then ordered an all out counter-attack by his forces. However, despite the confusion caused by the retreat of the elephants and a repeat of Qaqa's disguised camels, the Sassanid

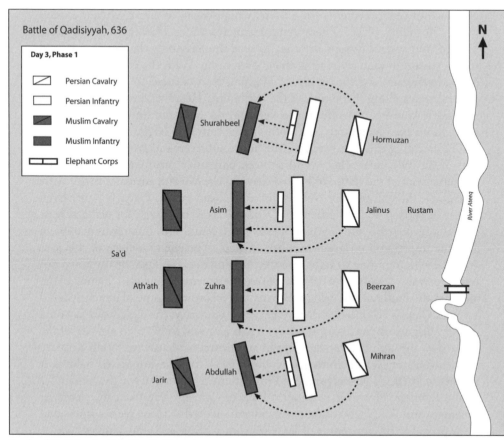

Battle of Qadisiyyah, 636: Day 3, Phase 1.

forces once again stood firm. With that, the battle settled into one of attrition as both sides inflicted heavy casualties on their opponent without being able to break the other, even as night fell.

Day 4 – 19 November 636

As the fighting of the third day continued into the early hours, breaking only at the first signs of daybreak, it might be expected that there was little or no fighting on the fourth day. Rustam and his army certainly seemed to think so. However, Sa'd and his increasingly prominent battlefield commander, Qaqa, saw this as an opportunity to force a decisive breakthrough. Addressing his troops, Qaqa proclaimed that, as the Persians were tired from the previous day and night's fighting, an unexpected attack so quickly after the break-off of hostilities would give the Muslim army victory. With that, Asim's left centre attacked Jalinus' right centre, followed by a general advance by the rest of the Muslim line. This took the Sassanids by surprise and, with the Muslim cavalry

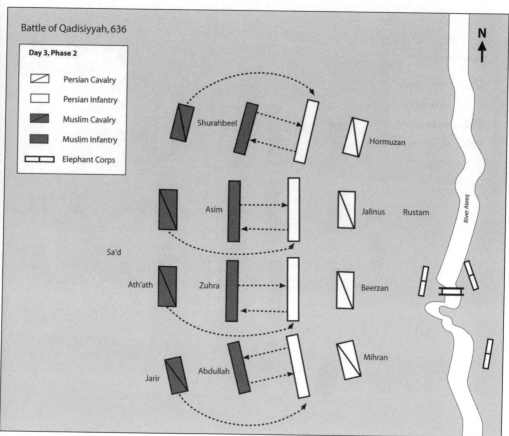

Battle of Qadisiyyah, 636: Day 3, Phase 2.

staging flanks attacks, the corps of Jalinus and Hormuzan were soon giving ground to those of Asim and Shurahbeel. Hormuzan stabilised the Persian right flank and, as Zuhra and Abdullah had been unable to match the progress of Asim, Hormuzan's successful counter-attack left both flanks of Asim's corps exposed, forcing it to also retreat.

However, it was at this point that news of the decisive move of the battle began to filter through to the Persian ranks. Taking advantage of Asim's early success against Jalinus, Qaqa had led his band of *mubarizun* through the Persian right centre and killed Rustam.[23] As news of the death of their commander spread amongst the Persian ranks, resolve began to dissolve as the weight of three days' hard fighting with little sleep the previous night began to weigh heavily. Recognising his opportunity, Sa'd ordered one last general attack from his own exhausted forces in the hope of taking advantage of the demoralising effect of Rustam's death. Under this renewed Muslim onslaught, the Persian line finally buckled and then broke.

Battle of Qadisiyyah, 636: Day 4, Persian Collapse.

With the death of Rustam, Jalinus took charge of the Persian force and, while he could do nothing to prevent their defeat, he does seem to have held the remaining Persian units together in an orderly retreat across the Ateeq and then the Euphrates back towards Ctesiphon. However, much like their compatriots in the aftermath of Yarmuk, Sa'd exploited his victory to its fullest. While Jalinus was able to establish defensive bridgeheads over the Ateeq and Euphrates, allowing a large proportion of his surviving forces to cross safely, once the Persian army was exposed on the alluvial plains of Mesopotamia they were ruthlessly pursued and cut down by Sa'd's cavalry. Much like Vahan's army, the force that Rustam led out from Ctesiphon ceased to exist.

There is some suggestion that Heraclius and Yazdgerd planned to coordinate their offensives of 635. They may even have cemented this understanding with a marriage alliance between the two. However, if such a marriage took place or was ever planned, the name of the female offered to Yazdgerd by Heraclius or her relationship to the emperor was not firmly established. Furthermore, whatever coordination the emperor and king hoped to accomplish aside from two individual victories is difficult to ascertain. Aside from Khalid's trek to Damascus in early 634, the possibility of Roman troops being at the Battle of Firaz and the arrival of Hashim at Qadisiyyah, the theatres in Roman Syria and Persian Mesopotamia were completely independent from each other. If such a dual venture did take place, it must have called for simultaneous action and decisive military victories. As it was, neither was achieved. The Roman and Persian counter-offensives were launched months apart and neither Vahan nor Rustam were able to defeat their Muslim opponents.

But, of course, the most important point about such proposed coordination was that not only did both Vahan and Rustam fail to achieve decisive victories, they both suffered catastrophic defeats that led to the complete undermining of the defensive positions of both Syria and Mesopotamia. By the end of the following year, the Romans would be forced back beyond the Taurus Mountains, attempting to establish some sort of defensive line capable of preserving their Anatolian provinces, while Qadisiyyah initiated a series of further defeats and retreats that would not only see the Persians lose Mesopotamia but over the course of the next twenty years lead to the virtual extinguishing of the Sassanid state.

Chapter 8

A Farewell to Syria and Mesopotamia

'Farewell; a long farewell to Syria.'

Heraclius
(Michael the Syrian, *Chron.* II.424)

23 Years Later – the Second Siege of Jerusalem and the End of Roman Palestine

The chronology of the Muslim exploitation of their victory at Yarmuk is uncertain and at times varying campaigns seem to overlap, making it appear as though the likes of Khalid and Abu Ubayda were simultaneously reducing cities in northern Syria and besieging settlements in Palestine. However, it appears as though the conquests in Palestine began before the Muslim force that had been victorious at Yarmuk split into two, for both Abu Ubayda and Khalid seem to have been present in the initial stages.[1] Given the options that Yarmuk had given them, the Muslim generals found it difficult to agree what they were to do next. At a council meeting called by Abu Ubayda, they decided that with their forces still combined they should complete the subjugation of Palestine before splitting up and attacking targets further afield. That narrowed the choice of their next objective down essentially to the two unconquered major cities of the region – Caesarea and Jerusalem.

The fall of the latter, with its religious significance, would be a massive blow to Roman morale. However, strategic and practical concerns must also have come into the reckoning. While both cities had formidable defences, Caesarea had the added advantage of being a coastal settlement. This meant that, no matter how tightly a Muslim blockade was enforced, their lack of any kind of sea power would mean that the Romans could continue to supply the Caesarean garrison indefinitely. Jerusalem, on the other hand, could be strangled into submission. However, with Caesarea still in enemy hands, it could provide the Romans with a beachhead from which to launch a potential recovery of the lands around the Jordan. Therefore, its capture would virtually secure the Muslim conquest of Palestine, including Jerusalem itself. The generals could not choose between these two objectives and therefore sent a messenger to Umar to make the decision for them. The caliph's choice fell upon Jerusalem.

With the decision made for them, the Muslim force marched through Pella towards Jerusalem, arriving before its walls in early-November 636. The Holy City appears to have been under some kind of partial blockade since the

Muslim capture of Pella in the autumn of 634, but each of the five commanders from Yarmuk – Khalid, Abu Ubayda, Yazid, Amr and Shurahbil – now took up positions surrounding the city, blocking off all routes in and out. The Jerusalemite leadership, headed by the Patriarch Sophronius, had had only around six weeks to prepare before the Muslim forces cut them off. Given that they had been abandoned by Heraclius and that the remaining garrisons were too busy organising their own defence, they could do little other than carry out minor repairs to the fortifications, gather supplies, and smuggle holy artefacts such as the True Cross to the coast for transportation to Constantinople.

Very little is recorded regarding the following four months' blockade of Jerusalem but it would appear to have been mostly bloodless as there were few if any assaults from the Muslims or any sallies from the garrison. Realising that further resistance was useless, sometime in March 637 Sophronius is thought to have intimated to the Muslim leadership that he was willing to surrender Jerusalem to them and pay the *jizya*, but only if the caliph came to the city and accepted its surrender in person. Not wanting to accede to such a demand or have to wait for the arrival of Umar, Shurahbil approached his fellow generals with a ploy for Khalid to impersonate the caliph. This was considered a realistic idea due to the strong family resemblance between the cousins and also due to the fact that they were both very tall. However, Khalid seems to have been famous enough to be recognised by some of the Jerusalem defenders and the ruse was a failure. It is also possible that some in the city may have known Umar by sight, as he had travelled through Palestine and Syria as a merchant in his pre-Islamic days, or they may have met either Umar or Khalid during their own travels to Arabia.

Knowing that they could not storm the walls without lengthy preparations and incurring heavy casualties, Abu Ubayda wrote to Umar to ask him to come to Jerusalem and treat with Sophronius. The caliph arrived in Palestine some-time in mid-637, ostensibly to deal with the administrative matters that had emerged from the conquests – dividing booty, distributing conquered land, establishing military defence, inheritances and the payment, reward and feed-ing of the soldiery. However, leaving Amr and Shurahbil to continue the blockade, Abu Ubayda, Khalid and Yazid all travelled to meet with the caliph to discuss the situation at Jerusalem. Ever the pragmatist, Umar agreed to meet directly with Sophronius. The Patriarch is said to have shown the caliph around the holy sites of the city, with the caliph being horrified by the state of disrepair and filth that places such as the Temple Mount had been allowed to fall into.

Sophronius then delivered Jerusalem into Muslim hands in late-April 637, marking the second time in a generation that the holiest city in Christianity had fallen to a non-Christian invader. However, while it had only taken fifteen years for Heraclius to retrieve it from Zoroastrianism, after Sophronius' capitulation it would be 462 years before Jerusalem would be wrenched from Muslim hands and only then through the almighty bloodbath of the First Crusade. The surrender of Jerusalem was not just important as the loss of the holiest city to Judaeo-Christians but to the future of Christian-Muslim relations.

The agreement of capitulation between Umar and the Patriarch was to become recognised as the Covenant of Umar, which recognised Christians as a protected people with freedom to practice their own religion in return for payment of the *jizya*. Even if the attributing of the treaty to Umar and its recording comes from decades later, that does not diminish its importance even to this day.

With the successful capture of Jerusalem, or perhaps even before, the Muslim army split into two groups. Amr and Shurahbil spent the rest of the year consolidating Muslim control of Palestine, including accepting the capitulation of Gaza, while Abu Ubayda, Khalid and Yazid moved off north to Damascus. There, while Abu Ubayda and Khalid moved further north, Yazid detached his corps and moved against those coastal towns that had yet to submit to Islam. Over the course of the next year, he was able to induce the surrender of Beirut, Sidon and Tyre, before approaching Caesarea from the north.[2]

Caesarea had already proven beyond Muslim siege craft during a month-long siege following the victory at Ajnadayn; a siege that was lifted by the need to concentrate forces in the face of the Roman counter-attack of 636. The strategic situation might have changed greatly in the intervening months but the walls of Caesarea and the Roman superiority at sea had not. Yet it still needed to be subdued if Muslim Palestine was to be completely secured, and Yazid set about investing Caesarea in a blockade. However, before he could make any inroads, plague erupted in his army and Yazid himself was afflicted and later died, and the blockade of Caesarea was lifted. This outbreak of 638/639, as will be seen below, caused a slowdown in the Muslim conquests.

It was not until the plague had subsided in 640 that Caesarea was again targeted by a Muslim force. This time it was under the command of Yazid's brother, Mu'awiya, by then the governor of Syria. Several skirmishes took place between the garrison and the blockading forces but the city continued to frustrate the Muslims through its links to the sea. However, Mu'awiya was able to take advantage of fractious in-fighting within the city. Despite being an early centre of Christianity, Caesarea had a sizeable Jewish community, leading to frequent clashes between the two. Encouraged by the increasing religious persecution of the Heraclian regime and the examples of tolerance displayed by the Muslims, the Jews seem to have decided to throw their lot in with the blockaders. To that end, a certain Yusef, probably Joseph, met with Mu'awiya and offered to deliver the city in return for fair treatment for the Jews. The Muslim commander readily agreed to this and Yusef then led a Muslim detachment through the sewers into the city, where they fought their way to the main gate and forced it open. With the entire Muslim force flooding in, the garrison surrendered on the usual terms of paying the *jizya*. With the fall of Caesarea, all of Palestine had fallen under Muslim control, something that would go largely unchallenged for nearly 450 years.

The Muslim Conquest of Northern Syria

While Amr, Shurahbil and Yazid were administering the last rites to Roman Palestine, Khalid and Abu Ubayda had struck north from Damascus. With the defeat and destruction of his army at Yarmuk, Heraclius seems to have decided that further resistance in Syria was largely futile and withdrew back to Anatolia. However, rather than a head-long flight in the face of a rampant foe, the emperor put strategic thought into his retreat. By passing through Edessa and Samosata, he hoped to keep lines of communication and retreat open as long as possible to allow what remained of his Palestinian, Syrian and Mesopotamian forces to escape north to the mountainous holdfasts of the Taurus, Armenia and Mesopotamia. Due to this strategic plan the likes of Damascus, Baalbek and Emesa were retaken by the Muslims in the wake of Yarmuk without much in the way of a fight. Epiphania, modern Hama in Syria, and Apamea also seem to have fallen without much resistance.

Yet despite being largely abandoned by their emperor, some of the garrisons of northern Syria were determined to resist the advance of Abu Ubayda and Khalid. As this northern arm of the Muslim conquest approached the Roman stronghold of Chalkis, probably modern Qinnasrin, it was intercepted by the Roman commander Menas, sometime in June 637. It is likely that Menas departed from the usual Roman tactic of avoiding battle because he recognised that there was no hope of relief from Heraclius in the event that he was besieged and that a retreat would see him overtaken by the rapid Muslim cavalry.

The numbers recorded for the subsequent Battle of Hazir are far from believable, as Menas is said to have had 70,000 men, while the Muslims reportedly had 17,000. Due to the mass evacuation of Syria ordered by Heraclius, it would be surprising if Menas had even a tenth of this recorded figure, while it is somewhat unlikely that Abu Ubayda and Khalid would have as many men as this with the detachment of the corps of Yazid, Shurahbil and Amr.

With Khalid's mobile cavalry probing the defences of Chalkis and the surrounding area, Menas launched a surprise attack, hoping to defeat this advance column before Abu Ubayda could bring up the rest of his forces. However, Menas had underestimated the abilities of Khalid and the resolve of the Muslim soldiers as the Romans proved unable to overcome this vanguard. The death of Menas early in the battle also disrupted the Roman effort and may have led the Romans to overcommit in their pursuit of vengeance. Therefore, once Abu Ubayda arrived on the battlefield, Khalid launched his cavalry in a flank attack that broke the Romans. While the suggestion that the entire Roman force at Hazir was killed to a man is almost certainly hyperbole, Khalid's cavalry attack and the likelihood of another post-battle chase meant that Menas' force

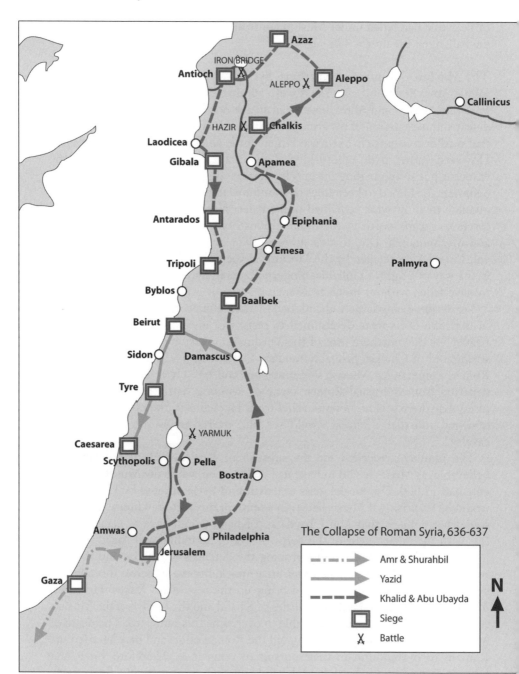

The Collapse of Roman Syria, 636–637.

probably did cease to exist as an entity. Abu Ubayda and Khalid then marched the short distance to Chalkis, which surrendered without a fight before the end of June 637, removing a major obstacle to the Muslim advance into northern Syria. It also prompted Umar to admit that he had misjudged Khalid in removing him from supreme command.[3]

The conquest of Chalkis opened northern Syria up to the Muslim advance, with Khalid and Abu Ubayda moving north-east against Beroea, modern-day Aleppo. A strong Roman garrison of perhaps 4,000 men under a certain Joachim was well established behind not just the large walls of the city but also in a moated fort not far from the city walls. Perhaps in a similar mindset to Menas regarding the lack of aid, Joachim decided to meet the approaching Muslim force in battle. However, despite the relative strength of his force, the Roman commander quickly found himself outmatched, outmanoeuvred and forced to take refuge behind the walls. While this defeat did not immediately break the spirits of the garrison, which launched numerous sallies against the Muslim blockade over the next three months, the futility of continued resistance became increasingly evident and in October 637 Aleppo accepted an offer to surrender. Joachim himself is thought to have converted to Islam, although the suggestion that 4,000 of his troops joined him makes this claim somewhat suspect. Abu Ubayda then sent a detachment under Malik b. Ashtar north-west to Azaz, which seems to have only offered token resistance before capitulating. This may seem like the capture of just another settlement but this move had strategic purpose given that Azaz protected the right flank of the Muslim army, which was about to turn west to attack the Roman eastern capital, Antioch.

Marching from Aleppo, the Muslim force reached the banks of the Orontes, a river that, along with Lake Amik and Mount Silpios, provided Antioch with strong natural defences.[4] It was at a large iron bridge crossing the Orontes that the seemingly sizeable Antiochene garrison chose to resist the Muslim advance. Unfortunately, the events of the subsequent Battle of the Iron Bridge are not recorded by the sources. As with many other Muslim battles on or near a river, perhaps the main battle plan of the Muslims entailed something akin to drawing the Romans away from the river and then striking around their flanks to capture the iron bridge. However, without even a whisper from the sources, it is difficult to make any conclusions about the battle. All that can be said is that in its aftermath the Romans retreated back to Antioch, and once the Muslims had encircled the city it was quick to surrender, on 30 October 637, with the garrison remnant allowed to retire north to Anatolia.

This capture of its third city once again saw the Roman Empire riven in two, much as Shahin and Shahrbaraz had done in the aftermath of their defeat of Heraclius at Antioch in 613. What remained of the Roman army in Anatolia and the isolated garrisons in Syria and Palestine were now completely cut off from each other by land. Abu Ubayda then split his force into several contingents to consolidate his control of northern Syria by reducing those garrisons that still held out. He himself drove south from Antioch to capture a string of coastal towns and cities, including Laodicea, Gibala and Antarados, against only limited resistance. Abu Ubayda may even have reached as far south as Tripoli, now in northern Lebanon. The importance in the subduing of such ports is the same as it was for the taking of Caesarea. As the Romans still commanded the seas, the Muslim conquests would not be completely secure while the Roman navy had a platform to strike through.

While Abu Ubayda headed south, Khalid scouted the passes of the Taurus Mountains. After driving eastwards towards the Euphrates and finding little opposition, he turned northward to drive into eastern Anatolia. There was some kind of skirmish at a place called Bughras where Habib b. Maslamah was victorious while Khalid drove towards Tarsus before turning north-east at the Pyramus/Ceyhan river and attacking Germanicia Caesarea, Kahramanmaras in south-eastern Turkey. A brief stand-off saw the inhabitants agree to leave without further fighting. The rest of Khalid's raid seems to have been largely uneventful even though he zigzagged first to the outskirts of Caesarea and then to just south of Sebasteia before returning to northern Syria through Melitene. This might be relying on an argument of silence given that there is little recorded information about Khalid's raid. However, it is possible that the lack of military challenge or overt success of Khalid's raid suggests that Heraclius had been successful in creating a no-man's-land between northern Syria and the Anatolian plain.

Muslim Raids and the End of an Era

As well as pulling back and congregating as many of his forces as he could in Anatolia whilst abandoning southern Syria and Palestine to their fate, Heraclius also seems to have briefly prioritised Armenia and Mesopotamia. This was hardly surprising given that Armenia was a valuable resource of military manpower, as well as the likely homeland of the emperor's family, while Mesopotamia controlled the remaining land links with Heraclius' Persian and Arab allies and contained increasingly valuable Roman units placed there during the Sassanid civil wars. Furthermore, from a strategic point of view, a continued presence in Mesopotamia diverted Muslim attention away from Anatolia and gave Heraclius time to implement something of a scorched earth policy, removing garrisons, farmers and workers, and destroying crops and fortifications, all the while preparing to repel any coming invasion.

Heraclius, therefore, ordered the commanders in Mesopotamia to stand firm as long as possible. However, if his advice, recorded later, to 'let no one engage in any more fighting with the [Arabs]; but let him who can hold his position remain in it' is any way truthful then the emperor's angry reaction to the actions of his governor of the Mesopotamian province of Osrhoene, John Kateas,

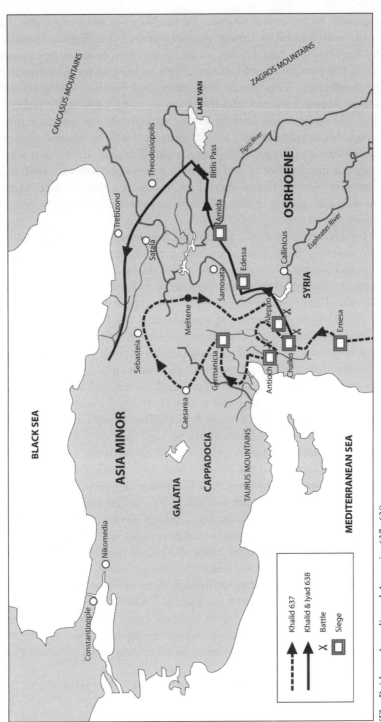

The Raids on Anatolia and Armenia, 637–638.

would appear to be somewhat strange.[5] As the Muslims advanced north, Kateas left his provincial capital at Edessa and approached the Muslim commander, Iyad, and negotiated a pact known as the Truce of Chalkis to pay an annual tribute of 1,400 pounds of gold to the caliph so long as the Muslims did not cross the Euphrates. This would have protected Roman Mesopotamia and perhaps even Armenia from Arab incursions, seemingly giving Heraclius what he wanted. However, upon hearing of this agreement, the emperor removed Kateas from his command and exiled him. It could be argued that, while Heraclius wanted to protect Mesopotamia and Armenia, he did not want the entire Mesopotamian front closed down as that would have allowed an even greater hammer blow to fall on Anatolia. On a more personal note, Heraclius may have seen the signing of this pact by Kateas as the governor overstepping his authority.

Whatever Heraclius' reasons, the annual tribute was not paid provoking an immediate reaction from Iyad, who struck across the Euphrates to capture Callinicus and Edessa with very little effort. Indeed, the lack of any major engagement to save Mesopotamia does seem somewhat peculiar given that Heraclius valued its preservation so highly. The rapidity of this collapse may be evidence of just how outnumbered and isolated the Roman army in Meso-potamia was and Ptolemaios, Kateas' replacement, may have decided not to waste what soldiers he had under his command in a futile gesture of resistance.

Despite the decisiveness of the Roman defeat in Upper Mesopotamia, Heraclius was still keen to slow the Muslim advance in any way possible. With the main Muslim forces driving north and along the Levantine coast, several major cities were left under-defended. Heraclius sought to exploit this by calling upon those Christian Arabs of the Syrian Desert and Mesopotamia who remained unconquered by Islam and remained allied to the Roman Empire to attack this soft underbelly of the Muslim lines, specifically the Muslim military headquarters at Emesa. However, Abu Ubayda seems to have gotten word of this sneak attack in its early stages and was able to gather a garrison force strong enough to resist the Christian Arab attack, which seems to have come in March 638. He then asked Umar for reinforcements, who sent men from Kufa, the newly founded military base near Hira, and raised new forces at Medina and from amongst the urban militias. Umar also sent orders to the Muslim forces in Iraq to attack the Upper Mesopotamian homes of these invading Christian Arabs and to cut off their retreat from Emesa. Unable to overpower the Emesa garrison and soon troubled by news of their homeland being ravaged, the Christian Arab force soon broke up. Upon seeing this, the hitherto patient garrison of Abu Ubayda sallied forth and crushed what remained of the besieging army.

With the Christian Arabs curtailed, the Muslims then returned to the job of subduing Roman Mesopotamia that they had started in 637 before then pressing on into Armenia and Anatolia.[6] Why the Muslims turned their attention away from Heraclius and Anatolia is not fully explained by the sources but there are several potential reasons for it. As already mentioned, Armenia was a valuable manpower resource for the Roman army and disrupting that could undermine its resistance. Also, as Heraclius' invasion of the Persian Empire had previously shown, the Armenian provinces provided a link between Constantinople and its Iberian, Laz and Turkic allies. Lastly, from an offensive point of view, Khalid's earlier raiding into Cappadocia and the fringes of Anatolia may have revealed that the hills and valleys of the Anatolian-Armenian frontier could provide the Muslims with an opportunity to circumvent Heraclius' defences by allowing them to emerge onto the Anatolian plains from the north-east on the Roman flank or even its rear.

At Edessa, modern-day Urfa in Turkey, the flying column of Iyad that had done so much damage in the wake of the breakdown of the Truce of Chalkis met up with Khalid's mobile guard. Together, these two Muslim generals and their fast-moving forces drove north-east towards Amida.[7] It is uncertain whether the city that had seen so much fighting between the Romans and Persians in previous centuries fell to this raid in 638 but it does seem to have been taken by the Muslims by 640. Driving further east, Khalid and Iyad may have approached Lake Van through the Bitlis Pass before turning north to attack Theodosiopolis. Again, it is unknown if this city was taken now or at some other time before 640. They then turned west, passing Satala and Sebasteia before crossing the Halys, the Kizilirmak River in Turkey, into northern Anatolia.

However, if Khalid was involved in these raids, they were to be his last campaigns. In the decade since his conversion to Islam Khalid had fulfilled his role as 'the sword of Allah', given to him by the Prophet himself, to an extent that no one would have predicted. However, his victories along the Euphrates and throughout Syria had not only brought vast territories to the Islamic state, they had propelled him to a level of fame and reputation beyond any other. Despite at no stage suggesting that Khalid might use his popularity to subvert the Islamic hierarchy, Umar saw such hero-worship as a danger to the importance of the position of the caliph and even Muhammad in the Islamic state. Therefore, despite their familial connection and having learnt his lesson in doubting Khalid's military prowess before Yarmuk, Umar began to actively seek some way of quietly deposing Khalid to highlight that the success of the Muslims came from the Will of God rather than the deeds of a select few.

This did not mean that Umar subverted the rule of law or distorted the truth to achieve his ends. One such incident brought to his attention was regarding Khalid bathing in alcohol. However, as the Muslim ban on alcohol applied to drinking it, Khalid felt he was well within his rights to use it for other purposes; as a warrior and duellist, Khalid may have had wounds that required attention and the use of alcohol as an antiseptic was long established and Umar accepted such reasoning as not transgressing Islamic law.[8] However, Umar found his opportunity in late-637/early-638. In the aftermath of his capture of Germanicia Caesarea, Khalid had handsomely rewarded a poet who had written a poem in praise of him and his exploits. That this led to the mere suggestion that he might have used funds from the state treasury sealed the end of his military career, for, even if the accusation of misappropriating state funds was proven false, as it would be, Khalid's gift to the poet meant he was guilty of extravagance. Even a personal appeal to Umar in Medina, protesting that extravagance was not punishable by military discharge, failed to save Khalid's military career.

However, despite it being cut short, it was a military career that was the envy of most. Perhaps undefeated in battle across scores of engagements of differing sizes, Khalid's strategic and tactical genius was demonstrated time and again as he manipulated the terrain and the dispositions of his opponents to turn over-whelmed Muslim armies into triumphant forces.[9] He pioneered much of the organisation and tactics of the Muslim army, a factor no less important than his mobile cavalry that provided immense manoeuvrability and striking power. The combination of hit-and-run tactics and massed flanking attacks proved irresistible to the more heavily armoured Roman and Persian cavalry. Recognising that he would usually be outnumbered, Khalid also made sure to give his men every advantage before the fighting began. To that end, despite his aggression and ruthlessness, Khalid would rarely if ever commit to an action without first reconnoitring the battlefield, allowing him to use the terrain to his benefit. He is credited as one of the main advocates of the *mubarizun* and using it to undermine an opponent's morale and leadership by targeting opposition officers in duels.

While Walaja demonstrated his tactical skills, and the tripartite victories at Muzayyah, Saniyy and Zumail showed his superior use of surprise, speed and decisiveness, it was at Yarmuk that Khalid's skills shone through most prominently. He not only rescued the situation on several occasions by rallying his demoralised men and striking at the gaps in the Roman lines, but also took full advantage of the geography of the plain of Yarmuk and its surrounding ravines. The engagement also demonstrated Khalid's willingness to risk everything in battle and ruthlessly press the advantages that this may present. His launching of the corps of Abu Ubayda and Yazid in a spoiling attack against Vahan's right wing on the fourth day could be argued to be one of the most important battlefield manoeuvres of Late Antiquity. Perhaps Khalid's greatest legacy to the Muslim army was that these aggressive yet diligent traits and tactical know-how were to permeate the Muslim command across the battlefields of Syria, Palestine, Mesopotamia, Iran, Northern Africa and beyond.

Despite the way in which his career ended, Khalid appears to have accepted Umar's arguments regarding the danger of his fame as relations between the two do not seem to have become particularly strained. Khalid did not attempt to gain any sort of revenge on the caliph even though his popularity could have presented great political and even military problems for Umar. After just four years of quiet retirement at Emesa, much to his own chagrin, Khalid died peacefully in his bed in 642, bequeathing his property to Umar. There can be little doubt that the Muslim cause and perhaps the world had lost one of its greatest cavalry commanders.[10]

War, Famine, Pestilence and Death – the 'Year of Ashes' and the Plague of Amwas

The dismissal of Khalid was not the only strange decision taken by Umar in 638. Despite being in a position to strike into Anatolia, it was at this point that Umar decided to focus on consolidation rather than further conquest. There was to be no decisive attempt to circumvent Heraclius' defensive line in Anatolia in the west and no crossing of what is now the Iran-Iraq border in the east. This begs the question as to why the caliph, who had been such a keen advocate of Islamic expansion, raising and sending reinforcements wherever and whenever they were needed, chose such an inopportune moment as mid-638 when supreme victory seemed at hand to call a halt.

Having spent a great deal of time and effort in establishing an administrative infrastructure, it is possible that Umar felt that a lull in the fighting was needed to consolidate Muslim rule in Syria, Palestine and Mesopotamia. This would have been an understandable motivation as Umar had the example of the collapse of the Persian conquests in the face of the Roman counter-attack of the late 620s. Adding infrastructural and administrative stability to his conquered territories will have helped make them more resilient in the face of any Roman or Persian counter-offensives. Strategically, the caliph may also have been somewhat concerned about his relatively few soldiers being spread too thinly across such a wide area; something highlighted by the Christian Arab attack on Emesa. Umar may also have wanted to give his armies some rest after over a decade of almost unbroken warfare.

However, the real driving force behind this consolidation probably lies in what Arab sources refer to as the 'Year of Ashes' – a nine-month period of drought in the Middle East. While this may have restricted recruiting and campaigning efforts in affected areas, by itself it may not account for the lull in the fighting in Syria, Mesopotamia and Iran. What exacerbated the problems caused by the drought, and may have been somewhat caused by it, was the outbreak of plague in Palestine in early 639. Known as the Plague of Emmaus or the Plague of Amwas, it is thought to have caused tens of thousands of deaths, including many high-profile Arab generals, namely Abu Ubayda, Yazid and Shurahbil.[11] The loss of such generals at the same time as Khalid's dismissal cannot have helped the Muslim military hierarchy and the morale of the common soldiery.

The exact nature of the Plague of Amwas is not certain, although it is most commonly associated with the bubonic plague cycle that had begun with the

Justinianic Plague in the 540s. That such an outbreak would have a profound effect on the Arabs that came into contact with it is hardly surprising given that they had been largely sheltered from previous outbreaks and therefore had failed to build up any real immunity or resistance to it. However, whatever its pathology, the plague did not become the kind of intercontinental pandemic that the initial Justinianic outbreak had been a century previously, or the Black Death would be 700 years later. The impact on the less-immune Muslims also seems to have been slight as the armies of Islam were on the move again in at least three separate theatres – Egypt, Iran and Anatolia – within a year.

These outbreaks of drought and plague within the Muslim ranks must have aided Heraclius' attempts to build a firm defensive position in Anatolia. Given that the defeat at Yarmuk had happened so far south and that the Muslims still had to deal with the garrisons of Syria, Palestine and Mesopotamia, it could be argued that the extent of Heraclius' abandoning of Chalkis, Aleppo, Antioch and even Anatolian cities like Adana and Caesarea was excessive. However, the Roman emperor does seem to have recognised the potential for further disaster that the ruthless rapidity of the Muslim cavalry represented. Had he sent the Roman army into northern Syria, it is possible that not only would it have suffered another defeat but, as the raids of Khalid and Iyad had shown, that a dynamic strike could have captured the escape routes through the Taurus, trapping the majority of the remaining Roman forces south of the mountains.

Therefore, while Heraclius' attempts to consolidate his forces in Anatolia may not have been overly successful in terms of getting garrison forces to leave their homes, and the abandoning of Syria, Palestine and Mesopotamia might have seemed drastic, such measures were not without positives. The time that these garrisons gave Heraclius by holding up the Muslim forces and the buffer zone he managed to establish were invaluable in 'the ultimately successful defence of what was to become the empire's Anatolian heartland'.[12] However, while Heraclius and his successors would be successful in defending Anatolia, this had little bearing on the future of Syria. Despite resistance from many of its towns and cities, once it became obvious that the Roman army would not be marching to their rescue the Muslim campaigns throughout the Levant took on the appearance of nothing more than a wide-ranging 'mopping-up operation'.[13] The Romans might have had ideas of retaking their Levantine provinces once the initial thrust of the Muslim storm had been weathered but 'Syria had become a land under Islamic rule' and would remain so to this very day, with few interruptions.[14]

The Fall of Ctesiphon and the Battle of Jalula
Syria, Palestine and Roman Mesopotamia were not the only regions in which the Muslims were steamrollering an increasingly desperate defence. Much like their victory at Yarmuk, their victory at Qadisiyyah and Sa'd's ruthless pursuit of Jalinus had exposed the entirety of Persian Mesopotamia and left the road

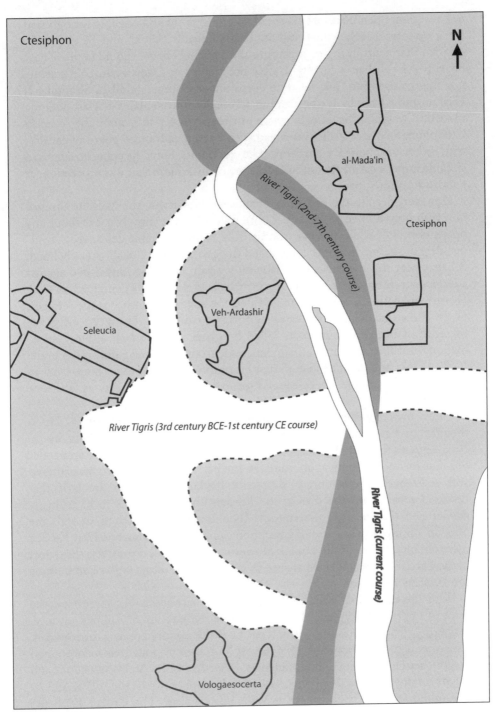

City Plans of Ctesiphon.

to Ctesiphon open. With its potential as a focal point and possible springboard for a counter-attack whilst still in Persian hands, Umar and Sa'd quickly decided that neutralising or capturing the Sassanid capital should be their next objective. Less than a fortnight after the victory at Qadisiyyah, Sa'd's army, now reorganised into five separate corps under Zuhra, Abdullah, Shurahbeel, Hashim and Khalid b. Arfatah, set out across the alluvial plains of Mesopotamia towards Ctesiphon. Seemingly aware of the garrison forces along the route to Ctesiphon, Sa'd sent Zuhra on ahead with a strong advanced guard of cavalry, with orders to subdue the garrisons if he could but, should he come up against a sizeable imperial army, he was to await the main column that was proceeding at a more restrained pace.

However, despite the mixture of caution and alacrity, the Muslim advance met with only limited resistance. Zuhra was able to occupy Najaf without any opposition and, while the garrison at Burs resisted, Zuhra defeated its commander, Busbuhra, in single combat and the garrison was quickly overwhelmed. A battle near the ancient site of Babylon is recorded in December 636 against a large concentration of Persian forces, which given that its commanders were Hormuzan, Mihran, Nakheerzan and Beerzan suggests that it was the remnant of the force that Jalinus had extricated from Qadisiyyah. However, given the presence of Beerzan, supposedly killed by Qaqa, and the lack of clear information regarding any battle at Babylon, aside from there being dissension in the Persian ranks and the information that Hormuzan retreated to his homelands in Khuzestan the whole event should probably be downplayed as a major engagement.

Zuhra then continued his pursuit of congregating Persian forces. He is thought to have defeated a Sassanid force at Sura before catching up to Nakheerzan's force at Deir Kab. Despite the killing of the Sassanid commander in a duel by one of Zuhra's subordinates, the Persian force seems to have offered stiff resistance. It was only a successful flanking manoeuvre by Jarir that captured a bridge to the rear of the Persian lines that seems to have finally encouraged the Persians to retreat.[15] The last Persian attempt to stall the Muslim advance to the gates of Ctesiphon came in early-January 637 at Kusa, a mere ten miles short of the capital. However, this time all it took was the defeat of the Persian commander, Shahryar, in a duel by one of the *mubarizun* to force the Persians to retreat.

With the capture of Kusa, nothing now lay between Sa'd's forces and the walls of the Persian capital. However, despite the rapidity of Zuhra's advance, properly defended, Ctesiphon would not be easily captured or even surrounded. This was because it was not a single city but a metropolis that incorporated several settlements including Seleucia, Veh-Ardashir, Vologaesocerta and others on the banks of the Tigris, as well as Ctesiphon itself. Indeed, in Arabic, Ctesiphon was and is known as al-Mada'in, meaning 'The Cities'. With the direction they were approaching from – the west bank of the Tigris – the

Muslims were to come to the sub-cities of Vologaesocerta, Seleucia and Veh-Ardashir first. Of these three, it appears that Yazdgerd and his generals focused their defensive efforts on Veh-Ardashir, probably due to it being the closest to Ctesiphon itself, digging ditches and placing ballistas and catapults. The presence of such siege engines forced the Muslims back from the walls but they quickly evened the odds by employing Persians to build siege engines for them.

By March 637, after almost two months of blockade, the Persian garrison was becoming desperate and sallied forth in an attempt to break the siege. In the subsequent fighting, Zuhra is said to have killed the Persian commander in a duel before being killed himself by an arrow. But one peculiar story stands out most from the siege of Veh-Ardashir: the Persians are said to have used a specially trained lion to disrupt the Muslim cavalry and infantry, with its rampage only being stopped by Hashim, who killed the beast with a single blow with his sword. One cannot help but suggest that this is a prime example of the corruption of the record of a Persian commander either called 'lion,' such as the Greek name Leo, or being described as fighting as fiercely as a lion.

As their sally proved ineffective, the Persians offered to recognise the Muslim conquest of all territory up to the banks of the Tigris in return for an end to the fighting. Sa'd replied by saying that peace would only come when Yazdgerd accepted Islam and paid the *jizya*. The next morning, the Muslims found Veh-Ardashir abandoned as the garrison had somehow managed to slip across the Tigris to Ctesiphon, destroying many of the bridges and taking any available boats with them.

Despite these measures and the fact that the river seems to have been in flood, the Persians failed to prevent the Muslims from crossing the Tigris. Taking advantage of local knowledge, Sa'd found a location where the river was fordable and sent a contingent of around 600 volunteers under Asim to force a crossing. These were intercepted by Persian cavalry, but Asim's men were able to fight off this attack, establish themselves on the eastern shore and hold their position long enough for Sa'd to get reinforcements to them. With the Muslim army safely across the Tigris, the Sassanid force in Ctesiphon under Mihran and Rustam's brother, Khurrazad, decided that any attempt to defend Ctesiphon itself was futile and prompted Yazdgerd to abandon the city with his army and treasury. With that, aside from small pockets of resistance, Sa'd and his Muslim Arab force took one of the ancient world's greatest cities, along with the large amounts of booty it possessed, without a fight.

This lack of an organised defence of their capital not only demonstrates the poor state to which the Persian military had fallen through its defeats by Romans, Turks, civil war and now Muslim Arabs, but also how unprepared the Persian defences of Ctesiphon were for an attack from the south. Centuries of warfare against the Romans and the nomadic tribes of the Eurasian steppe had concentrated Persian defensive efforts to the north of Ctesiphon. The contrast between the destruction of the bridges over the Nahrawan canal to block Heraclius' approach in 627 and the ease with which Sa'd approached Veh-Ardashir and then took Ctesiphon in 637 demonstrates the direction in which Persian defences were facing. It could be argued that, by leaving troops in Mesopotamia to slow the advance of the Muslims on Ctesiphon, Yazdgerd assured the capture of his capital by depriving its defence of much needed man-power. However, without garrisons at the likes of Burs, Babylon and Kusa, Zuhra's advanced guard would have arrived at Ctesiphon before any defensive measures were implemented. Therefore, after the defeat at Qadisiyyah, the Sassanid king and his generals were left with what was a no-win situation with regard to defending Ctesiphon.

However, this Persian evacuation of their capital without a fight meant that there were still sizeable Sassanid armies in the field that needed to be defeated before Muslim control of Mesopotamia could be consolidated. The main Persian force under Mihran and Khurrazad retreated north to Jalula, which, as well as being near the modern site of Baghdad, lay on a strategically impor-tant route between the Persian provinces of Mesopotamia, Khurasan and Atropatene. There were also forces congregating to the north at Birtha, usually identified with modern-day Tikrit, as well as the significant garrison of the fortress further up the Tigris recognised as modern Mosul. Its governor, Intaq, appears to have moved south to Birtha with his garrison and along with some survivors from Ctesiphon and new recruits from the local Arab tribes formed a sizeable force.

The relative proximity of Birtha to the main Sassanid force at Jalula meant that Intaq could move to join his forces to those of Mihran and Khurrazad as well as providing a potential route of retreat for the Persian force should it be defeated at Jalula. Therefore, whilst Sa'd sent the majority of his force against Jalula under Hashim in April, he also sent about 5,000 men under Abdullah to preoccupy if not neutralise Intaq. Upon arriving, Abdullah attempted to storm the walls with a lightning attack. However, Intaq's men held firm and it appears as though Abdullah became concerned about the size of the garrison. To deal with this perceived strength, the Muslim commander attempted to drive a wedge between the elements of Intaq's force. Muslim spies made contact with the Christian Arab contingent and persuaded them to side with Abdullah rather than Intaq. The Persians seem to have gotten wind of this betrayal or at least suspected it, as they attempted to abandon Birtha along the river. However, they found themselves trapped between the attacking Muslims and their former Arab allies and the Persian garrison was quickly overrun. A few days later, a small Muslim force received the surrender of Mosul without much of a fight.

While Abdullah was cutting off a potential route of retreat and reinforce-ment for the Sassanids, Hashim had squared up to the Persian forces at Jalula. While the strategic position of Jalula as a crossroads for the Sassanid state meant that it was vital for Mihran and Khurrazad to try to defend it, the position of the town with the Diyala River to the west and foothills of the Zagros Mountains to the east also offered an excellent defensive position. Knowing that the naturally narrow plain in front of Jalula would funnel the Muslim army towards the town and protect their flanks, Mihran prepared diligently for the Muslim attack he knew would come. Jalula itself was turned into a fort, protected by a line of trenches stretching from the broken ground of the Zagros foothills to the Diyala and caltrops to further hinder the Muslim infantry and cavalry. Archers and artillery were also positioned on the fortifications to bleed the Muslims as they approached the walls. Only after inflicting crippling damage on the Muslim ranks would Mihran then leave this defensive position in order to win a decisive victory.

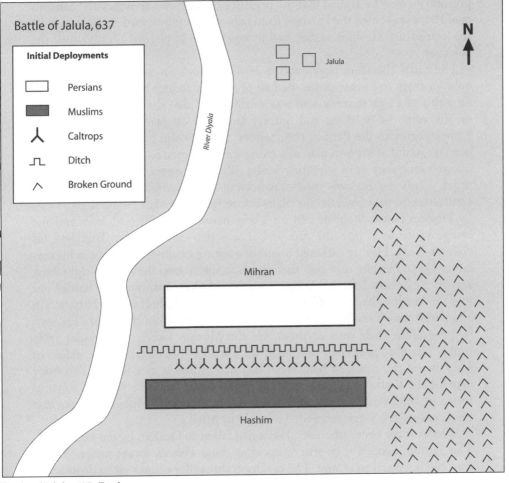

Battle of Jalula, 637: Deployments.

Upon surveying the disposition and defences of the Persian force, Hashim recognised Mihran's ploy in presenting the Muslims with only one offensive option – a costly frontal assault. This was something that he could ill afford given that the size of the forces arrayed at Jalula were likely very similar, around 12,000 each. Therefore, Hashim decided to draw the Persians away from their defences by employing one of the riskiest manoeuvres in battlefield tactics – the feigned retreat. The danger of this tactic is that a feigned retreat can quickly become an actual one if the morale and discipline of those attempting it is not strong enough and a counter-attack from the opponent is so well pressed and coordinated as to be impossible to resist. Clearly, after the numerous victories they had won up to the battlefield of Jalula, Hashim had every reason to believe in the discipline and prowess of his men to even attempt such a tactic. While there is no evidence to suggest that Mihran's counter-attack was not well pressed, it could be argued that the presence of their own trenches and caltrops could have prevented the Persians from launching a fully coordinated assault on the 'retreating' Muslims as they had to waste time in placing a bridge over the defences.

The battle therefore began with a Muslim attack on the defences of Jalula, only for them to retreat under the hail of Persian archers and artillery. Mihran took this as a sign that his plan was working and that the Muslim forces were on the verge of breaking and quickly launched his planned counter-attack. Unbeknownst to the Persian commander, his opposite number will have also been pleased that his own plan was going well. His men had fooled the Persians into thinking they were retreating whilst still retaining their own discipline and order. With the Persians now drawn away from their defences, an infantry confrontation took place on the plain before Jalula. Further staged withdrawals by Hashim's men then opened up a gap between the Persian lines and the bridge route back into the fort and it was then that Hashim launched his counterstroke. Having gathered together a strong cavalry contingent in his rear under Qaqa, Hashim now sent them in an attack around the Persian right flank against the lightly defended bridge. Once word filtered through the battlefront that the Muslims had cut off the only escape route, Hashim ordered his men in a full-scale attack on the Persian lines while Qaqa attacked their rear. Trapped by geography, their own defences and the Muslim forces, the Persian army broke. Despite many men making it back to the fort of Jalula, the defeat of Mihran and the death of Khurrazad had neutralised it as a threat. The exact date for the Battle of Jalula is difficult to pin down from the sources, some of which place the battle at the end of a seven-month siege while others say that the seven-month siege succeeded a battle in April 637.

Whatever the order of events, Jalula had fallen to Hashim by the end of 637. The Muslim general then sent Qaqa after those Persian forces under Mihran who had managed to escape. The cavalry commander caught up to them at the city of Khanaqin, some fifteen miles to the east. Some reinforcements from

Hulwan may have reached Mihran but they were not enough to prevent a further defeat and the capture of Khanaqin. It is recorded that Qaqa defeated Mihran in a personal duel, removing one of the more capable Persian commanders as an obstacle. Qaqa was now within 100 miles of Yazdgerd III's base at Hulwan and was to appear before its walls before the end of January 638.

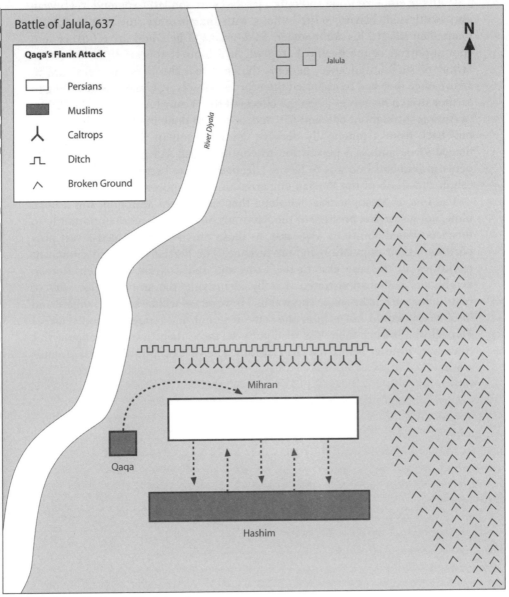

Battle of Jalula, 637: Qaqa's Flank Attack.

However, upon hearing of the defeat of Mihran at Khanaqin, Yazdgerd had retreated further east into the Iranian heartland of his empire, reaching Qom, around 100 miles south of modern Tehran. This hopping from Ctesiphon to Hulwan to Qom was to become a repeating pattern for the rest of Yazdgerd's life as he attempted to outrun the Muslim advance whilst at the same time trying to bring together an army strong enough to retake his lost lands.

With the emperor gone and only a modest garrison left to defend it, Hulwan also swiftly fell. Having settled affairs with the citizenry, the ever ambitious Qaqa then sent to his commander, Sa'd, asking if he could drive further into Iran in pursuit of the fleeing Yazdgerd. Sa'd himself appears to have been in favour of such an advance, perhaps thinking that the Persians were sure to return once they had reorganised their forces. However, Umar was unwilling to further stretch his forces given the effects of the 'Year of Ashes' and the Plague of Amwas throughout 638 and 639 and, as he had done in ordering his men to pull back from a potentially decisive confrontation in Roman Anatolia, he denied Qaqa and Sa'd permission to continue east. What is now the border between Iran and Iraq was to be the effective frontier between the lands of the caliph and those of the Persian emperor, albeit temporarily.

The loss of Mesopotamia, let alone their capital at Ctesiphon, was a huge blow, not just to the prestige of the Sassanids but perhaps more importantly to their continued ability to wage war, as those provinces contained a vast proportion of their population and tax revenue. The Persians still held significant territories all the way east to the Oxus and Indus rivers and their Roman neighbours had demonstrated that by identifying the strategic necessity of regrouping such losses were survivable. However, as will be seen, Yazdgerd and his advisers would not exhibit the same restraint and strategic good sense of Heraclius, allowing their loss of dignity to force them into challenging this 'Iran-Iraq' frontier before they had laid any defensive or infrastructural groundwork.

Chapter 9

Stealing Roman Bread and Persian Heart

There is scarcely any important event in history of which the accounts are so vague and so discrepant as the capture of Alexandria. The whole history of the irruption of the Saracens into the [Roman] empire is indeed dark and obscure: but of all the events of this dark period the conquest of Egypt is the darkest.

Brooks (1895), 435

Amr's Great Egyptian Enterprise[1]

While the likes of Khalid, Abu Ubayda, Iyad, Sa'd and Qaqa were winning great renown for their exploits in Syria, Mesopotamia and beyond, another of the Muslim commanders was chaffing under his lack of action and glory. Despite having led the first real invasion of Roman territory, won the first engagement at the Battle of Dathin and played an important role at Yarmuk on the Muslim right wing, Amr b. al-As had been largely overshadowed by his colleagues. However, as an ambitious and capable commander, after forcing the capitulation of Gaza and other isolated garrisons that continued to offer resistance across Palestine following the capture of Jerusalem, Amr was determined to find some venture to help redress this imbalance.

He found his target by looking to another continent, and, when journeying to Caesarea to help in its capture in the autumn of 639, Amr is thought to have approached the caliph with an audacious plan to invade the breadbasket of the Roman Empire – Egypt. It is possible that Amr had conceived this plan and may even have approached Umar about it at an earlier date but it was only now, with most of Palestine subdued, that the caliph was willing to give more thought to further campaigning. Amr urged Umar to act quickly for, while large parts of Egypt lay undefended, the former governor of Jerusalem, Aretion, who had escaped the Holy City before its capitulation, was now in Egypt attempting to rally Roman and local forces. However, Umar prevaricated. He believed, quite rightly, that Amr was underestimating the difficulties involved in such an undertaking, especially as the ongoing struggles in Syria, Mesopotamia and Khuzestan along with the lasting effects of drought and plague meant that Amr would probably only have a force of between 3,500 and 4,000; a figure that Amr thought would be enough for the initial surprise attack.

However, despite being seemingly rebuffed, on his way to Caesarea Amr received a letter from Umar. The lure of one of the oldest and richest regions in the world had proved too much for the caliph, as he now authorised Amr's plan.

To maintain the strictest secrecy, Amr and his small force left Caesarea in the dead of night, heading straight for the Egyptian border. However, upon reaching Raphia, just short of the frontier, messengers arrived in Amr's camp from the caliph. It seems as though Umar's earlier doubts, spurred on by the counsel of the future caliph, Uthman, had gotten the better of him and the messengers brought orders for Amr to not cross into Egypt. This would appear to have torpedoed Amr's adventure before it had even begun; however, Umar's regard for honour left Amr with an opportunity. Not wanting to order a Muslim army to retreat from enemy territory without meeting them in battle, Umar gave the proviso that if Amr had already crossed into Egypt by the time the messengers reached him, he was to continue with his plan of invasion.

Recognising that the caliph's letter was not going to bode well for his enterprise even before reading it, Amr refused to do so before crossing into Egypt. Once in the valley of Arish, he read the letter and then asked the officers present: 'Is this place in Syria or in Egypt?' When he received the answer 'in Egypt', Amr then read Umar's letter to them and declared that the caliph's orders to continue on would be obeyed. Whether or not the Muslim column was actually in Egypt is open to some interpretation, as some scholars place the ancient boundary of Egypt further to the west than the valley of Arish. The celebration of the *Eid al-Adha* Festival of Sacrifice by Amr and his men when they arrived in Egypt, which takes place between the tenth and twelfth day of Dhu al-Hijjah, which in 639 equates to 12–14 December, gives some kind of timetable for their early movements.

The Muslim sources for Amr's invasion of Egypt are much like what they are for the rest of their conquests – chronologically tangled and at times contradictory. The Romano-Greek sources are in an even worse state. John of Nikiou, an eyewitness to the invasion, is the most useful but he does not detail the entire invasion while the rest 'neither examined nor understood what they recorded, and their confusion of dates and perversion of truth are such that they have served only as false lights, luring into quagmires nearly every modern writer who has followed them.'[2]

Theophanes claims that the Romans paid annual tribute to the Muslims to stave off Amr's attack for three years. Nikephoros places the invasion of Egypt prior to Heraclius' departure from Syria and perhaps even before the Battle of Yarmuk. He also records Amr fighting battles against a certain John, Duke of Barcina, and then negotiating a treaty that would have seen the Muslim commander become a Christian and marry a daughter of the emperor. The author of the *Chronicon Orientale* has Heraclius remove all troops to Syene, modern-day Aswan in southern Egypt, and pay tribute to the Muslims for ten years.

There is no record amongst the Muslim sources of any kind of negotiations so early in the invasion beyond the surrender of individual towns and cities.

From Arish, Amr marched along the main road of Egypt, the same road that Biblical characters like Abraham, Jacob and Joseph and rulers such as Cambyses, Alexander the Great and Cleopatra had used. Despite the importance of this road to trade, pilgrims, communications and the military, Amr met no Roman soldiers before reaching Pelusium, the city guarding the eastern-most approaches to the Nile Delta and the site of many important events in Egyptian history: Sennachrib, king of Assyria from 705 to 681 BCE and the antagonist of Lord Byron's 1813 poem, *The Destruction of Sennacherib*, retreated from before its walls; the Battle of Pelusium in 525 BCE had seen all of Egypt fall under the yoke of Achaemenid Persia; while more recently Pelusium had seen the first recorded appearance of the Justinianic Plague in 541 CE.[3]

Approaching the walls of this important city unmolested, Amr then settled into the now-customary Muslim blockade. In a peculiar way, the lack of numbers in his force played into the hands of Amr as the Pelusium garrison were not afraid to launch numerous sallies against the blockaders. Not only did this allow the Muslims to inflict casualties they otherwise would not have been able to, the constant opening of the gates to permit the exit and return of the sallying forces presented Amr with an opportunity to capture the city. After at least a month of such fighting, the Muslims repelled a sally so forcefully that a contingent was able to chase the Romans back to their walls and seize one of the open gates. Recognising this breakthrough, Amr launched his forces in an all-out attack that broke Roman resistance and delivered the city to the Muslims sometime in late-February 640. Some Roman sources claim that Egyptian Copts aided Amr in his capture of Pelusium, but this was likely an example of looking for a scapegoat to detract from Roman incompetence and deficiencies, and John of Nikiou, an eyewitness of much of the invasion, defends the Copts from such accusations.

The capture of Pelusium was vitally important for the future of Amr's adventure as it secured his lines of communication, reinforcement and potential retreat. However, the difficulty and time involved highlighted to the Arab com-mander how much he would need the reinforcements that Umar had promised him. If he had required some good fortune to overcome an under-defended city like Pelusium, how was he going to deal with the much larger Roman garrisons of the Nile Delta? The size of those Roman forces present in Egypt is diffi-cult to pin down for no source goes into any detail on them after the *Notitia Dignitatum* of the late-fourth/early-fifth century, which suggested that the Egyptian provinces, along with Libya, had perhaps over 60,000 regular, semi-professional and militia troops at the turn of the fifth century.[4] Furthermore, as Egypt remained largely unmolested militarily in the intervening two centuries, its garrisons had significantly dropped in size. By the time of Justinian, if not before, it relied solely on locally raised, *limitanei* forces for its defence rather than the regular field armies stationed in Syria, Armenia, Constantinople or the Balkans. The campaign of Nicetas and the subsequent Persian conquest in the 610s will have done further damage to an already weakened Egyptian military infrastructure and Heraclius seems to have done little to encourage rebuilding after his victory in 627, with his representatives focusing more on forcing religious unity through persecution rather than repairing the region's defences and repopulating its military forces.

The extent of this damage may be best highlighted by the lack of reaction to the possibility of an Arab incursion. The Muslim victories in Syria and Palestine should have provided ample warning to the Egyptian hierarchy that they would be next. Indeed, Amr's initial Muslim raids towards Gaza and the Battle of Dathin in February 634 had taken place less than fifty miles from Arish. However, instead of taking heed of these warnings and the examples that they must have been made increasingly aware of taking place in Syria, the Roman authorities in Egypt appear to have done nothing to prepare themselves. There were no observation posts established along the road from Gaza to the Delta and therefore no army sent to help defend the walls of Pelusium. While the previous thirty years may not have been kind to the forces of Egypt, an army of even comparable size to that of Amr, together with the defences of Pelusium, may have been more than capable of fighting off this initial Muslim thrust. Another seeming consequence of Roman inactivity and poor organisation with regard to the arrival of Amr was the joining of local Bedouin tribesmen with the Muslim army. After the fall of Pelusium, these tribesmen seem to have viewed the coming invasion of the Nile Delta as an excellent opportunity for immense plunder.

Suitably buoyed by military success and now reinforced, Amr struck out across the desert for the fortress of Bilbeis, on the eastern edge of the Delta. It was here that the first real signs of any prepared Roman resistance can be seen due to the presence of Aretion, the former governor of Jerusalem. Rather than surrender and pay the *jizya*, Aretion launched a surpise night attack on the Muslim camp. This gambit failed as the Roman force appears to have broken as news spread that Aretion himself had been killed in the opening stages of the attack. However, retreating back behind the walls, the garrison remained defiant throughout March 640, fighting off assaults and refusing to capitulate despite overtures from Amr. However, after a month of such fighting and realising that there was no reason to believe that a Roman relief force was on its way, Bilbeis finally surrendered. In doing so, it cost the Romans not just a valuable fortress but also some 4,000 men – 1,000 dead and 3,000 prisoners. This victory also put Amr within a day's march of the Delta and he seems to have wasted little time in forging ahead with his invasion, bypassing the fortress of Heliopolis and its sizeable garrison to arrive at the fortified position recorded by the Arabs as Umm Dunain, on the banks of the Nile north of Babylon. This site has been identified as the fort of Tendunias recorded by John of Nikiou and was the harbour and docks of the much larger settlement of Misr, which is now in the heart of modern-day Cairo.

Finally, with the enemy having already established a firm foothold, the Romans presented a more sturdy defence. Cyrus, the Patriarch of Alexandria, who had exercised vast control over Egypt since it was recovered from the Persians, and the overall commander of Roman forces in Egypt, Theodore, assembled an army capable of meeting the Muslims in the field and marched to the fortress of Babylon, which was Amr's main target in the region. The arrival of this army, the defences of Tendunias and the presence of the Nile meant that Amr quickly found himself in a potentially disastrous situation, surrounded by garrisoned Roman settlements at Tendunias, Babylon, Misr and Heliopolis.

Despite sending an urgent missive to Umar calling for reinforcements, Amr realised that he could not risk waiting for any such reinforcements to arrive before the Roman forces converged on his exposed army. Instead, Amr decided that his army would have to extricate itself from this predicament through military victory. Given that his force was not large enough to invest Misr, Heliopolis or Bablyon, Amr launched the full might of his modest force against the walls of Tendunias. Unfortunately, neither the Roman nor Arab sources give any indication as to how this Muslim attack played out or how they were able to overcome its defences. Whatever way it was accomplished, it established Amr and his men in a highly defendable and strategically important position and greatly diminshed the likelihood of Cyrus and Theodore being able to deliver the crushing victory that they had hoped to secure upon arriving at Babylon.

Yet despite this victory, Amr was still faced with well-established Roman forces at Heliopolis, Misr and particularly Babylon. Again, not willing to wait for them to converge on his position, in May 640 Amr showed himself to be as bold as the other prominent Muslim commanders by using the boats he had captured at Tendunias to cross the Nile. In threatening the richest parts of Egypt, he hoped to draw the garrison forces into the field where he would have a better chance of defeating them. As Amr's contingent passed through the ruins of Memphis, the ancient capital of the Pharoahs, and surveyed the defences of Misr and Babylon from across the river, a Roman force of archers and cavalry appeared. The harrassment by this mobile column and the stiffening of Roman organisation by the governor of the Fayum, Domentianus, the provincial prefect, Theodosius, the prefect of Alexandria, Anastasius and a certain John, despatched by Heraclius to take overall command in Egypt, forced Amr to move away from the river. In capturing a small town called Bahnasa in the desert hills, the Muslims became aware that a small Roman force was following them, gathering intelligence on their movements. Knowing that surprise and anonymity was one of his greatest allies in such hostile territory, Amr quickly set about ridding himself of this unwanted shadow. Marching by night and making use of information from local Bedouin, Amr was able to fall upon this isolated scouting party, killing them all. The success of this counterstrike was heightened when Amr found that Heraclius' hand-picked commander, John, and his lieutenant were amongst the dead, removing a skilled military practitioner from the field.

The loss of John seems to have greatly unnerved the remaining Roman leadership, with Theodore ordering a congregation of his forces at Babylon rather than perhaps attempting to surround Amr at Bahnasa or threatening his recrossing of the Nile when the garrison of Fayum proved capable of resisting a Muslim attack.

While Theodore might have thought that his outlook on the strategic situation had been proven correct by the Muslims turning away from Fayum, Amr's retreat was not solely dictated by the strength of the garrison. The prevailing reason was that, after having extricated his forces from a difficult situation before the walls of Tendunias and gaining more time by crossing the Nile, word had reached the Muslim commander that reinforcements from Medina were finally on their way and he needed to move back towards the fort in order to meet up with them.

The Battle of Heliopolis and the Siege of Babylon
In the first week of June 640 a force of about 4,000 men under Zubayr b. al-Awwam arrived in the vicinity of Heliopolis, having marched from Medina through Tabouk, Aqaba and Suez. Zubayr's force seems to have been accompanied or quickly followed by another force of similar size. This gave the Muslims perhaps 12,000 men in Egypt, a force that could cause the Roman garrisons of Babylon and Heliopolis some serious trouble.[5] However, the Romans were still in a strong strategic position as the forces of Amr and Zubayr were still separated by the Nile and the Romans appeared to be taking advantage of that situation as Theodore not only reoccupied the fort at Tendunias but he also put his forces into the field near Babylon, seemingly blocking the direct route between the two converging Muslim forces. However, inexplicably, the Romans then failed to prevent Amr from recrossing the Nile further north of Tendunias at Trajan's Canal, which joined the Nile to the Red Sea. Even worse, they seem to have stood idly by as Amr then marched to Zubayr's camp near Heliopolis to unite the Muslim forces.

The exact size of the force that the Romans had been able to bring together is nowhere recorded, although it is suggested that, while Theodosius and Anastasius commanded the Roman cavalry, the majority of the Roman force was made up of spearmen and archer infantry. However, as Theodore and his commanders seem to have hoped to lure the Muslims into a decisive pitched battle and decided that neither Amr nor Zubayr would fight such a battle until they had united, they must have had numerical superiority over the 12,000 Muslims. However, this is mere speculation based more on the idea that the Romans would not be foolish enough to allow Amr and Zubayr to combine

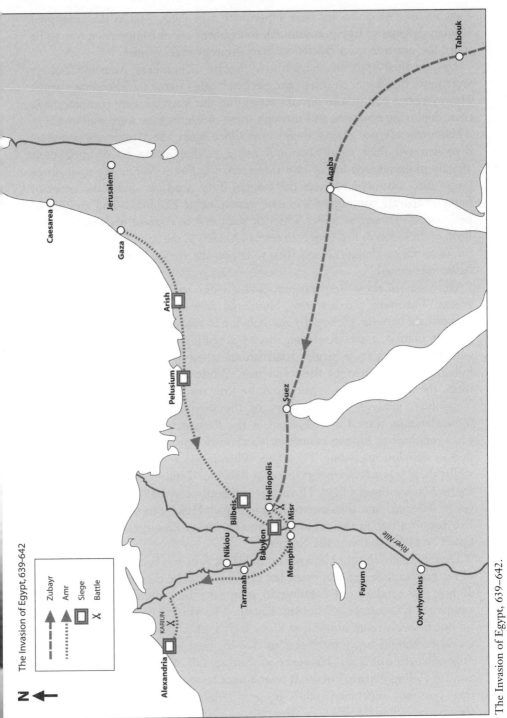

The Invasion of Egypt, 639–642.

their forces if they did not have superiority over them. And as the attempted Roman defence of Egypt continued, foolishness and incompetence was to be more the norm than calculated military strategy and logistics.

Despite their apparent comparative paucity of numbers, Amr and Zubayr were more than eager to accept the pitched battle offered by Theodore's army. However, this enthusiasm did not mean that the Muslims were complacent in their deploying of scouts and through these measures they were well aware of Theodore's advance against their camp. Once again, the Muslim commanders demonstrated their confidence and belief in their cause by dividing their already outnumbered forces into three separate forces. While the main force under Amr advanced to meet the Roman force head on, under the cover of night a separate contingent was sent west towards Tendunias and another of perhaps 500 horsemen under Kharijah went east to conceal itself in the hills. Both of these forces had orders to remain hidden as the Roman army passed by on its march to Heliopolis and then to fall on the enemy flanks and rear when battle was joined.

Oblivious to these preparations, perhaps due to not deploying their own scouts, Theodore and his army blundered forward to meet Amr head on. Somewhere between Heliopolis and Babylon in mid-July 640 there was a fierce infantry contest in which neither force was willing to give ground. However, with the fighting at its height, Kharijah launched his attack from the eastern hills on the Roman right flank and rear. While it was not enough to break them, the disorder it wrought caused the Romans to began to retreat towards Tendunias, straight into the jaws of the second Muslim flanking force. 'Disorder now turned into disaster' as the Roman force disintegrated.[6] The exact numbers of Roman casualties is unknown but there were survivors who fled to Babylon, including Theodore, Theodosius and Anastasius. However, whilst there was an effective garrison at Babylon, Tendunias and then Misr fell to the Arabs without a fight. Having gained control of the river both above and below Babylon, Amr then moved his camp from Heliopolis to the north-east of Babylon to a region that would become known as Fustat, the fore-runner to Cairo, in order to invest the fortress.

Despite establishing a blockade on Babylon, Amr was keen to take advantage of the growing spectre that preceded his forces and he therefore spent the rest of July 640 sending out columns to subjugate the regions surrounding the conquered settlements of Misr and Fayum. The Muslim commander was careful not to overstretch himself, as cities such as Nikiou still possessed sizeable garrisons behind heavy fortifications that his men would find difficult, if not impossible, to overcome. However, as word spread of the defeat of the Roman army at Heliopolis many of the Roman forces remaining in the field abandoned their positions, most importantly those of Nikiou, and retreated back to what they perceived as the safety of Alexandria.

This combination of consolidation and retreat allowed Amr to focus solely on reducing Babylon. At first glance, the defences and position of the fortress would appear to have been beyond the siege capabilities of the Muslims. Its walls were a formidable eight feet thick and at places sixty feet high, with numerous projecting bastions all around. The seventh-century course of the Nile flowed beside the north-western wall and, despite the cursory Muslim control of the river to the north, a quay provided a connection to the nearby fortified island of Raudah and onwards north to Alexandria. Another obstacle for Amr was the fast-rising waters of the Nile, which had already flooded the moat that surrounded the walls of Babylon. Combined with the catapults the Romans had placed on the walls, the moat gave the Muslims little chance of approaching the fortress unmolested. Despite the removal of vast numbers of the leadership, soldiery and the citizenry up the river towards Alexandria, Patriarch Cyrus was still present alongside a military commander called al-Araj by Arab sources, which is likely a corruption of George, who may have been able to call upon up to 6,000 soldiers, supported by large stores of food and water.

With the siege probably not beginning in earnest until September 640, the rest of the year seems to have been spent with the Romans able to repulse any Muslim assault with relative ease. However, Cyrus appears to have lost faith in the continued ability of the garrison to resist, becoming convinced that God had given Egypt to the Arabs. He therefore called a council of war at which he championed a plan to attempt to pay off the Muslims. George would not countenance surrender but does not seem to have stopped Cyrus from carrying out his plan. The Patriarch used the pontoon bridge, which was destroyed behind him to prevent the garrison fleeing in his wake, near the quay to steal out of the fortress across to Raudah, from where he sent an embassy headed by the Bishop of Babylon to Amr's camp. The terms Amr replied with were by now well established – accept Islam, surrender and pay the *jizya* or fight to the death. Despite the lack of room for negotiation, Cyrus did not reject or accept any of the terms and sent back to Amr asking for a delegation to come to Raudah. The leader of this delegation, Ubadah b. al-Samt, overcame the inherent racism of his hosts due to his black skin by impressing Cyrus with his eloquence and the strength of his faith – enough to encourage the Patriarch to argue for the acceptance of the *jizya*.

However, George and his garrison refused to surrender without a fight and as the time for the fortress to surrender expired they launched a surprise attack on the besieging Muslim forces. Despite making some initial inroads against the Muslim positions, the inferiority in numbers gradually took its toll on the Romans as they were first fought to a standstill and then forced back behind the walls of the fortress once more. This defeat strengthened Cyrus' hand and he was able to convince the demoralised garrison that honourable surrender was the only option. However, despite informing Amr of the willingness of the garrison to capitulate, Cyrus also told the Muslim commander that only the Roman emperor could approve such a treaty.

While Amr seems to have been happy to maintain the siege as Cyrus travelled to Alexandria to relay the situation to Heraclius in Constantinople, there is confusion over what exactly the Patriarch intended for this treaty to entail – a sole focus on the capitulation of Babylon or the securing of peace for Egypt by surrendering it all to Amr? These mixed messages together with a decade of mismanagement saw Heraclius look upon these developments with scorn and in mid-November he summoned the Patriarch to Constantinople to explain himself. Despite a spirited defence of his actions and an in-depth description of the Arabs and their fighting prowess, something that must have touched a nerve in the emperor given what he had overseen in Syria and Palestine, Cyrus found himself the target of intense ridicule from the emperor and leveled with charges that were tantamount to treason. Stripped of his position and humiliated, Cyrus was then banished into exile; his treaty with Amr in tatters.

Word that there would be no surrender probably reached Babylon before the end of 640 and for the defenders it could not have come at a worse time, as the Nile floods were receding, leaving their defensive moat dry. Attempts were made to fill it in with caltrops and the Muslim lack of nouse in siege warfare meant that only slow progress was made. While exchanges of missile fire, the use of battering rams, repulsed sallies and assaults are recorded throughout the winter, by the time spring of 641 came around, the morale of the defenders had begun to waver. Tiredness, past defeats and perhaps even disease saw to it that, while the Muslims continued to make slow progress against the fortifications, they were doing so under ever decreasing pressure.

Yet as the spring wore on and the Nile floods continued to recede, the chances of a Roman relief force increased and Theodore, who must have escaped Babylon at some stage, did attempt to put a sizeable army into the field. Not wishing to be caught against the walls of Babylon and eager to deal the already beleaguered Roman forces another blow, Amr once again split his forces, leaving enough men to maintain the siege whilst sending a force north into the Delta to disrupt the assembling of Theodore's troops. Amr's detachment caught up to a Roman force near Samanoud on the eastern Damietta branch of the Nile and were met with one of the few reverses to be suffered by a Muslim army. However, any benefits gained from this victory were quickly squandered by the tentativeness of Theodore, who failed to make any real attempt to relieve Babylon or to keep the pressure on Amr's retreating column, a failure once again blamed on the desertion and treachery of the Copts.

With the failure of Theodore to even approach Babylon, the fate of the beleaguered garrison was sealed. The Romans continued to resist throughout February and March 641, even with word of Heraclius' death in early February 641 filtering through, but eventually the slow progress of the Muslims bore fruit. In the early days of April, sometimes recorded as 6 April, which happened to be Good Friday, with a section of the moat successfully filled in, Zubayr managed to get a scaling ladder to the walls unseen under the cover of night. By the time the defenders were alerted Zubayr was established on the walls and a volley of arrows from supporting archers prevented the Romans from dislodging him. There was still some fighting to be done as Zubayr and his men had unwittingly assailed a section of the wall that was cut off from the rest of the defences, but the presence of this small Muslim force within the fortress was enough to finally break the defenders' already eroded resolve. At first light George called for a parley with Amr and offered to surrender Babylon on terms. Despite some objection from Zubayr that he was about to capture the citadel by force, Amr agreed to this surrender on 9 April 641.

While both Babylon and Memphis had long been surpassed by Alexandria as the capital of Egypt, the position and defences of the fortress gave the Arabs an almost immovable foothold along the Nile that granted easy access to its upper reaches and the Delta. By re-establishing the bridge of boats from Babylon's quay to the abandoned Raudah and then on to Jizah on the western bank, the Arabs were also able to take control of all traffic travelling north down the Nile. That the Romans had summarily failed to even attempt to save Babylon was yet another nail in the coffin of Roman Egypt.

The 'Siege' of Alexandria and the End of Roman Egypt

From this secure position, Amr then moved against Nikiou, one of the major cities of the Delta. A Roman force anticipated that the Arabs would approach Nikiou up the western bank of the Nile in order to take advantage of the more wide open spaces of the fringes of the Sahara, but knew that they would have to recross the river to approach Nikiou itself, which was on the eastern bank. Therefore, there was a Roman cavalry force defending Amr's chosen crossing point at Tarranah. While this force was easily brushed aside, such repeated crossings of the river could have put Amr in a difficult position due to the strength of Nikiou's defences. A well-pressed sally from its sizeable garrison could have proven disastrous for the Muslims as they crossed.

Yet once again the Roman leadership proved unwilling to stand up to the invaders, as Theodore retreated from Nikiou long before Amr approached, taking the majority of the garrison with him. And when the Arabs did reach Nikiou, the remaining defenders under Domentianus fled towards Alexandria only to be cut to pieces as Amr launched his cavalry against them. Amidst such slaughter, on 13 May Nikiou, another great city of Roman Egypt, fell to the Muslim invaders. The Arab cavalry, under Sharik, then chased after Theodore's men, catching them about sixteen miles north of Tarranah. The sheer numbers of Romans were able to force Sharik onto the defensive but just the rumour of the approach of Amr's main force was enough to break the nerve of Theodore and once more he retreated from this opportunity to destroy a sizeable portion of Amr's valuable cavalry.

Brushing aside another small Roman garrison force at a place called Suntais, the Muslims were now within striking distance of Alexandria. Only the fortress of Kariun stood in the way and it was here that Theodore decided to finally make a stand and unsurprisingly Amr took up this challenge. The sizes of both the Roman and Muslim forces arrayed at Kariun are unknown. Theodore seems to have commanded the garrison of Alexandria and those other forces that had managed to retreat to the provincial capital along with some reinforcements from Constantinople, although no specific numbers can be extracted. By the time he approached Kariun it is likely that Amr also had received additional reinforcements either from Medina or the local Bedouin as it would have been unwise, if not impossible, for him to march on Alexandria in any strength after detaching garrisons for Pelusium, Bilbeis, Heliopolis, Babylon, Misr, Fayum, and Nikiou from the 12,000 men he and Zubayr had brought together at Heliopolis.

The Battle of Kariun seems to have involved significant localised fighting and several engagements stretching out over a period of up to ten days with neither side able to force a decisive outcome. However, as had seemingly been the norm since entering Egypt, fighting the Roman army to a standstill was all that was required for Amr to claim a strategic victory, so low was morale amongst the Roman leadership. Kariun was no different and, despite not being defeated, the Romans withdrew leaving Amr in control of the battlefield and yet another fortress.

However, despite their successes in Mesopotamia, Palestine and Syria, the Arabs were about to face a task greater than anything they had yet faced – a truly immense coastal city that was heavily fortified, well-garrisoned and surrounded by canals and Lake Mareotis. The magnitude of that task was quickly demonstrated by the fierce artillery barrage that welcomed the Muslims when they ventured close to the walls. Having little avenue of response, either in siege craft or naval strength, Amr was reduced to the most ineffectual of blockades, given that supplies were easily brought in by sea and quite possibly by land as well. Perhaps in an attempt to lure the garrison into a rash sally, in late-June 641 Amr led a small detachment eastward to effect the subjugation of the Delta, although it appears that he was able to achieve little aside from the burning of some crops.

The 'siege' of Alexandria now entered a rather peculiar phase, with the Muslims unable to effect any kind of offensive and the Romans seemingly unwilling to meet them in battle, despite the supposed size of the Alexandrene garrison and its unbroken naval supply lines. However, rather than before the walls of the city itself, the fate of Alexandria was about to be decided 1,000km to the north in Constantinople where another bout of imperial politicking was about to break out.

As will be seen, when Heraclius died on 11 February 641 he left his eldest son, Heraclius Constantine, and his eldest son by Martina, Heraklonas, as joint emperors, and as part of his final request asked that they recall those he had exiled. As the senior emperor, Constantine III attempted to take charge of the increasingly dire situation in Egypt and sent for Cyrus from exile as well as Theodore from Alexandria. Constantine seems to have agreed to send a large army to Egypt in the summer of 641 but his untimely death on 25 May and the revolt of Valentinus, in support of Constans II and against the machinations of Martina and Heraklonas, saw to it that these reinforcements did not appear, at least not in any sizeable numbers.

This split in imperial politics also greatly affected the proposed negotiations regarding the future of Egypt. It appears that exile had not changed Cyrus' thoughts regarding the divine mandate of the Arabs to take control of Egypt and he appears to have won the backing of Martina and Heraklonas. However, Valentinus and Theodore refused to surrender Egypt without a fight. This split spread to the Egyptian populace as a whole, for when Cyrus and Theodore arrived back in Alexandria they found the citizenry and even the military more intent on fighting each other than the Muslim forces on their doorstep. Indeed, Domentianus and a certain Menas were essentially fighting a proxy war within the walls of Alexandria through the Blue and Green circus factions over who was to be the supreme Roman military commander. The return of Theodore put an end to this squabble but perhaps only through the formal deposition of Domentianus in favour of Menas and even direct military action on the Alexandrian streets.

The Muslims had not been inactive during this period of Roman self-destruction. Despite the lack of progress against the walls of Alexandria or in bringing the rest of the Delta under control, Amr was quick to exploit the socio-political and religious divisions undermining what was left of the Roman defences in Egypt. A small Muslim force marched up the Nile to the province of the Thebaid but upon reaching its capital, Antinopolis, it appeared that it was going to face a similar problem to that which had been faced in the Delta, as it seemed that the garrison forces were resolved to fight. However, much like several other Roman provincial governors and garrison commanders, the local prefect refused to take the field, choosing instead to retreat north across the desert towards Alexandria, leaving the Thebaid undefended. There is some suggestion that the example of how the Fayum had quickly settled into its status as a tributary province of the religiously tolerant Muslims may have encouraged other parts of Egypt to view Arab overlordship as better than the persecution and heavy taxation of the Romans.

As the Thebaid was being successfully subjugated, Amr received an unexpected visitor on an even more unexpected mission at Babylon in the autumn of 641. Having won over Martina to his 'peace at all costs' policy, the ex-Patriarch

Cyrus arrived at Babylon for the express purpose of buying off Amr, even if it meant surrendering Alexandria and recognising the Muslim conquest of all of Egypt. What amounted to virtually an unconditional capitulation will have surely taken Amr by surprise, for, despite the at-times calamitous attempts by successive Roman commanders to defend parts of Egypt, Roman resolve and resistance had stiffened greatly since the Battle of Heliopolis. An assault on Alexandria in particular was well beyond the capabilities of the Muslims and could serve as a launch pad for a Roman counter-attack. Therefore Amr was quick to accept terms, which included a substantial tribute of two dinars for every able-bodied adult living in Egypt and the complete evacuation of all Roman military forces from Egypt, including Alexandria, within the next twelve months.

This humiliating treaty was signed on 8 November 641. Despite some initial anger, the Alexandrians seem to have accepted the almost eschatological arguments of Cyrus that Islam had been given Egypt by God and continued opposition them could only lead to disaster. While there were still large areas of Egypt not under Muslim control, there was very little organised resistance from what remained of Roman Egypt. Some towns and fortresses of the Delta and coastal regions such as Damietta did not formally surrender until a Muslim force approached their walls and some may even have attempted to resist. However, while these mopping up operations may have taken the best part of a year to complete, Roman rule in Egypt had ended.

Whilst the people of Egypt had plenty of reason to shy away from further conflict – the continuing hangover from civil war and the Persian conquest, Roman mismanagement, Cyrus' persecution, the invincible reputation of the Muslims and the demoralising effects of Heraclius' passing – why the Romans were so willing to hand over their richest province without a final battle is difficult to explain. For over 600 years Egypt had been the breadbasket of the Roman Empire, while its large population had long provided vast amounts of tax revenue. War weariness will have played a part but it is more likely that the defence of Anatolia was prioritised over that of Egypt due to its proximity to the capital. Events in and around Constantinople will also have had their effect, with the deaths of Heraclius and Constantine III and then Valentinus' revolt coming at inopportune moments.

However, it must be highlighted that, despite the whimper with which Roman authority ended, Roman forces had fought hard against the Arab invaders; hard enough for Muslim sources to comment on it. The Romans had also not completely given up on Egypt as Constans II would make several attempts to regain it. Roman forces even succeeded in retaking Alexandria in 645 only to be ejected again the following year. However, after a large flotilla was defeated off the Egyptian coast in 654, the Romans were finally forced to give up on ever regaining their lost province.

The Conquest of Southern Mesopotamia and Khuzestan

Egypt was not the only territory where fighting continued on in spite of the effects of drought, famine, plague and Umar's policy of consolidation. In Mesopotamia, throughout 638 and 639, there were still pockets of resistance to the Muslim conquests. Yet the most intense fighting came in a hitherto less well-known theatre – the river delta of the Tigris and Euphrates and Khuzestan. After Khalid moved north from Ubulla and won his victory at the Battle of the River in April 633, the fighting in southern Mesopotamia devolved back into the raiding that had preceded his arrival. However, upon his accession in August 634 Umar sent reinforcements to the regional Muslim commander, Suwayd b. Qutba, perhaps with the strategic aim of opening up a second front to divert Persian attention and resources from the middle Euphrates and the movements of al-Muthanna, Jarir and Sa'd.

Surprisingly, this first force under Shurayh b. Amir was destroyed by a Sassanid garrision force near Ohrmazd-Ardashir, modern Ahwaz in the Khuzestan province of Iran. A second force, mostly made up of Thaqif tribesmen, under Utba b. Ghazwan, a veteran of the battles of Badr, Uhud, the Trench and Yamamah, appears to have been of no great size, with the sources suggesting that it was at most 2,000 strong or as small as a mere 40 men. Nevertheless, Utba moved against Ubulla and its garrison of perhaps 500 cavalry in the summer of 635. Camping nearby, he drew the Persians into a fight, defeating them to such an extent that the city fell. Throughout the rest of 635 and into 636, using Ubulla as a base of operations, several Muslim contingents took advantage of what was a complete collapse of Persian authority in the region, with entire districts falling without any real resistance. It was on this captured territory that in 636 Utba was to establish a further forward base along the confluence of the Tigris and Euphrates, called the Shatt al-Arab or 'Stream of the Arabs', that would later become Basra.[7]

The exact timeline of the events after the establishing of Basra is difficult to ascertain but there seems to have been a quick turnover in governors of the new military camp. After Utba died falling from a camel on his way back to Basra after performing the *Hajj*, the man he had sent to aid Sa'd at Qadisiyyah, al-Mughira b. Shuba, succeeded him as governor. This could have happened as early as late-636/early-637 or as late as 639. Whenever it was, al-Mughira did not last long in his new position for he was removed in order to defend himself from accusations of fornication. Despite being acquitted, he was not restored to Basra, although he did later become the governor of Kufa. al-Mughira's replacement at Basra was Abu Musa, who oversaw much of the Muslim campaigning into Khuzestan.

With the capture of Ubulla and once established at Basra, the next target for the Muslim forces in southern Iraq was the garrison city of Ohrmazd-Ardashir on the east bank of the Karun River, north-east of Basra. By this time it was being defended by a force commanded by Hormuzan, one of the Persian corps commanders at the Battle of Qadisiyyah, who had returned east to defend his own estates in Khuzestan. With an experienced commander now in the field, Persian resistance seems to have stiffened somewhat and local counter-attacks may have briefly driven the Muslims back from Ohrmazd-Ardashir and maybe even back to Basra. However, when the Muslim commander received reinforcements from Sa'd at Ctesiphon and was able to raise more men from the local Arab population, Hormuzan found himself outmatched. A two-pronged Muslim strike towards Ohrmazd-Ardashir forced the Persian commander to retreat across the Karun and, when the Muslim forces then confronted Hormuzan, he agreed to pay the *jizya* tax in return for a ceasefire that recognised Muslim control of the lands of the Shatt al-Arab and the Karun, essentially cutting the Persians off from the northern reaches of the Persian Gulf.

However, this ceasefire was not meant to last, at least not on Hormuzan's part. Almost immediately after extricating his army from potential disaster along the banks of the Karun, he was recruiting from amongst the Persian and Kurdish populations to challenge the Muslim hold on Shatt al-Arab. These preparations did not go unnoticed and, after consulting with Umar, Abu Musa led his army back to Ohrmazd-Ardashir. Despite the presence of Hormuzan's new forces, the Muslims forced a crossing of the Karun and, after a fiercely contested battle, drove the Persians back to Ramhormuz, leaving the Muslims to take Ohrmazd-Ardashir unopposed. A well-pressed pursuit by Abu Musa's cavalry forced the Sassanids to retire even further east and prompted Hormuzan to again offer a ceasefire, this time in return for recognising the Muslim conquest of Ohrmazd-Ardashir and again Abu Musa accepted.

Once again Hormuzan used this cessation of fighting to build up his forces for another counter-attack. This time he appears to have been directly assured and reinforced by Yazdgerd. However, again Muslim spies brought news of Hormuzan's imminent treaty-breaking to Abu Musa. A Muslim column then set out from Ohrmazd-Ardashir for Ramhormuz and, when it delivered a sharp rebuke to a Persian force sent to dispute its crossing of the Arbuk River, Hormuzan was obliged to retreat once more and regrouped at the fortress of Tustar to the north. This allowed Abu Musa to occupy not just Ramhormuz but also Izeh, one of the easternmost settlements of Khuzestan.

Yet the strength of the fortifications at Tustar worried Abu Musa. He recommended to the caliph that further reinforcements would be needed if he was to take the fortress. The call was answered not just by the governor of Kufa, Ammar b. Yasir, who at first dispatched 1,000 men under Jarir, only to then lead up to half of his army to Ohrmazd-Ardashir, but from a more unexpected source. Yazdgerd had followed through on his promise to send military aid to Hormuzan; however, he could not have foreseen that a sizeable contingent of those reinforcements would defect to the Muslim camp. Suitably reinforced, Abu Musa and Ammar now marched on Tustar from Ohrmazd-Ardashir, collecting further manpower from the garrisons already established at Ramhormuz and Izeh.

Despite the strength of his fortifications, Hormuzan was confident enough that his forces gathered together at Tustar were capable of defeating Abu Musa's army. Therefore, as soon as the Muslims arrived outside his walls, he wasted little time in challenging them to open battle, only to suffer another defeat and be forced back into the city. Abu Musa then settled into a blockade, sealing off all routes in and out of Tustar. This siege reportedly dragged on for months, although there is no way to be sure. Finally, running low on supplies, Hormuzan led a desperate sally in an attempt to break out but, in the process of being beaten back, the Persians lost the outer defences of the city. This further demoralisation encouraged an unknown traitor to lead a small band of Muslims through the sewer to open the main gate. With the Muslims flooding into the city, the Sassanids fought valiantly and were able to maintain control of the citadel. However, Hormuzan knew that the situation was hopeless and, the following day, he surrendered himself and the city.[8]

From Tustar, the Muslims advanced to the ancient city of Susa, which was quickly invested. While there were several sallies and assaults, it was to be a gambit using another traitor and a religious prophecy that won Susa for the Muslims. A Persian priest within the city exclaimed from the walls to both defenders and attackers that only a *dajjal* was fated to capture Susa, a term used by Islamic eschatology in relation to the Day of Judgement with the *al-Masih ad-Dajjal* – the false Messiah – being similar to the Antichrist of Christianity. However, in a more general sense, the term *dajjal* means 'deceiver' or 'impostor' and the Persian general, Siyah, who had defected to the Muslim camp in the run up to the siege of Tustar and was present at Susa, claimed that his turning his back on Zoroastrianism in favour of Islam made him a *dajjal*.

Abu Musa agreed to allow Siyah to try out his proposed ruse. One morning soon after, the Sassanid sentries of Susa noticed a bloodied individual in a Persian officer's uniform prostrate before the main gate. As there had been a skirmish the previous day, they believed that this man had been left outside the walls overnight and rushed to help him. However, as the gate opened and the sentries approached the fallen officer, he jumped to his feet, revealed himself to be Siyah and slew his intended saviours. Proclaiming that the *dajjal* had come to conquer the city, the Persian turncoat, along with a group of hidden Muslim soldiers, then charged through the open gate. The Persians attempted to oust them from within the city walls but the attackers were quickly reinforced by regiments of the main Muslim army and the ancient city was soon captured without much resistance.

The capture of Susa left Junde Sabur as the only military position of any importance in Khuzestan unconquered, and while the Muslim attack on it by Aswad b. Rabeea followed the same pattern as many others – the routes in and out of the city were blocked and neither the defenders nor the attackers could force a decisive conclusion before an almost amicable surrender – there was some peculiarity about the ending of the siege. One day, with the blockade still being enforced, the gates of the city opened but, instead of a sally, the inhabitants of the city emerged to go about their daily business. Confused by this, the Muslim forces asked why they thought that hostilities had ceased. The Persian citizens replied that they had accepted their offer of peaceful surrender in return for the payment of the *jizya* . Aswad contacted the Persian commander to inform him that no such terms had been offered. However, the Persians then produced an arrow complete with a note offering peaceful surrender and a quick inquiry found that a slave from the Muslim army had been responsible.

This left both sides in a quandary as the Persians had surrendered to terms that carried no authority. An uneasy truce prevailed while Aswad sought confirmation on what he should do. Needless to say, Umar was more than happy to reward peace to those who so eagerly sought it as to agree to a slave's offer. The successful captures of Tustar, Susa and Junde Sabur confirmed Muslim control of not just the entire region from the Persian Gulf to central Mesopotamia but also of the Iranian province of Khuzestan.

Around this time, there is some suggestion that an abortive attempt was made by the Muslim governor of Bahrain, Ula b. al-Hadrami, to conquer a large part of Fars, despite Umar's order not to invade Iranian territory. Perhaps overconfident and desperate for some personal renown, despite some early success Ula quickly found that his planned attack on Persepolis was beyond his men without reinforcement. Attempting to retreat back to Bahrain, Ula's army found itself stranded in Fars as the Persians managed to overtake them and burn the boats with which they had crossed the Persian Gulf. Surrounded by superior forces, the Bahraini army was only saved by the timely arrival of a relief force sent from Basra, which then led a prompt withdrawal from Fars.

The exact chronology of these campaigns in Khuzestan and the extent to which this theatre was disrupted by the 'Year of Ashes' and the Plague of Amwas are not altogether clear. However, Tustar, Ramhormuz and Susa would appear to have fallen after the battles of Qadisiyyah and Jalula but certainly before the climactic showdown that was to come at Nahavand in 642. Any attempts to paint a more comprehensive chronological picture than this would 'demand more of the sources than they can reasonably be expected to provide'.[9] However, despite the misadventure of Ula, it is fair to say that by the end of 641 the Muslims not only had a firm grip on Syria and Mesopotamia and a strong foothold in Egypt, they also had a launching pad for an attack on the Iranian plateau should they be prompted to use it.

'The Victory of Victories' – the Battle of Nahavand, 641/642

The capture of such an ancient city as Susa, along with a considerable quantity of booty and artefacts such as the coffin of Daniel, considered a prophet by

Islam, seems to have been viewed by many Muslims, including Umar, as the culmination of the war with the Persians. However, while Umar displayed some reticience in continuing the war, Yazdgerd did not. As his empire had been greatly humiliated and weakened by the loss of Mesopotamia and Khuzestan, rather than accept the lull offered by Umar and take time to stabilise and consolidate his position in Iran – as Heraclius had done in Anatolia – Yazdgerd could not abide a cessation of the war.

While the most obvious reasons for this continuation were how injurious the loss of Mesopotamia and Khuzestan had been to the Sassanid state both in terms of prestige and material resources, perhaps the most pressing was the weakness of Yazdgerd's own position. He had come to the Sassanid throne during a period of relentless civil war and, while he had eventually become recognised as the sole ruler of Persia, he did not enjoy the same autocratic control over his empire as many of his predecessors had enjoyed. The power and influence of Persian generals, governors and warlords therefore obliged Yazdgerd to challenge the Muslim conquests as quickly as possible before his own right to rule was challenged from within. In the simplest terms, Yazdgerd had to risk the continuation of war with the Muslims and the potential for destruction it entailed in order to prevent the Persian state from descending back into the anarchy that had plagued it since the death of Khusro II.

Having retreated to Qom, Yazdgerd put out a call to all his remaining forces to congregate at Nahavand, about fifty miles south of Ecbatana, the modern Iranian city of Hamadan. The size of the forces that gathered there is variously recorded as anything from 50,000 to 100,000. While such large numbers are usually cause for concern and the forces available to the Persians will have been drastically reduced by the wars of the seventh century, that Yazdgerd portrayed the upcoming battle as being for the future of the Sassanid state and its Zoroastrian faith means that it is entirely possible that he was able to bring together a vast host from across all of Persian society – soldiers, clergy, farmers, artisans and peasantry.[10] It is therefore possible that the Persian army that was to fight at Nahavand was in the order of several tens of thousands.

However, such a congregation of troops did not go unnoticed by the Muslims scouts deployed in the frontier lands and word soon reached Ammar at Kufa and then Umar himself that the Persians were planning a massive attack. Suspecting that the Persians planned to attack Basra and Kufa, Ammar advised the caliph that they should gather together the bulk of their forces and attack the Persians whilst they were still congregating at Nahavand. In Medina, Umar sought the advice of his council and, while they all agreed that a pre-emptive strike against Nahavand was the best course, there was some disparity on what forces should be sent. Uthman proposed the most drastic action of gathering the full might of their forces and sending them against Yazdgerd, although Ali suggested that such a move would only provoke extensive counter-attacks from the Romans. Therefore, he suggested that the forces of Kufa,

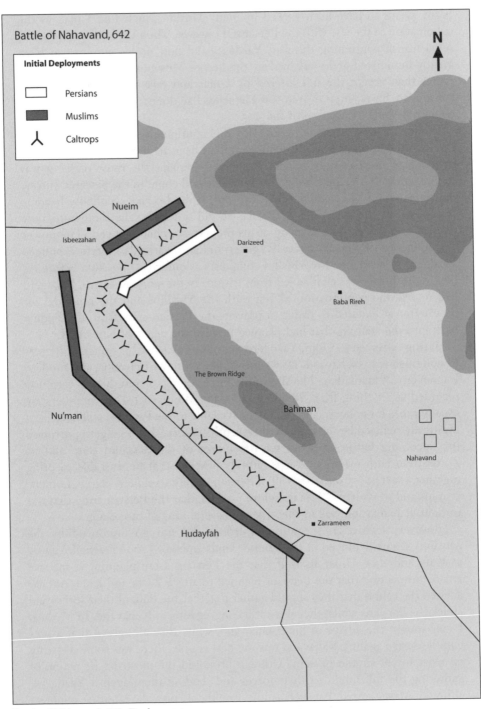

Battle of Nahavand, 642: Deployments.

Basra and along the frontier, reinforced by a levy of new recruits and veterans, would be enough to defeat Yazdgerd if a surprise attack was launched. Umar agreed with the assessments of both Ammar and Ali, issuing a call to arms from amongst the peoples of Arabia. He was also swayed from leading the attack on Nahavand in person and appointed Nu'man b. Muqrin, a subordinate of Sa'd, to command the combined Muslim forces.

Collecting together the Muslim forces posted on the frontier, Nu'man advanced to Tazar, a few miles west of Kermanshah, to await the arrival of the forces from Basra, Kufa and Medina. This coming together was seemingly completed by the beginning of December 641 and seems to have provided Nu'man with up to 30,000 men.[11] The Muslims then set about scouting the land ahead of them to see if the Persians had noted their mobilisation. When the report came back that there were few or no Persians between the Muslims and Nahavand, Nu'man ordered a rapid advance to Isbeezahan, a small town about ten miles from Nahavand. The land that lay between the Muslim and Persian forces was framed by high ridges to the north-east and south-west with the gap between these two dominated by a stream and a smaller outcrop known as the Brown Ridge. Once they realised that the Muslims were upon them, the Persian commander, Bahman, quickly established this ridge and the stream as the backbone of his dispositions, deploying his forces in an 'L' shape in order to follow the path of the stream and to have the ridge to their rear. The Persian lines were anchored on their right by the town of Darizeed and on their left by the divergence of the stream and the town of Zarrameen. Bahman was also careful to place a large number of caltrops on the shore of the stream to impede the Muslim cavalry.

It is possible that his advantage in numbers and the strength of his position may have made Bahman somewhat overconfident, as he was willing to allow the Muslim forces to deploy in front of his men unhindered. However, it is also possible that he was more than aware of the events of Jalula and how the Persians had suffered defeat by leaving a well-fortified position. Nu'man took up the challenge laid down by Bahman and deployed his men opposite the Persian lines with his brother, Nueim, taking command of the section of the Muslim line between Darizeed and Isbeezahan; Nu'man himself commanded the Muslim centre, the left flank of which began near Isbeezahan, and the Muslim right that reached to a position opposite Zarrameen was commanded by Hudayfah b. al-Yaman.

Relying on the strength of Muslim morale and the momentum of repeated victories, Nu'man launched an all-out attack across the stream along the entire length of his battle lines. However, the combination of the stream, the ridge and the caltrops disrupted the Muslim attack, allowing the Persian lines to stand firm throughout the first day of fighting. The second day played out along similar lines with neither side able to force any kind of breakthrough and the only tangible results being the casualties suffered by both sides. While it is

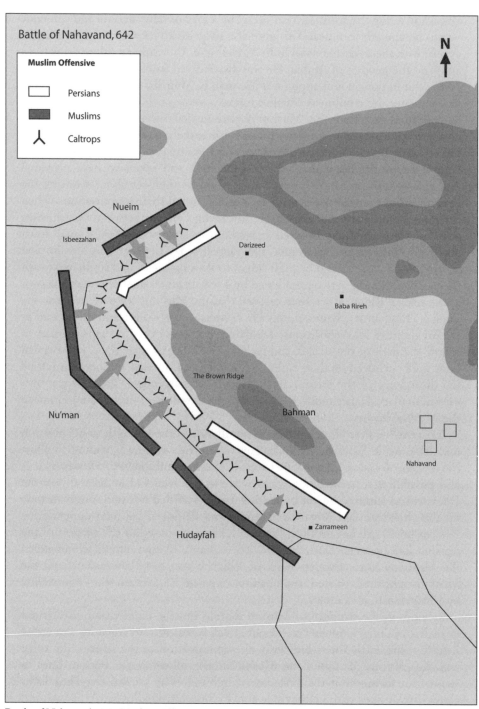

Battle of Nahavand, 642: Muslim Offensive.

easy to be critical of Nu'man for such unimaginative attacks in the opening forty-eight hours of the fighting, this was a testament to the defensive position that Bahman had been able to take up in spite of the lack of preparation that the Muslim advance on Nahavand had given him.

Recognising the strength of the Persian position, Nu'man now took a more passive stance, daring the Persians to leave the safety of their defences to attack his army. However, Bahman refused to be drawn in to such a rash attack, determining instead to use the increasingly cold weather to further sap the Muslim strength. For the next two days there was little fighting aside from some minor Persian raiding parties. Mindful that time was not on the side of their army, as the Persians were using the proximity of Hamadan to receive reinforcements and supplies, the Muslim leadership decided on the same risky tactic that had worked so well at Jalula – the feigned retreat. However, perhaps wary that Bahman might not take the bait, the Muslims added an extra layer to this ruse. The rumour was put about that Umar had died and was given perhaps a week to seep into the Persian camp. At the end of that week, the forces of Nu'man and Hudayfah withdrew north-west to join Nueim at Isbeezahan.

Buoyed by the rumour of Umar's passing, the week of Muslim inactivity, and now their retreat, Bahman felt the time was right for a decisive counter-attack. Leaving the security of his defences and gathering his forces opposite Isabee-zahan, the Persian commander ordered his men to advance after the retreating Muslim forces. However, as soon as the Persians moved onto the obstacles of the stream and their own caltrops, Nu'man ordered his forces to turn and attack. As with the first days of the battle, it was a brutal and bloody contest, one that claimed the life of Nu'man himself. Hudayfah's quick assumption of command meant that there was little disruption to the Muslim force; although, while the Muslims do seem to have pushed the Persians back somwhat, there was no decisive breakthrough throughout the vast majority of the daylight hours.

However, before he had been incapacitated, Nu'man had put in place the mechanisms for a Muslim victory. He knew that as the Persians advanced on Isbeezahan they would not only move away from their defences around the Brown Ridge, they would also detach their right flank from the security of Darizeed and its surrounding hills, exposing it to an attack from the north-east. To take advantage of this, Nu'man had gathered together his cavalry and sent it under the command of Qaqa to hide in the foothills north-east of Isbeezahan, a move that went unnoticed by Bahman. Now, as the sun began to set on a hard day's fighting, Qaqa struck hard at the Persian right whilst Hudayfah and Nueim ordered a renewed assault along the entire Muslim line. Attacked head on, in the flank and disrupted by the stream and caltrops, the Persian line began to pull back. The death of Bahman in the early stages of the retreat proved to be fatal as the large numbers of raw recruits meant that any sort of ordered with-drawal under concerted Muslim pressure was impossible. As they had always done, the Muslims pressed their advantage to the fullest. The next day

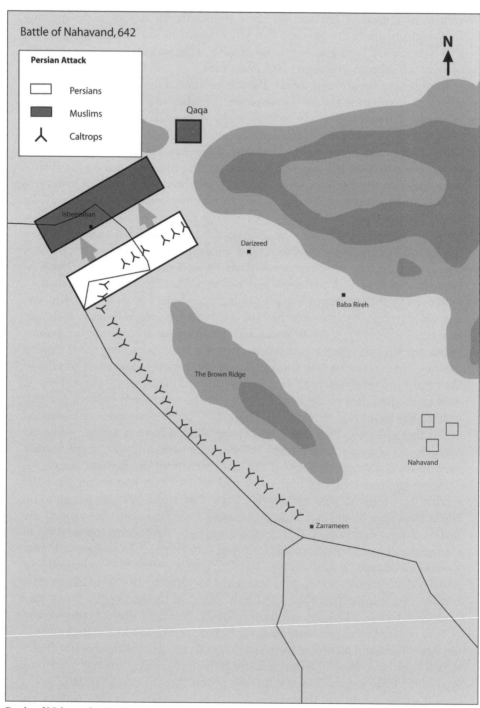

Battle of Nahavand, 642: Persian Attack.

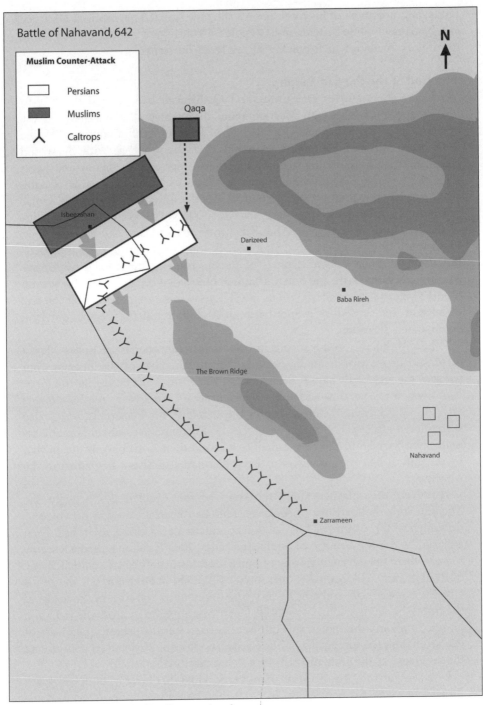

Battle of Nahavand, 642: Muslim Counter-Attack.

Hudayfah took most of his force against the now isolated garrisons at Darizeed and Nahavand while Nueim and Qaqa led a contingent after those retreating towards Hamadan, which quickly surrendered on terms.

The End of the Persian Empire

Much like the victories at Yarmuk and Qadisiyyah had opened the way to the conquests of Syria and Mesopotamia, the victory at Nahavand and the destruction of Bahman's army opened all of Iran to Muslim conquest. While there were still large numbers of undefeated garrisons, as with Syria and Palestine these were unable to come together to present any significant threat since there was no Sassanid field army for them to gravitate towards. Taking advantage of this situation and perhaps under the advice of Hormuzan, Umar sent several armies in different directions to accelerate the conquest of the lands of the Sassanids. Abdullah b. Abdullah drove straight into the heart of Iran, capturing Ray through betrayal after a week-long siege before then approaching another of the ancient capitals of Persia, Isfahan. Reinforced by further contingents from Basra and Kufa, Abdullah blockaded this large city for several months before it surrendered on terms. There is some suggestion that the fate of Isfahan was settled by a duel between Abdullah and the Persian garrison commander, Fazusfan.

While Abdullah was advancing in central Iran, another force under Maja'a b. Masud drove east from Basra along the north coast of the Persian Gulf towards the city of Bishapur, near modern Kazerun. After besieging the fortified town for several weeks before accepting its surrender, reinforcements arrived under Usman b. Abi al-Aas for the attack on the Persepolis, which also surrendered after several weeks of blockade. Further waves of reinforcements under first Sariyah b. Zuniem, Suhail b. Adi and then Asim b. Amr meant that by the end of 643 the provinces of Fars, Kerman and Sistan had fallen to the Muslims.

However, this advance along the coast of the Arabian Sea brought the Muslims into the territory of Makran. This had been a Sassanid province or dependency for centuries but in the aftermath of Qadisiyyah it had been annexed by the Rai Empire of Sindh. Its leader, Raja Rasil, marched a sizeable force to meet the advancing army of Suhail and Usman. The subsequent Battle of Rasil in early 644, probably near modern Karachi in Pakistan, saw the Arabs victorious once more and able to carry their conquests right up to the banks of the Indus. Suhail is said to have asked Umar's permission to cross the river and invade Sindh and the Indian subcontinent beyond but the caliph, again wary of overstretching his forces, denied this request, choosing instead to consolidate the conquest of the Iranian lands before looking further afield.

Umar had already given a similar answer to Ahnaf b. Qais earlier in 644 when Ahnaf had asked for permission to cross the Oxus River. Appointed to command the invasion of Khurasan, a vast Persian province that today includes

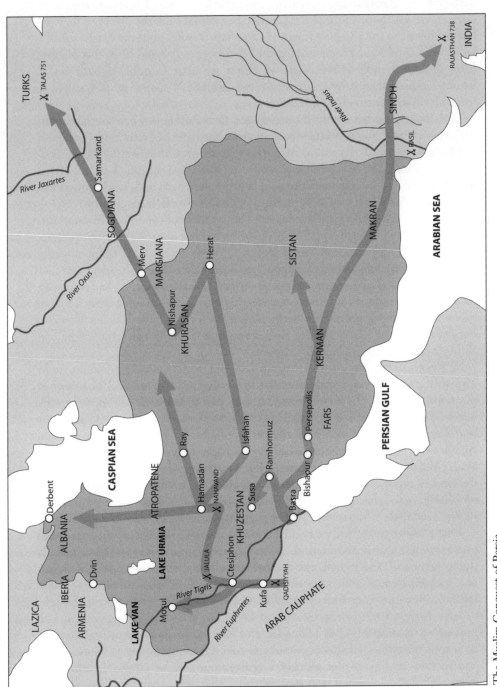

The Muslim Conquest of Persia.

parts of Iran, Afghanistan, Turkmenistan, Uzbekistan and Tajikistan, instead of skirting the southern shore of the Caspian Sea Ahnaf took the direct route from Isfahan between the Dasht-e Kavir – Great Salt Desert – and the Dasht-e Lut – Desert of Emptiness. After covering the vast distance in rapid time, this Muslim force appeared outside the walls of Herat in what is now Afghanistan in late-643. Ahnaf then drove north-west and induced Nishapur and Mashhad to surrender without much of a fight.

At this point Ahnaf received intelligence that the biggest prize was perhaps within his grasp. Since fleeing Qom in the aftermath of Nahavand, Yazdgerd had been resident in Merv, now in Turkmenistan, and Ahnaf sniffed the opportunity to capture the Sassanid king. However, Yazdgerd was quick to flee across the Oxus at even the slightest hint of a Muslim approach and, while Ahnaf was able to take Merv without a fight, he was unable to catch his quarry.

Despite this city-hopping, the Sassanid king had not been idle in his attempts to bring together an army to stave off his Muslim pursuers. Whilst the advance to Isfahan and into Fars and Sistan had cut him off from a large number of the remaining Persian garrisons, Yazdgerd had been able to not only bring together some of the remaining frontier garrisons of his failing empire, he had also been able to draw military aid from the neighbouring Hephthalite and Turkish tribes.[12] The most important of Yazdgerd's allies was the Turkic Khan of Ferghana, who will have clearly seen the potential for great advancement in aiding a Persian king regain his throne.

However, notwithstanding crossing the Oxus to join Yazdgerd in northern Afghanistan with a large army, it seems that, after hearing tales of the extent of the Arab conquests, the Khan quickly had second thoughts about incurring the wrath of Islam. Therefore, by the time the forces of Ahnaf squared up to this last 'Persian' army in mid-644, the task at hand for the Muslims had been significantly reduced. However, once again, despite winning the Battle of the Oxus, Ahnaf was unable to capture or kill Yazdgerd, who managed to flee into the land of the Turks and perhaps even to that of the Chinese emperor. It was now, looking to continue his chase of Yazdgerd and maybe to deliver a warning to the Turks, that Ahnaf was denied permission to cross the Oxus by Umar.

There seems to have been good reason for Umar's wariness of overly rapid expansion without consolidation, as both Hamadan and Ray, in concert with the governor of Tabaristan, the region along the south coast of the Caspian Sea, had rebelled not long after the bulk of the Muslim force had moved against Isfahan. Nueim was quickly dispatched to deal with the rebels and is thought to have fought a bloody battle against Isfandiar, a brother of Rustam, in the process of recapturing both Hamadan and Ray by the end of April 642. Umar then took advantage of this re-establishment of Muslim forces at Hamadan to add further prongs to the already extensive number of armies in the field. Nueim's brother, Suwayd, was sent against Tabaristan where numerous minor victories and the capture of several settlements throughout 643, including

Damawand, now part of the modern Iranian capital of Tehran, were enough to force the tribal families of the region to accept Muslim rule for now.

While Suwayd was in Tabaristan, Hudayfah was sent north-west against Atropatene, an area which covers modern Azerbaijan and north-western Iran. He quickly defeated the sizeable garrison of Zanjan in the field, and then drove up the Caspian coast before being recalled, which allowed the remaining Persian forces under Isfandiar and his brother Bahram to reclaim some of the lost territory. However, this was rectified with a two-pronged attack that defeated both brothers, bringing virtually all of Atropatene under Muslim control by the end of 643.

It should be noted that, while there are virtually no numbers recorded for either the multitude of Muslim armies sent to conquer Sassanid territory or the Persian garrisons they encountered, the likelihood is that they were not of any great size. This is almost certainly because of the overwhelming nature of the victory at Nahavand and the capitulation at Hamadan, which effectively destroyed the Sassanid army and isolated the remaining garrisons. The exact timeline of these monumental campaigns is also similarly muddled. Whilst attention was focused elsewhere, the final conquests of parts of Fars and Khurasan might not have taken place until much later than 643/644 and it is even possible that large parts of Persia were not 'conquered' until the death of Yazdgerd in 651, although these might point to reconquests after a string of uprisings that took place across former Persian territory in the aftermath of Umar's assassination in 644.

However, regardless of the numbers involved and their exact chronolgy, it should take nothing away from the dynamism and extent of the achievements of Umar's commanders. While Ahnaf had failed to bring about the capture of Yazdgerd, it was clear that by the end of 644 the twenty-ninth Sassanid monarch was a king without a kingdom, for in the eighteen-month period after the victory at Nahavand the armies of Islam had outstripped the eastward expansion that the Roman legions had managed in centuries by over 2,000 miles. And when added to the conquests of Syria, Mesopotamia, Palestine and Egypt, the Muslims could boast that they had retraced almost all of the steps of Alexander the Great.

Chapter 10

Three Deaths, Two Gods, One Winner

In the first and last years of a long reign, the emperor appears to be the slave of sloth, of pleasure, or of superstition, the careless and impotent spectator of the public calamities. But the languid mists of the morning and evening are separated by the brightness of the meridian sun; the Arcadius of the palace arose the Caesar of the camp; and the honour of Rome and Heraclius was gloriously retrieved by the exploits and trophies of six adventurous campaigns . . .

Gibbon (1788), V.46 on Heraclius

Under his reign and that of his predecessors, the conquerors of the East were the trusty servants of God and the people; the mass of public treasure was consecrated to the expenses of peace and war; a prudent mixture of justice and bounty maintained the discipline of the Saracens, and then united, by a rare felicity, the despatch and execution of despotism with the equal and frugal maxims of a republican government.

Gibbon (1788), V.51 on Umar

The grandson of [Khusro] was betrayed by his servant, insulted by the seditious inhabitants of [Merv], and oppressed, defeated, and pursued.

Gibbon (1788), V.51 on Yazdgerd

The Death of Heraclius and the Troubled Succession

By the beginning of 641, Heraclius will have known that his days were numbered. He was well into his sixties, had faced numerous personal and imperial problems, and had been ill for a large part of his adult life. The exact nature of his illness has never been fully diagnosed, with dropsy the most likely but also prostate problems and even epispadias being suggested.[1] However, more recently, it has been put forward that much of Heraclius' somewhat erratic behaviour late in life was down to the effects of Post-Traumatic Stress Disorder. He will no doubt have seen some horrendous things throughout his lengthy military career and, when added to the grief he had experienced in losing so many family members during his life and the paranoia inspired by the plot of Athalarichos, PTSD might well be a strong possibility.[2] Perhaps the most depressing thing for Heraclius was that his age and poor physical health affected his ability to take an active role in the Roman reaction to the Muslim conquests, which were undoing his reconstituting of the Roman Empire.

Another area that will have contributed to Heraclius' depression was the results of his efforts in the realm of religion. While he had been incredibly successful in incorporating religious ceremony and belief into the moral fabric of his imperial office and the Empire as a whole, and had been able to convert the pagan Croats and Serbs, Heraclius had been far less successful in dealing with existing Christians. In his attempts to bring about religious unity through the promulgation of Monothelitism, he had caused civil and religious strife across his lands at a time when the Empire required unity in order to repel the Muslim invasions. It could be argued that some of those he employed to encourage or enforce such religious unity, such as Cyrus, overstepped their bounds and were overly zealous in their efforts, alienating large sections of the populace in Armenia and Egypt. However, as the emperor who had appointed these individuals, even if he does seem to have shown shock at some of their methods, ultimate responsibility for this failure lies with Heraclius. Ironically, it was to be the Muslim conquests themselves that were to force religious unity on the Roman remnant by removing the Monophysite populations from the Empire and by extension of the entire reason for the Monothelite doctrine.

The appearance of religious figures such as Cyrus and Paul with high political and military authority also demonstrates not just how far Heraclius had promoted religion as a way to galvanise the state but also how far the leadership of the army had declined. Relying on his family to help run the state, even when they were perhaps not fit for the jobs assigned, demonstrates how little trust Heraclius had in others with military ability. However, there are instances during the Arab wars that would suggest that this mistrust of non-Heraclians led to a lack of clear delegation of military authority and the undermining of the positions of those who were appointed to high positions within the military hierarchy. The most apt example of this was at Yarmuk, where the squabbles between Vahan, Theodore Trithurios, Buccinator, George and Niketas undermined Roman strategic planning and the Romans' ability to react to Khalid's movements.

The deposed and soon-to-be-killed Phocas had challenged Heraclius on whether he would do any better than him, and, despite the victories over the Persians, it is clear that in purely geographical terms Heraclius should ultimately be judged a failure. By 641 the Empire had been stripped of its Asian provinces by the Arabs, seen its authority in the Balkans smashed by the Avars and Slavs, its Italian holdings dwindle in the face of Lombard dukes, and Spain lost to the Visigoths, with Armenia, Egypt and even Africa soon to follow suit. However, while the last years of Heraclius' reign may have seen things take a dramatic turn for the worse, this should not detract from his achievements.

Despite being faced with one of the most dire periods ever to rock the Roman Empire, at the time of his death, Heraclius still ruled over an empire that stretched from Gibraltar to the Caucasus and while his armies had been pushed back they were still resisting in Egypt, Syria, Armenia and Anatolia. For the most part, this resistance proved to be a forlorn hope but it still could be argued that he left the Empire in a better position than he had found it in 612 or at the height of Persian success in 620 and all of this was to do with the energy and organisational skills exhibited by Heraclius himself.[3]

While no longer thought to be the creator of the administrative and military districts that made up the *theme* system, a development now attributed to his grandson Constans II in the 660s, Heraclius' own short-term reforms enabled the Empire to survive and largely overcome the fiscal crises and corruption that had overtaken it during Phocas' reign.[4] Along with his successful integration of Christianity into the fabric of the Empire, his reorganisation of the military saw it show greater resilience in the face of defeat than it might have done otherwise, not only recovering the provinces lost to the Persians but also, ultimately, halting the Muslims in Anatolia. Without his galvanising personality and organisation, swimming against the tide of history, the Roman Empire would probably have been washed away by the Persian waves in the 620s and almost certainly by the Muslim torrent of the 630s.

However, perhaps Heraclius' most impressive personal achievement came at the head of his reorganised army. As the first emperor to lead the eastern Roman army in person in over 200 years, the dynamism of his campaigns in the 620s that lead to the defeat of Khusro II were something rarely, if ever, seen in the antique world, resulting in the proclamation that 'since the days of Scipio and Hannibal, no bolder enterprise has been attempted than that which Heraclius achieved for the deliverance of the empire'.[5] His dealing with Comentiolus and Priscus, repeated but limited strikes into Persian-held territory to rebuild Roman morale and harden his rebuilt army, and clever exploitation of the ambitions and suspicions of Persian generals and Turkic khans, eventually led to a series of increasingly decisive blows against the Persian king. These demonstrated that, while he may have had little political or military experience upon taking the throne in 612, Heraclius was a quick learner and had a sound grasp of the political and military strategies involved.

The victory over Khusro II alone qualifies Heraclius to be ranked amongst the highest echelons of Roman emperors. It also means that the question will always be asked as to whether a fit and healthy Heraclius could have defended the Empire any better from the Muslim invasions. However, while it is possible that Heraclius might have added some much needed stability to the leadership of the Roman army and would not have needed to demonstrate his authority through such a decisive yet destructive move as Vahan made on accepting battle on the plain of Yarmuk, such 'counterfactual speculations are dangerous'.[6] Given the difference in the type of opponent that the Muslims presented when compared with the Persians, there is little or no evidence that Heraclius could have done any better than his generals in stemming the Muslim tide in Syria and Egypt had he been able to take the field, or adopt a more hands-on approach in the mid-630s.

In the end, it is difficult not to feel sympathy for Heraclius. Few would have passed the first Persian test, let alone been able to withstand the Muslim on-slaught that followed, but when he died on 11 February 641, mired in physical and emotional turmoil, the great emperor will have been deeply sorrowed by having had to sit on the sidelines and watch as 'his life's work collapsed before his eyes. The heroic struggle against Persia seemed to be utterly wasted, for his victories here had only prepared the way for the Arab conquest.'[7]

However, despite the regard in which he was held, Heraclius very nearly undid a lot of the stabilising work he had done at the centre of imperial politics when it came to his addressing of the succession. His death was not unexpected given his advanced years and longstanding illness so he had time to arrange matters; however, in his final years, Heraclius fell increasingly under the thrall of Martina, who was determined to see her own sons advanced with or even beyond those from Heraclius' first marriage to Eudocia. Normal procedure would have seen Heraclius' eldest son, Heraclius Constantine, who had been elevated to co-emperor as early as 22 January 613, succeed as emperor. How-ever, on 4 July 638, Martina persuaded Heraclius to elevate her eldest son, Heraklonas, to *Augustus* alongside Heraclius himself and Constantine. This caused, or more likely exacerbated, the animosity between Constantine and his stepmother enough for it to become obvious enough for Heraclius to set aside money with the Constantinopolitan Patriarch, either Sergius or Pyrrhus, 'on behalf of Empress Martina so she would not be lacking funds if she were driven out of the palace by her stepson'.[8]

However, despite seemingly recognising this animosity, Heraclius failed to do anything about it and, therefore, when he died in 641 Heraclius left the Empire in a precarious political position by passing power to both Constantine III and Heraklonas, with Martina as *Augusta*. So wary was Constantine of his scheming stepmother, and of his own mortality given the illness that must have been presenting itself, that he took pre-emptive action in order to secure the support of the army. Writing to its leaders and playing on the wide-spread dislike of Martina, he expressed concern regarding his own safety and asked them to champion the rights of his children in the imperial succession should the worst occur. Whether or not Constantine truly believed his life was in danger from Martina is unknown but it could be argued that he was manipulating the situation of his illness, laying the suggestion that the hated *Augusta* was responsible for his impending demise, while at the same time seeking protection for his children. Whatever Constantine had planned, it was soon to be put to the test for in late-May 641, after a reign of just four months, he died of tuberculosis.

This seemingly left Heraklonas and Martina in supreme control of the Roman remnant. However, persuaded by Constantine's plea, Martina's con-tinued unpopularity, and the rumour that she had had her stepson poisoned, the army took up the cause of Constantine's young son, Constans. It is also

important to note that Constantine and his adviser, Philagrius, had appropriated the funds set aside by Heraclius for Martina with the Patriarch and used
them to buy the support of much of the military's leadership. This opposition
quickly flared into open revolt when Martina banished Philagrius to the
remotest part of the Roman Empire, the city of Ceuta, perhaps for his part in
taking the nest egg left to her by her late husband. The Anatolian army under
Valentinus marched to Chalcedon, opposite Constantinople, and demanded
the elevation of Constans to the position of his father. When confronted with
such military opposition, along with the popular support shown for Constans
by the Senate and people of Constantinople – or was it dislike of Martina? –
Heraklonas had little option but to agree to the promotion of his nephew in
late-September 641.

This setback did not deter Martina from further plotting, but, whether she
realised it or not, the balance of power had shifted decisively towards the supporters of Constans. Therefore, when she attempted to alleviate the damage
Constans' elevation had done to her and Heraklonas' position by promoting
another of her sons, the *Caesar* David Tiberius, to the rank of *Augustus*, Martina
found herself and her sons forcibly deposed by the irresistible combination of
the Senate, people and army of Rome. The ignominious end of this branch of
the Heraclian dynasty was sealed when all three fell victim to mutilation –
Martina, rather symbolically, had her tongue removed – before being exiled to
Rhodes.

With Constans II now recognised as sole *Augustus*, it might be expected that
the Empire could focus on recovering some of its lost territory. However, the
death of Constantine III and the deposition of Heraklonas had left an eleven-
year-old boy on the throne and prone to exploitation. The almost inevitable
challenge came from Valentinus himself. Benefitting from his brief alliance
with the Senate, Valentinus saw himself appointed *comes excubitorum* and
supreme commander of the Roman army and married his daughter Fausta to
Constans. However, after suffering a defeat at the hands of the forces of
Mu'awiya in northern Syria, Valentinus saw his position crumble as quickly as
it had been built. In a desperate move, he marched into Constantinople with a
contingent of troops and demanded that Constans crown him as co-emperor.

However, without the vast military and popular support he had enjoyed
against Martina, Valentinus' usurpation was doomed to failure almost before it
had begun. The Senate and people of Constantinople firmly backed their
emperor, despite him being still only 13 in 644, and Valentinus was lynched in
the streets. This finally brought the debacle of Heraclius' dynastic arrange-
ments to an end, with a cadre of senators led by the Patriarch Paul II determined to re-establish firm rule in Constans' name until he matured. Despite the
failed coup of Valentinus and this senatorial backing, due to the military
support that had led to its creation the regime of Constans II would prove to be
far more progressive in attempting to regain the territories lost in the previous

decade and, as already mentioned, would build upon the administrative foundations provided by Heraclius to restructure the Roman Empire by way of the *theme* system.[9]

Despite this ropey transfer of power from its founder to the second and then third generations, the Heraclian dynasty was to survive throughout the seventh century and guide the Roman Empire through its transition into what is recognised as the Byzantine Empire of the medieval period.[10] However, it would not be a smooth transition by any stretch of the imagination. Constans II and then his son Constantine IV were faced by the continuation of the Muslim conquests, the emergence of the Bulgars as successors to the Avars, and the religious disputes that had dogged Heraclius. Eventually, the stresses and strains that such troubles involved saw the deposition and exile of Constantine IV's son, Justinian II, in 695. This saw a decade-long interruption in the Heraclian dynasty as first Leontius and then Tiberius III, both military commanders, sat on the imperial throne. An alliance with the Khazars, Bulgars and Slavs saw Justinian returned to the throne in 705, even though his nose had been removed, but he seems to have learned no lessons from his first deposition and in 711 his increasingly tyrannical rule provoked another rebellion. This time there was to be no exile and the execution of Justinian II and his son Tiberius outside Constantinople in late-711 brought about the extinguishing of the Heraclian line, just over a century after Heraclius and his father had rebelled against Phocas to save the Empire.

The Assassination of Umar, the Election of Uthman and the Establishing of the Umayyad Dynasty[11]

It was fortunate for the Roman Empire that, whilst it chose this time to descend into such a pantomime of imperial politics and powerplays, the Muslims themselves were distracted from delivering a decisive hammerblow against the Anatolian frontier by their own internal political wranglings. The first of these internal problems seems to have arisen from the importation of prisoners of war and slaves into the Arabian Peninsula. From amongst this population a conspiracy to assassinate Umar emerged, supposedly led by Hormuzan, the Persian commander who had surrendered at Tustar in 642. As part of the terms of surrender, Hormuzan is said to have negotiated a personal audience with Umar at Medina, whom he then persuaded to spare his life and give him a pension by embracing Islam.

Despite advising Umar in fiscal, political and even military matters, it seems that Hormuzan never forgot that he was a virtual prisoner of those who had brought the Sassanid state to ruin. There are other suspected members of the plot but the most important is the man chosen to carry out the deed, another former Persian soldier, now a slave called Firuz, also known as Abu Lu'lu'ah. His presence in Medina seems to have been due to the recognition of his exceptional skill in carpentry, iron-working and painting by his owner, the governor of Basra.[12] There is some suggestion that Firuz was frustrated by Umar's decision to uphold the taxation that the slave had to pay to his master but, whatever his reasons, it is recorded that on 3 November 644 Firuz attacked Umar whilst he was leading morning prayers in the Al-Masjid al-Nabawi mosque in Medina. The caliph was reportedly stabbed as many as six times before Firuz, having wounded or killed several people in attempting to escape, was then cornered outside the mosque, where he committed suicide. Umar survived the incident but would eventually succumb to his wounds on 7 November 644.[13]

There can be little underestimating of the importance of Umar's reign to the history of Islam. While Muhammad and Abu Bakr were able to extend its teachings across Arabia and take the first steps in spreading it abroad, it was under Umar's auspices that the caliphate expanded in almost every direction. He is also responsible for the strong administrative organisation that allowed the caliphate to consolidate its hold on its newly conquered territories. The process of codifying Islamic law was begun with ministries established to ensure its implication. The conquered territories across Syria, Palestine, Mesopotamia and Persia were divided into provinces, with each provided with their own provincial hierarchy to provide law, order and justice, and collect taxes with a governor selected on merit by Umar himself at the top.[14] These provinces were also further subdivided into over 100 districts and urban units with their own governor to further enforce the law. Umar went as far as to discourage corruption amongst his officials by not only paying them well but also by providing the population with a legal avenue to appeal against their actions. He is also credited with decreeing in 639 that the Islamic calendar would begin with the *Hijira*, Muhammad's flight from Mecca to Medina.

However, much like Heraclius, Umar seems to have been in something of a quandary as to who would succeed him as caliph. He is said to have originally favoured Abu Ubayda or even Khalid as his successor, but once they had both predeceased him Umar seems to have given little indication as to whether he was going to name his successor as Abu Bakr had done; an act of appointment that had been considered controversial. Even on his deathbed, the caliph refused to make a decision, perhaps going as far as to lecture those present when it was suggested that he nominate his own son. At length he chose instead to name a council of six men – Uthman, Sa'd, Ali, Abdur-Rahman, Zubayr b. al-Awwam and Talha b. Ubaydullah – who would choose the next caliph from amongst their number. Umar is also said to have given these men three days to come up with a unanimous decision. Such a limited period of time meant that Talha, who was not present in Medina, was unable to take part in the discussion. Of the remaining five, only Uthman and Ali were willing to accept the position of caliph, with Zubayr favouring the former and Sa'd the latter. After the council agreed to support the majority decision, this left Abdur-Rahman with what was essentially the casting vote. Having chosen to back Uthman, there is some suggestion that Rahman stage-managed the presentation of his decision, waiting until he was at a public meeting in the mosque to give Ali no option but to immediately pledge his allegiance to Uthman.

Throughout his subsequent twelve-year reign, Uthman was able to build on the firm basis that Umar had created. Using his own skills as a trader, Uthman expanded on the agricultural and trading infrastructure through deregulation, the establishing of trade routes, the building of canals, allowing loans and the purchase of land, enabling the peoples of the caliphate, Muslims and non-Muslims alike, to enjoy far-reaching economic prosperity; prosperity that allowed for large building projects across the empire. Hundreds of new mosques were built, along with the beautification of existing ones such as the Kaaba and the Al-Masjid al-Nabawi at Medina, whilst numerous encampments, barracks, training and recruitment facilities were built to house and expand the growing Muslim army. Uthman also confronted the problems that the spread of Islam and Arabic oral traditions had had on the transmission of the text of the Qur'an. As various Muslim communities began to flourish, their own local languages, dialects and writing styles began to produce slight differences. To prevent such corruptions taking hold and potentially developing into something that might be considered schismatic, Uthman brought together a committee to transcribe large numbers of copies of the Qur'an from one of the original manuscripts belonging to Hafsah, one of the Prophet's wives.

However, while the development of the Islamic state and the spread of its faith through conquests would continue during his twelve-year reign, it was perhaps Uthman's dynastic appointments and the discontent they caused that were to have the greatest impact. It appears that many of the governors Uthman appointed were overly fastidious, perhaps even tyrannical, in their rule, with the discontent that this caused exacerbated by the fact that the four most important governorships – Egypt, Basra, Kufa and Syria – had been given by the new caliph to members of his own tribe. This nepotism was viewed by many as an attempt by Uthman to not only increase his own personal power but also to establish control over the caliphate for his Umayyad clan. Such accusations of dynastic plotting were latched onto in particular by those who supported Ali's claim to be the true caliph and by individuals such as Amr, who had been removed from his governorship of Egypt by Uthman.

Investigations into this discontent suggested that it was largely anti-governmental propaganda or relatively small in scale. However, by 656 it had spread throughout the caliphate and could count on large support from within the provinces of Kufa, Basra and Egypt, if not their governors. This gave the rebels their chance to strike at Uthman. Neutralised by anti-Umayyad propaganda, the main population of Medina refused to back either side and looked on as an ever-tightening siege of Uthman's house began. After numerous skirmishes, some of the rebels were eventually able to sneak into the house and kill Uthman on 17 July 656.[15] The squabble over his right to a proper burial and the limited size of his eventual funeral suggests just how unpopular

Uthman had become amongst those who had managed to take tacit control of Medina in mid-656. However, despite this ignominious end and the 'doting love for a corrupt and rapacious kin' that not only destroyed Uthman himself but also in time the meritocratic heart of the caliphate, much like Umar, Uthman had played an important role in building upon the successes of his predecessors.[16] The prosperity his reforms had brought made the caliphate even more resilient in the face of the internecine conflict that was to follow.

The day after Uthman's assassination, a meeting in the Al-Masjid al-Nabawi mosque saw Ali declared the new caliph over Zubayr and Talha. Given the circumstances of his accession, it might be expected that Ali would be cautious about his opening political moves. However, convinced of his religious mission and unwilling to compromise against the advice of several of his supporters, Ali quickly attempted to remove Uthman's kinsmen from their high-profile governorships.[17] While all but one governor acceded to Ali's orders, the one who did not was perhaps the most powerful – the governor of Syria, Mu'awiya, who withheld his recognition of Ali's succession due to Ali's failure to punish the assassins of Uthman. This failure, along with Ali's decision to then make war on Mu'awiya, was met with disdain by several leading Muslims, not least Zubayr, Talha and Abu Bakr's daughter, Aisha. These three fled to Basra and raised an army to challenge Ali's caliphate. Having somewhat belatedly secured the support of the garrison of Kufa, Ali marched from Medina to relieve Basra, where his forces decisively defeated the rebels in the the Battle of Bassorah, also known as the Battle of the Camel.

Yet this battle represented not just the first time that Muslims had fought against one another but also the initiating of the Islamic civil war that was to last the entire length of Ali's caliphate, known as the First Fitna. This was because, despite this decisive victory over Zubayr and Talha, Mu'awiya remained un-bowed. Ali tried to settle the dispute through diplomacy but the governor of Syria, who had built up a powerful and loyal following in his province through success against the Romans, was determined to force an armed conflict. After numerous skirmishes throughout Mesopotamia and Syria, the two forces, recorded as being of suspiciously large proportions – Ali with 90,000 and Mu'awiya with 120,000 – met at the Battle of Siffin on 26–28 July 657 on the plains between Aleppo and the Euphrates. The momentum of the battle seems to have swung back and forward over the course of three days of carnage before the two leaders agreed to arbitration to settle the dispute over who should be caliph.

As it would appear that Mu'awiya was on the back foot when the battle ended, Ali's agreement to enter arbitration caused great dissension in his camp, especially when that arbitration resulted in Mu'awiya's representative, Amr, out-manoeuvring Abu Musa, Ali's arbitrator. This dissension quickly erupted into violence as a group, later known as Kharijites, declared that all parties involved at Siffin had deviated from the true path of Islam. This forced Ali to divert his attention from a proposed invasion of Syria to fight and win the Battle of Nahrawan in mid-658. However, once again military victory did not bring overall victory for Ali as Mu'awiya was quick to take advantage of the caliph's distraction, conquering virtually all Islamic territory west of Kufa.[18] These conquests do seem to have strengthened support for Ali, as they portrayed Mu'awiya more as a war-monger than a man looking to avenge his kinsmen, but, before such increased support could bare fruit for the Alid cause, Ali himself was assassinated at Kufa on 26 January 661 by a Kharijite.

Ali's son, Hasan, was elected as his successor by his remaining supporters, but with the military superiority now enjoyed by Mu'awiya he was fighting a lost cause and soon capitulated. This allowed Mu'awiya to use the power and loyalty his successes in battle had inspired to take full advantage of the foundations laid by Uthman. By appointing his son Yazid as his successor on his death in 680, Mu'awiya replaced the elective caliphate with a monarchical dynasty. While such dynastic organisation can and did have positive effects on loyalty and solidarity, when such hereditary autocracy is forced upon a state that has enjoyed an elective theocracy it can have detrimental effects. Indeed, from the death of Uthman to the beginning of the ninth century there were four Islamic Civil Wars. The Umayyad dynasty established by Uthman and Mu'awiya would rule the Muslim world for much of the next century, before being removed from power following their defeat at the Battle of the Zab on 25 January 750 during the Third Fitna.[19]

The End of the Sassanid Dynasty: The Death of Yazdgerd III and the Wanderings of Peroz II

While both the Roman and Muslim hierarchies descended into in-fighting, the third major head of state of Late Antiquity was facing an altogether different problem. With the destruction of his imperial army at Nahavand, the loss of all of his territory in the aftermath, and his defeat on the Oxus, by late-644 Yazdgerd III was a king without a kingdom. However, he had fought incredibly hard to establish himself as the sole king of that kingdom in the mid-630s and he was not going to give it up now a decade later without a fight. For the next seven years he proved himself remarkably proficient in evading capture by Muslim forces. In his attempts to bring together an army capable of challenging the Muslim grasp on Iran he travelled back and forth across the frontiers of his former Khurasan province and the neighbouring lands of the Turks, and even beyond the Jaxartes into the Pamir Mountains and the Tarim Basin, territories in which the dynasty of Tang China held interests.[20] It is even possible that during Yazdgerd's lifetime he made direct contact with the Chinese emperor, which may in turn have led to the Muslim leadership sending an emissary to the Chinese court in around 650.[21] This is the traditional date for the establishment of Islam in China; although the concurrent belief that it was Sa'd b. Abi Waqqas who led the embassy has been questioned.[22]

To further aid Yazdgerd's efforts, it has been suggested that the recording of the capture of the likes of Persepolis and Merv as late as 650 rather than in 644 meant that many of the territories conquered by the Muslims rebelled sometime after the death of Umar. The fact that Tabaristan, a territory supposedly subdued by Suwayd before the end of 643, would see Sassanid loyalists cling on for grim death along the southern coast of the Caspian Sea for more than a century – its final conquest would elude the Umayyads and be left to the Abbasids in 759–761 – may give some credence to the idea of a large-scale revolt within the caliphate. However, whatever attempts Yazdgerd made to take advantage of this unrest and forge an anti-Muslim/pro-Sassanid alliance between Turkish tribes, the Chinese and the meagre forces still left under his control, they came to very little and 'the end of [Yazdgerd], was not only unfortunate but obscure.'[23] There are several different retellings of the final end of the last Persian king. By far the most popular is that a local miller, not recognising him, killed Yazdgerd for his purse; however, it is also suggested that he was killed trying to cross the Oxus by Muslim or even Turkish cavalry, while the connivance of the local governor of Merv, Mahui Suri, is also heavily suspected.

Whatever the circumstances, Yazdgerd III was dead by 651. However, while his death marked the official end of the imperial rule of the Sassanid dynasty, which had in truth ended at the Battle of the Oxus in 644, if not before, it did not bring to an end his family history. His position was inherited by his eldest son, Peroz, who is thought to have escaped through the Pamirs to arrive at the court of the Chinese emperor, Gaozong. Despite the earlier arrival of the embassy of Sa'd, perhaps wary of the scale and rapidity of the Muslim advances beyond the Iranian plateau, the Chinese seem to have been willing to offer Peroz aid in regaining his father's kingdom. With this help, between 658 and 663, Peroz established something of a 'kingdom in exile' at Zarang, now in Afghanistan near the Iranian border but then considered to be part of the province of Sistan. However, when he next appeared at the Tang capital, Chang'an, in 674/675, it would appear that Peroz had suffered a crushing defeat.[24]

A military escort led by the Chinese general, Pei Xingjian, returned Peroz to Suyab, near Tokmok in Kyrgyzstan. Whatever the objectives of this expedition, they seem to have been abandoned with the death of Peroz in around 679, which might explain Pei Xingjian's return to China. Peroz's own son, Narseh, a hostage at Gaozong's court, then succeeded as the Persian king in exile, but for the next three decades he seems to have been left largely to his own devices in Suyab, too weak to make any real attempt at challenging Muslim control of Persia. It is possible that the Chinese regarded Narseh as more a governor of part of their Anxi Protectorate rather than an ally. By the time Narseh returned to Chang'an in 708 it would seem that he had abandoned his attempts to retake his grandfather's throne. Having married a Tang princess, over the course of the next century their descendants became more and more integrated with the

Chinese hierarchy, collecting numerous military titles and taking the Tang imperial name of Li. By the ninth century what remained of the Sassanids were seen as the military governors of Guangzhou in south-eastern China.

Peroz and Narseh were not the only descendants of Yazdgerd to attempt to reclaim Persian lands. Another of his sons, Wahram, is also thought to have launched unsuccessful attacks on the Muslims with forces raised from amongst the tribes of Central Asia. Wahram is thought to have died in 710, but his cause was taken up by his own son, Khusro, who with a large force of Turks invaded Muslim Persia only to once again face defeat.[25] This is considered the last attempt by the house of Sasan to regain the throne of Iran. Other members of the Sassanid family faired much better, with two of Yazdgerd's daughters recorded as having married high-profile men – Shahrbanu may have been one of the wives of Husayn, the second son of Caliph Ali, whilst Izdundad married Bustanai ben Haninai, the first Jewish exilarch under Muslim rule. Through these marriages it was possible for the nineteenth-century Bahá'í religious leader Bahá'u'lláh to trace his ancestry back to Yazdgerd III.[26] However, in the world of ruling politics, the Sassanid race had been run and they had trailed in a distant third. And, as they blended in with other cultures, the religion of the Sassanids, Zoroastrianism, went into a slow decline. It still survives today in India, Iran, Afghanistan and in other parts of the world but its adherents only number in the thousands.

Chapter 11

The Feast Continues: From the Atlantic to the Indian Ocean

I shall not cease from the struggle with Constantinople until I force my way into it or I bring about the destruction of the entire dominions of the Arabs.

Sulayman, Umayyad caliph 715–717
(*Chronicle of Zuqnin*)

The Conquest of North Africa and the Iberian Peninsula

Despite the interruptions the deaths of Heraclius, Umar and Yazdgerd caused or put in motion within their respective camps and dynasties, they should in no way suggest that military operations had ceased. Despite having already built an empire comparable to the Romans at their second-century CE height, the Muslim wave of conquest was far from a spent force and would continue to advance east and west for another century after the assassination of Umar in 644. The most spectacular of these successes came in the west. Before the death of Umar and perhaps even before the ink was dry on the treaty that acknowledged Muslim control of Egypt, Amr had turned his attention on securing its western borders against the continued Roman presence in North Africa in the guise of the provinces in Cyrenaica, Tripolitania and Africa province itself.[1]

Before the end of 642, Amr appears to have moved west from Alexandria against the urban region called the Pentapolis. One of its major cities, Barca, seems to have submitted without a fight, along with large parts of Cyrenaica and Fezzan. However, Amr met more stubborn resistance as he approached Tripoli. The city contained a Roman garrison and ready access to the sea so Amr, due to his lack of any siege equipment, was forced into an incomplete blockade. However, this aquatic avenue of expected relief turned into the harbinger of the Roman garrison's doom. After a month of fighting, the aid they had hoped to arrive from the sea failed to materialise and the Muslims were able to force an entrance through the harbour to capture Tripoli. Amr then followed up this victory with a lightning attack that captured Sabratha, near modern-day Zawiya, without much resistance. Yet despite Amr wishing to carry the attack to the Exarchate of Africa, Umar seems to have recalled his ambitious general for fear that he had over-reached himself before consolidating the

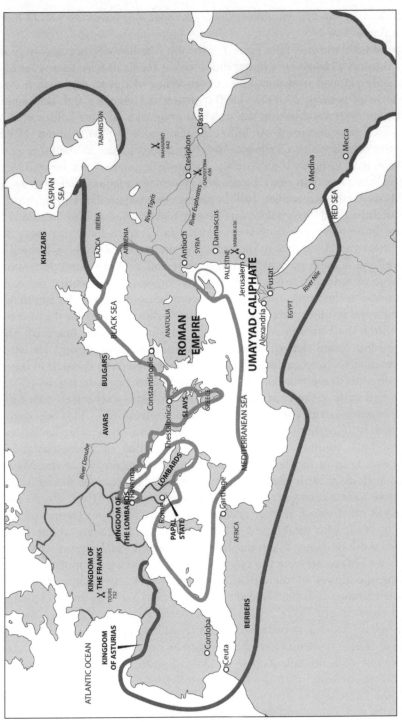

The Umayyad Caliphate and the Roman Empire in 750.

conquest of Egypt. Obeying his orders, Amr seems to have returned to Fustat before the end of 643.

It would be another four years before the Muslim advance across North Africa resumed. However, when it did in 647 it seems to have been a far more thoroughly planned invasion. The new governor of Egypt, Abdullah b. Saad, led a force of perhaps 20,000–40,000 men across Cyrenaica and Tripolitania, confirming or re-establishing the previous conquests of Amr before crossing into Africa province itself. At Sufetula, near modern Sbeitla about 250km/ 150 miles southwest of Carthage, Abdullah forced battle on the army of the African exarch, Gregory the Patrician. A year earlier, in 646, encouraged by the failure of the Heraclian central authority to provide adequate defences against the Muslim advance whilst still imposing the unpopular combination of Monothelitism and heavy taxation, Gregory had rebelled against Constans II.[2] Despite gaining support from across Africa and even in Italy, this usurpation made little or no difference to the unfolding situation and Gregory himself did not live long enough to benefit from it as he and his army were destroyed at the Battle of Sufetula. It has been stated that this defeat signalled the end of Roman Africa;[3] however, such a pronouncement overshadows the fact that the Exarchate and its allies were able to fend off Muslim conquest for the next forty years. After their victory at Sufetula the Muslims did raid much of Africa province but found that they could make little headway against the strong defences of cities like Carthage. This stalemate enabled the Romans to buy the Arabs off with heavy tribute, Abdullah returning to Egypt in late 648.[4]

The civil strife of the First Fitna gave Roman Africa a seventeen-year respite before another attempt to capture Carthage began in 665. This was perhaps instigated by Gregory's successor as exarch, Gennadius, who having been expelled by a military and civil rebellion travelled to Damascus to seek Mu'awiya's help in recovering his position. Once again, while the Muslims were victorious in battle near Carthage, they failed to scale the fortifications of the city or induce it to surrender. However, this time the Muslims were not to be bought off. Instead, further reinforcements arrived from Damascus under Uqba b. Nafi, who established a forward base at Kairouan, about 130km/ 80 miles south of Tunis. From this base Uqba raided widely across what is now Algeria and Morocco over the course of the next decade or more, eventually reaching the shores of the Atlantic. On the other hand, Uqba had under-estimated Roman resistance and the armies of the Exarchate and its remaining Berber allies caught Uqba's column unprepared at Vescara, modern Biskra in north-eastern Algeria, in 682 or 683 with Uqba himself killed and the Muslims forced to retreat from much of the territory he had traversed. His replacement as governor at Kairouan, Zuhair b. Qais, despite some success against the Berbers, was defeated with the help of a relief force from Constantinople.

Yet the Exarchate of Africa could not build on the respite that its victories over Uqba and Zuhair and the distraction of the Muslims by the Second Fitna between 680 and 692 had provided. The Muslim raids, heavy tribute and the increasing defection and desertion of its tribal allies had drained away too many of its resources. As a result Zuhair was able to regroup his forces and win a victory over a Romano-Berber alliance near Kairouan before the end of the 680s, and his successor as governor, Hasan b. al-Nu'man, was finally able to capture Carthage sometime between 695 and 697. There was a brief Roman revival as a naval expedition sent by the emperor Leontius succeeded in recapturing Carthage in a surprise attack in 697. However, the next spring Hasan concentrated his superior forces before the Carthaginian walls and overwhelmed the Roman defenders. The subsequent Muslim sack marked the second and final destruction of Carthage.[5]

However, the victory was not to mark the final conquest of North Africa. There were still other Roman garrisons and the unpredictable element of the Berber tribes to deal with. Indeed, soon after his conquest of Carthage, Hasan is said to have suffered a humiliating defeat at the hands of Dihya, a Berber queen and prophetess also known as Kahina, near Tebessa. Supposedly, this defeat forced the Muslims to retreat from large parts of the province of Africa for the best part of five years. If there was such an interruption in Muslim control, they used it to plan a far more definitive conquest and Hasan returned in late-702/early-703 to inflict a crushing defeat on the Berbers, killing Kahina. Hasan's successor, Musa b. Nusayr, then not only completed and consolidated the conquest of the Maghreb, more importantly he encouraged the conversion of large sections of the Berber population to Islam. This provided the Muslim armies with a fresh supply of recruits at a time when they had shown some signs of running out of steam.

With the successful completion of the conquest of North Africa, these new recruits brought a new thirst for conquest that naval expeditions against the Balearics could not quench. Therefore, when Musa's armies moved against the Romano-Gothic enclave at Ceuta in 711 they needed very little persuasion to cross to Hispania, ostensibly to interfere in a Visigothic civil war that seems to have been raging since the death of the Visigothic king, Wittiza, in around 710. However, given that Wittiza and his father, Ergica, had sent forces to help the Romans defend Carthage in 698, it is possible that the Muslims believed that a state of war with the Visigoths already existed.

There are several different sources for the Muslim invasion of Hispania but few of them agree on the dates and locations of the major events. Under the command of Tariq b. Ziyad,[6] and perhaps with ships provided by the exiled family of Wittiza and Julian, the Roman commander at Ceuta, an Arab-Berber force, recorded as being of any size from a few hundred up to 15,000, crossed to the Iberian Peninsula in mid-711, landing at what is now called Gibraltar, a corruption of Jebel al-Tariq – the Mountain of Tariq. This Muslim force then marched north towards Hispalis, modern-day Seville, and may have reached Cordoba before the Visigothic king, Roderic, who had usurped the throne on Wittiza's death, was able to march south from campaigning against the Basques. The date, site and course of the subsequent battle between these converging forces are heavily disputed. Sometime in July 711 is the most common dating, although its postponement to the following year is not infrequent. The lack of consensus even on what to name the battle – Battle of La Janda, Battle of the Rio Barbate, Battle of the Transductine Promontories, or the Battle of Guadalete – demonstrates the difficulties involved in the identification of its location, while the lack of consensus on the size of the forces involved also makes it difficult to give a clear narrative of how the battle played out.

However, the outcome is undisputed. It is suggested that Tariq's cavalry and the divisions within Roderic's ranks led to a bloody battle that ended in a decisive Muslim victory. The rout of the Visigothic force, the death of Roderic and the arrival of Musa with reinforcements led to the rapid and unopposed conquest of virtually the entire Iberian Peninsula for the armies of Islam within the next three years. Dislike of Visigothic leadership or Roderic specifically is usually pointed to as one of the main reasons for the rapidity of the collapse of resistance. However, Muslim willingness to negotiate and their general tolerance of other cultures must also have played a part as several Visigothic nobles who surrendered without a fight were allowed to retain their semi-independent status, merely changing their suzerain from the Visigothic king to the Umayyad caliph.

The only part of Hispania to avoid coming under direct Muslim control was a strip of land running across the northern coast, where the inevitably independent Basques continued to fight alongside the emerging Kingdom of Asturias, which would secure its existence with a victory over a Muslim force at Covadonga in either 718 or 722, a victory that is seen as the first step in the near-800-year reclaiming of the Iberian Peninsula for Christianity known as the *Reconquista*.

The Battle of Tours and the Salvation of Europe

The Muslim inheritance of most of the lands of the Visigothic kingdom included Septimania, a region on the northern side of the Pyrenees, which today includes the cities of Perpignan, Narbonne and Montpellier. By 719 the governor of al-Andalus, the Muslim name for the Iberian Peninsula, al-Samh b. Malik, had claimed that inheritance with the capture of Narbonne. This brought the Muslims into contact and conflict with another western European state – the Kingdom of the Franks. While on the surface it was divided into just two states, Austrasia and Neustria, in reality this Frankish kindgom was far more heavily subdivided into dukedoms and baronies. Yet the Franks presented the Muslims with a far tougher military challenge than the Visigoths, as these dukes and barons were so accustomed to fighting each other for control over what remained of the Merovingian dynasty that their lands were highly militarised and contain well-defended positions and large forces.[7] Frankish resistance was also strengthened by the fact that the power behind the throne in Austrasia, the Mayor of the Palace, Charles, had in 719 been able to take control of Neustria as well.

However, the first Frankish warlord to square up to the armies of Islam was Odo, the duke of Aquitaine, when in 721 al-Samh attacked Odo's capital at Toulouse. After a siege of about three months, just as al-Samh was about to break into the city, Odo returned with a relieving force and inflicted a heavy defeat on the Muslim army. While this defeat seems to have sparked some disputes amongst the Arab, Syrian and Berber elements in the Muslim forces, it did not prevent them from raiding deeply into France throughout the 720s, getting as far north-east as Autun in 725. Having attempted to aid the Berber rebels operating in Catalonia against the new governor of al-Andalus, Abdul Rahman, Odo once again found his lands the target of invasion in 732. However, this time, unable to surprise his enemy, the duke of Aquitaine suffered a heavy defeat along the Garonne River and was a powerless bystander as Bordeaux was ruthlessly sacked.

The Muslim column then drove further north towards the Loire, seemingly disdainful of Frankish military strength. They were soon to learn that, while Odo had been one of the more powerful Frankish dukes, he was not the most powerful. That title lay with Charles and, while he had refused to send aid to the Aquitainians before the battles at Toulouse and Bordeaux, he had not been idle in the face of this new threat seeping across the Pyrenees. Gathering together a strong infantry force, Charles correctly surmised that Abdul Rahman would head for the Abbey of St Martin at Tours and interposed his force between the abbey and approaching Muslim column without the latter's knowledge in October 732. It was therefore a complete surprise to the governor of al-Andalus when he found a large Frankish army blocking his path, not only commanding the high ground but also well protected from the dangerous Muslim cavalry by trees and broken ground.

Recognising the strength of his opponent's position, Abdul Rahman called together the rest of his army in France, most of which had dispersed on raids after the victory over Odo. As he had decided to fight a defensive battle hoping to draw the Muslims onto his strong defensive phalanx square, for a week after the two armies first made contact Charles maintained his position and allowed the Muslim army to congregate. This delay also ramped up the pressure on Abdul Rahman to fight in spite of the literally uphill struggle his forces would face. Having marched so far north, he could not return south without fighting this army that was arrayed against him; so in a way the decades of success worked against the Muslims at Tours.

On the seventh day, Abdul Rahman launched his cavalry in an attack on the Frankish position but, despite forcing some breakthroughs, the Muslims were repeatedly thrown back by the well-disciplined Frankish infantry. With the Muslim army fully deployed, it appears that Charles sent the scant few cavalry scouts he had in his force to threaten the Muslim camp, which was heavily laden with plunder from Bordeaux. Fearful of losing their hard-fought gains, sections of the Muslim cavalry returned to defend the camp. The core of the Muslim force saw this as a retreat by its cavalry support and therefore began to retreat itself. A swift Frankish counter-attack left Abdul Rahman dead and forced the Muslim force to retreat back across the Pyrenees.

Long thought one of the most important victories in history, the importance of Charles' victory at Tours in 732, for which he received the sobriquet 'Martel' meaning 'the Hammer', has been played down in recent years, giving way instead to the argument of it being just one part of a larger series of campaigns upon which the real importance should be laid.[8] It is easy to see why, given that there was a second substantial Muslim invasion of France by Abdul Rahman's son Yusuf in 736. This seaborne invasion required Charles to win further victories at Avignon, Nîmes and the River Berre throughout 736 and 737 and he even had to ask Liutprand, King of the Lombards, for aid.[9] It would not be until 759 that the Muslims would be conclusively driven back beyond the Pyrenees with the capture of Narbonne by Charles' son, Pepin.[10] However, there can be no overlooking that, had this main Frankish army been defeated at Tours with the decisiveness of other Muslim victories such as Yarmuk, Qadisiyyah or Nahavand, the future of France and all of western Europe – devoid of the achievements of Charles Martel, his son Pepin and his namesake grandson, known as Charles the Great or more famously as Charlemagne – might have looked very different.

Even with their ejection from France in the mid-eighth century, some Frankish gains in Catalonia and the consolidation of the Kingdom of Asturias before the end of the century, in various guises there would be a Muslim presence in Iberia for the next 700 years. It would not be until the unification of the kingdoms of Castile and Aragon in the late-fifteenth century that the last Muslim state of Iberia, the Emirate of Granada, would be removed.

The Eastern Front – China, Pakistan and India

Distracted by civil wars at the centre of the caliphate, military expansion in the far west and rebellions throughout Iran, Muslim expansion in the east seems to have ground to something of a halt. However, after the successful consolidation of the authority of the Umayyads by the end of the seventh century by Caliph Abd al-Malik and his most able general and administrator, al-Hajjaj b. Yusuf, the wheels of conquest began to roll again under Abd al-Malik's son, al-Walid I. Under the auspices of al-Hajjaj, who was made governor first of Iraq and then Iran, a cabal of highly skilled generals were sent forward to add new lands to the caliphate, including Qutayba b. Muslim, Muhammad b. Qasim and Musa b. Nusayr, the man who had completed the conquest of North Africa and initiated the invasion of Hispania.

As governor of Khurasan from 705, Qutayba spent the next decade expanding and consolidating Muslim control of large parts of Central Asia that now form regions of Turkmenistan, Afghanistan, Uzbekistan, Kazakhstan and Tajikistan at the expense of Turkic and Iranian tribes, many of whom were acting under the direction of the Chinese, whose Anxi Protectorate the Muslim armies were fast approaching. However, after Qutayba's death in 715 it quickly became obvious how important his diplomatic and military skills, along with his sheer strength of personality, were to the maintenance of these conquests. Rebellion and the emergence of the Turgesh Khaganate as a military threat saw the gradual undoing of Qutayba's advances in Transoxiana over the next twenty years. When a Muslim army marched against Ferghana in 724 to reassert its authority, it found itself surrounded by superior Turgesh forces and had to retreat back across the Jaxartes; a retreat remembered as the Day of Thirst. This defeat marked a serious role-reversal in Central Asia, with the Muslims now firmly on the back foot. Heavy casualties suffered during the drawn Battle of the Defile in 731, an Iranian rebellion and the defeat of Syrian reinforcements at the Battle of the Baggage in 737 saw to it that by 738 the Muslims were driven back beyond the Oxus and Khurasan itself was being raided by Turkic columns.

It was only the appointment of Nasr b. Sayyar and the institution of a more inclusive and conciliatory policy towards the Turkish and Iranian populations beyond the Oxus, along with the death of the Turgesh khagan, that allowed the Muslims to recover. The growing internal dissent felt towards the Umayyad caliphate that finally erupted in the Third Fitna of 747–750 prevented Nasr from enforcing more direct control beyond the Oxus than a system of alliances and tributaries. However, his placatory policies were well remembered in 751 amongst the peoples of Transoxiana when the confrontation that had been threatened for nearly a century finally occurred when a Muslim army met a Chinese-led force at the Battle of Talas.

Despite the failure of their backing of the survivors of the Sassanid dynasty, the Chinese had not retreated from their western provinces and the combination of wariness of an alliance between the Muslims, Tibetans and Uyghur Turks and the potential opportunity posed by disruption of the Third Fitna finally encouraged them to put a sizeable force into the field. In July 751, eager for a notable success to enshrine his new dynasty, the first Abbasid caliph, Abul Abbas al-Saffah, sent a large force to the borders of the Chinese Anxi Protectorate. On the banks of the Talas river, alongside allied Tibetan and Uyghur contingents, this Muslim force attacked a Chinese-Turkic force. In the heat of the battle the good relations fostered by Nasr bore fruit as the large Turkish contingent in the Chinese army either retreated or defected, giving the Muslim forces a decisive victory that, when coupled with the outbreak of the An Lushan Rebellion in China in 755, marked the disengagement of China from Central Asia.

While Qutayba had been establishing the Muslim presence in Central Asia, another of al-Hajjaj's triumvirate, Muhammad, had been looking to build on the success won at the Battle of Rasil in 644. After Umar had decided that there was nothing worth conquering beyond Sindh, Muslim military involvement in the subcontinent had declined from seeking conquest to raids on Sindh and the Punjab. However, by the turn of the eighth century it seems that the Muslims were encouraged to launch punitive campaigns against the peoples of the northern subcontinent due to aid they gave to the Sassanids and numerous piratical raids carried out on Muslim territory.

Marching east from Shiraz, Muhammad reinforced Muslim control of Makran and gathered allies for his invasion. Crossing the Indus, the Muslim force met the army of Raja Dahir, the Hindu ruler of the Sindh. The subsequent victory at Ar-rur in 712 delivered virtually all of what is now Pakistan into Muslim hands. Yet, much like Qutayba's death in Central Asia, the recall of Muhammad to Kufa gradually undermined much of what the Muslims had been able to achieve. His successors were faced with numerous rebellions and raids and it was only in 738 under Junayd b. Abd al-Rahman that the Muslims were again able to take the offensive, driving into what are now the Rajasthan and Gujarat states of India. In a series of battles cumulatively known as the Battle of Rajasthan, an alliance of several Hindu kingdoms forced Junayd to retreat back to Sindh. Further Muslim attempts to expand across the Indus were frustrated and the river would remain the boundary between the Indian kingdoms and successive Muslim states until the opening of the eleventh century.

The Central Front – Armenians, Khazars and Constantinople

While the east and west had seen the continuation of the spectacular gains that had characterised the earliest successes of the caliphate, progress on the central front was much slower. Despite the raids of Khalid, the capture of several cities by Iyad, and the penetration of a Muslim column perhaps as far as Ararat or even Dvin, large parts of Armenia remained free from Muslim domination for at least another decade after the death of Heraclius. Backing from Constans II may have played a role in this continued independence of Armenia but it also seems to have sealed its fate. Such imperial interference and attempts to impose Monotheletic Christianity rankled with the Armenians, leading them to take an increasingly independent approach to negotiations with their Muslim neighbours. One Armenian leader, Theodore Reshtuni, is thought to have played a major role alongside a Muslim force in removing a Roman army from Dvin in 653, after which he agreed to accept Muslim overlordship in return for limited autonomy in a treaty with Mu'awiya.

As a result, Armenia essentially reverted somewhat to the quasi-independent status it had 'enjoyed' for centuries between the Roman and Persian empires, with both sides continually looking to gain the upper hand politically and militarily. A Roman army was defeated near Dvin in 654 while a Muslim invasion in 656 removed Reshtuni from power and replaced him with Hamazasp Mamikonian, a man already recognised by Constantinople as the governor of Armenia. This was a peculiar choice, especially when Hamazasp showed himself as favouring the Romans. However, the succession of his brother Grigor in 661 represented the definitive loss of Armenia for the Romans, as the principality fell firmly under the suzerainty of the Muslims. The Armenians were not the only Caucasians to offer stout defence against Muslim advances. The Iberians and Laz accepted Muslim overlordship at the same time as the Armenians but would rebel frequently throughout the second half of the seventh and the eighth centuries, using their mountain holdfasts to maintain some limited autonomy. It was only with the imposition of a Muslim governor in the 730s and a ruthless crackdown that much of Iberia and Lazica were brought under more direct Muslim control.

The reason for this ramping up of pressure on the Caucasians was the emergent power of the Khazar Khaganate of the Russian steppe. In the aftermath of the Turkish invasions that aided the downfalls of Khusro II and Shahrbaraz, it appears that the Khazars were able to achieve pre-eminence amongst those Turkish tribes between the Caspian and Black Sea, and their continued raids through the Caucasus brought them into conflict with the advancing Muslims. It is possible that the first battle between the Khazars and Muslims took place as early as 642, perhaps as part of Hudayfah's advances into Atropatene, but it is more likely that the Battle of Balanjar took place in 652 instead, with the Khazars being victorious.[11] This marked the beginning of a century-long Khazar-Arab War, which involved punitive, retaliatory raids rather than large scale battles and definitive territorial changes, with the Khazars reaching Mosul in 730–731 and the Muslims sacking the Khazar capital at Atil in 737.

For the Romans themselves, whether through fortune or design, the Heraclian defensive line in Anatolia managed to preserve Asia Minor throughout the 640s and provided a respite that allowed them to regroup their forces. However, the energetic governor of Syria and future caliph, Mu'awiya, was to prove that these Anatolian defences were not as solid as the Romans might have hoped. After the effects of plague, drought and famine abated, Mu'awiya built up the military strength of Syria to not only repel Roman attacks in 644 and 647, and Armenia in 653, but also to penetrate deeply into Anatolia with seeming impunity for the rest of the next century.

Even more worrying for the Romans was that Mu'awiya also began the building of a fleet to challenge Roman control of the waves. This opening of a new front bore fruit as early as 649 when a Muslim force raided Cyprus and then again in 654 when Rhodes was briefly occupied, a campaign perhaps best know for Mu'awiya's selling of the remains of the Colossus of Rhodes, one of the Seven Wonders of the World, to a Jewish salesman from Edessa. Recognising the seriousness of this development, Constans gathered together a large

Roman fleet to destroy the burgeoning Arab navy. The two fleets met off the coast of southern Turkey in 655 in what became known as the Battle of the Masts. Both sides suffered heavy casualties but it seems that the Romans were the first to retreat, with the emperor barely escaping with his life. While the Roman navy was still to remain a force, its supremacy across the Mediterranean was no longer secure. With the combination of land and naval forces, it seems that Uthman ordered Mu'awiya to prepare for a decisive attack on Anatolia and even Constantinople. However, to the relief of the Romans, the governor of Syria was then dragged into a civil war with Ali.

Constans did take some advantage of this Muslim distraction in rebuilding his power base. He inflicted defeats on the Slavs and Avars in the Balkans, enrolling some of them in his army, and attempted unsuccessfully to rebuild the Roman position in Italy by attacking the Lombard dukes. However, in 661, with Mu'awiya now firmly secured as caliph, when large-scale Muslim raids into Anatolia recommenced, Constans' distraction with the Balkans and Italy severely undermined his position. So much so that, in 667, the commander of the Armenian *theme*, Saborius, rebelled and, although this rebellion was soon ended by Saborius' accidental death, it further encouraged the Muslims by demonstrating to them that the Roman hierarchy was ripe for attack. Soon raiding parties had begun wintering in Roman territory and were driving all the way to the Bosphorus. Already unpopular due to his religious and tax policies, the rumour that he planned to combat this reinitiated Muslim aggression by moving the imperial capital from Constantinople to Syracuse sealed Constans' fate. On 15 September 668 he was assassinated in his bath, to be succeeded by his son, Constantine IV.

Yet the accession of a new emperor did nothing to stem the Muslim tide. By early 669 a Muslim army had repeated the feat of Shahin and Shahrbaraz, encamping before Chalcedon across from Constantinople, and when a naval strike took Cyzicus by 671 it was clear that Mu'awiya was planning an attack on the Roman capital. After careful planning and the capture of several coastal bases, such as Smyrna and Rhodes, to serve with Cyzicus as a string of supply points, in April 674 a Muslim force landed on the European side of the Bosphorus and attacked Hebdomon. This began the four-year siege of Constantinople between 674 and 678, although in truth it was less a siege and more a series of assaults on the city's land walls with the Arabs crossing from Cyzicus in the spring before retreating back across the Marmara for the winter.[12] Distracted by Slavic attacks on Thessalonica and Lombard advances in Italy, the Romans had to once again put their faith in the Theodosian walls to preserve Constantinople. This faith proved to be well placed and in late-677 Constantine IV launched a counter-attack with his fleet, using Greek fire – which was essentially an ancient version of napalm dispensed like a flame-thrower – to destroy the Muslim fleet while the Roman army inflicted a heavy defeat on the Arab army in Pamphylia.

This successful defence, coupled with religious upheaval in Syria and the outbreak of the Second Fitna on Mu'awiya's death, served as something of a crescendo for the first period of Romano-Arab warfare with a peace treaty being agreed. This peace and the continued distraction of the caliphate allowed the Romans to focus on recovering other lost territories. Much of Armenia and Iberia were brought back into Roman alliance in the 680s while the Roman armies of Constantine IV and his son Justinian II campaigned extensively in the Balkans against the Avars, Slavs and the emergent threat of the Bulgars. Whilst not always successful – the Bulgars inflicted heavy defeats on Constantine's forces at Ongal in 680 and on those of Justinian at Anchialus in 708 – these campaigns restored a modicum of Roman prestige and control over parts of the Balkans, most importantly the hinterlands of both Constantinople and Thessalonica.

Buoyed by these successes, Justinian broke the treaty with the Arabs in 692 and attacked Sebastopolis only for a large portion of conscripted Slavs to desert, leaving the Roman army to face a heavy defeat. Not only did this defeat allow the Muslims to establish tighter control over Armenia and Iberia, along with Justinian's heavy-handed exactions regarding land, tax and religion, it led to a rebellion under Leontius, the general defeated at Sebastopolis, inaugurating a period of twenty years of political and military chaos with six different men ruling as *Augustus* between 695 and 717. While the Romans fought amongst themselves, the Umayyads emerged from the Second Fitna stronger than ever and using Sebastopolis as a *casus belli* again raided deeply into Anatolia. The Romans contained the main thrust of this attack with a victory near Tyana in the early years of the eighth century. However, this led to a nine-month siege of the Roman fortress at Tyana, which drew large numbers of Roman forces into a largely futile situation against the main Muslim army. The subsequent defeat of the restored Justinian II's relief force and the fall of Tyana by 709 was a military disaster for the Romans and left Anatolia open to virtually unchecked Muslim raiding.

With the increasingly feeble resistance of the Roman army in the wake of Tyana, successive caliphs, al-Walid and Sulayman, began the planning and organisation of a second attempt to capture Constantinople. Informed by spies of the build-up of Muslim naval and military forces, the Romans attempted to disrupt these preparations but their efforts were forestalled by the army choosing instead to initiate another round of fractious infighting, replacing Anastasius II with Theodosius III.

In late-715 the Arabs made their move. A large force advanced methodically through Anatolia, securing its lines of communication by capturing numerous cities and castles along the route, including Akroinon, Sardis and Pergamon. However, the Muslim advance was hindered by the double-dealing of the governor of the Anatolic *theme* Leo the Isaurian, who was currently rebelling against Theodosius III and would soon be recognised as Leo III. Because of this, it would not be until the beginning of summer 717 that the main thrust against Constantinople would take place. This allowed the Romans to make further preparations and perhaps most importantly secure an alliance with Tervel, the Bulgar Khan.

Upon arriving opposite Constantinople, the Muslim general, Maslamah b. Abd al-Malik, crossed to Thrace and proceeded to deploy his forces in a much more systematic blockade of the land routes into the city than in 674–678. However, the Muslim fleet once again proved to have no defence against the Greek fire of the Roman navy, allowing Constantinople to be resupplied by sea, and, while the Arab army had brought plenty of supplies with them, the severity of the winter of 717–718 quickly depleted these stores. The defeat of two Muslim relief fleets by the Roman navy, the ambush of a Muslim army near Nikomedia and the timely arrival of a large Bulgar force to attack Maslamah's lines before the Theodosian Walls broke the back of the siege, and the Muslims retreated on 15 August 718 after a siege of thirteen months.

The defeat of this second Arab attack on Constantinople was to have a significant impact on the military interactions between the Romans and the Muslims. The costliness of the defeats, along with the overextension of their forces against Berbers, Visigoths and Franks in the west, Turks, Chinese and Hindus in the east, and Khazars to the north, encouraged the caliphs to pull back from further attempts to conquer Constantinople and even Anatolia. Therefore, while Muslim raids continued to take place virtually every year, there was a marked decline in attempted conquest as the eighth century wore on, and a large-scale Roman victory at Akroinon in 740 essentially marked the definitive establishment of the Romano-Arab border along the Taurus Mountains; a frontier that would remain mostly unchanged for over 200 years until the conquest of Antioch and Aleppo by Nikephoros II Phocas and his generals in 969 and, more definitively, the Roman disaster at Manzikert in 1071.[13]

Epilogue

In the name of God, and praise to Him. The earth is God's; He causes to inherit of it whom He wills among His servants, and the result thereof is to them that fear Him ... Build, and God bless you!

al-Mansur, Abbasid Caliph
(ordering the foundation of what would
become Baghdad on 30 July 762)
(Tabari 622)

The Three Empires – Truncated, Terminated and Triumphant

From dominating virtually the entire Mediterranean in 600 and dealing a decisive defeat to its traditional Persian rival, even with the successful defence of Constantinople and the cessation of Muslim attempts at the conquest of Anatolia, by the mid-eighth century the Roman Empire was cutting a rather sorry figure. Not only had the Muslims taken its African, Egyptian, Palestinian, Syrian and Armenian provinces and begun to nibble at hitherto-untouched islands such as the Balearics, Sardinia, Sicily and Crete, aside from the hinterlands of major cities such as Constantinople, Thessalonica and Athens and several fortresses along the Adriatic coast, virtually the entire interior of the Balkans and the Greek peninsula had been lost to the influx of Slavic tribes. To make matters worse, just as there were some signs that the Roman army was starting to get to grips with the Slavs, the arrival of the Bulgars south of the Danube greatly hindered the attempts of successive emperors to reclaim the lost lands.

It was a similar situation in Italy where, with their capture of Ravenna in 751, the Lombards had eroded Roman territory down to the hinterlands of Naples and Venice, along with the heel and toe of the Italian peninsula. This left the Papacy to assume greater temporal control over not just Rome itself but also the erstwhile Roman province, roughly corresponding to the regions of Romagna, Marche and Umbria – although it did require a Frankish invasion in 756 to prevent this emergent Papal State from also falling to the Lombard king. With political independence came a greater degree of religious freedom from the emperor at Constantinople, which was perhaps best seen in the comparison of the reaction to religious controversies. Constans II had been able to forcibly remove Martin I from the Papacy in 653 when he had dared condemn Monothelitism; however, when Leo III took drastic action to prevent the over-veneration of religious icons, initiating the first period of Iconoclasm, the Papacy responded by excommunicating all 'those who broke icons' – iconoclasts – including the Patriarch of Constantinople and the emperor himself. The only response open to Leo was to transfer his territories that had been under the religious jurisdiction of the Pope to the patriarch. How the mighty had fallen.

However, despite the poor state to which they had declined, at least the Romans were still in the fight. Aside from token Iranian resistance in Tabaristan and the continued existence of the Sassanid family under Chinese protection, for all intents and purposes the Sassanid kingdom was gone; washed away by the Muslim tide. Yet the removal of the Sassanids did not lead to the permanent excising of Iranians from power politics. Much as the old pagan Roman aristocracy had reinvented themselves as the early papal families, within a few generations of converting to Islam the Persian elite were able to establish themselves in the upper echelons of provincial power within the Umayyad and Abbasid caliphates. The foundation of Baghdad in 762 as the capital of the Abbasids close to the former centres of Persian power in Mesopotamia and the Iranian plateau further encouraged this integration. So successful were they in doing so that one Muslim historian wrote in the ninth century that 'the Umayyad dynasty was an Arab empire; the Abbasid dynasty, a Persian empire'.[1] So well placed were families such as the Samanids, Tahirids and Saffarids that not only did they help run the caliphate, they were in positions to take over large parts of it with the decline of the central authority of the Abbasids in the second half of the ninth century. While these first Muslim Persian states proved ephemeral, Persian culture itself would prove remarkably resilient even in the face of centuries of domination by Turkish and Mongol invaders from the Central Asia steppes, exerting a great deal of influence on the development of Islamic culture and on the linguistic and artistic make up of many non-Persian dynasties such as the Seljuks, the Timurids and the Ottomans.

Of course, the real winners by the middle of the seventh century had been the Arabs. Armed with the words and deeds of the Prophet Muhammad, enshrined in the Qur'an,[2] they had burst forth from their humble beginnings in the desert oases of Arabia and within a century had converted their largely peripheral position in the Late Antique world into what was the largest empire in history to that point, a title they would hold until the establishment of the Mongol Empire in the thirteenth century. Their success had certainly been aided by the destruction wrought in the war between Heraclius and Khusro and the civil wars of both the Romans and the Persians, but to place too much emphasis on the fall out of the last Romano-Persian war would be to do the Arabs a disservice. Both the Romans and the Persians may not have fully recovered by the early 630s but they both still commanded the resources of vast territories and were more than capable of putting significant military forces into the field, forces that the Muslim armies had to defeat. The Arabs could also be said to be fortunate with being able to find a cabal of highly skilled battlefield tacticians and strategians such as Khalid, Amr, Iyad, Sa'd and more, but fortune only gets you so far in warfare. The way they wielded the combination of highly mobile cavalry and the religiously fortified Arab infantry, a much overlooked work-horse of the Arab conquests, enabled the Arabs to repeatedly out-manoeuvre Roman, Persian, Berber, Visigoth, Frank, Indian, Turkic and Chinese commanders across the world.

However, while 'morale and mobility may be the main reasons for Muslim military success', just as important, if not more so, was the ability of the caliphate to implement a government by the minority.[3] While there were revolts in the aftermath of the deaths of Umar and Uthman, retaining local non-Muslim governors in cities and regions and not attempting to impose religious unity in the way that Heraclius and his successors had done with Monothelitism was vital to building upon the successes of the armies. Muhammad had deduced from an early stage that his cause needed the support of, or at least the neutrality of, non-Muslim communities and he was not going to get that by threatening forced conversion or religious conflict. His caliphal successors recognised that such religious tolerance needed to be extended to the Christian, Jewish, Zoroastrian and pagan populations that their victories brought under their control and these instances of tolerance and fair treatment of conquered lands made other opponents more willing to capitulate. This tolerance continued long after the conquests as well, as seen by the fact that 'Italian pilgrims travelled comfortably to Jerusalem'.[4] The abilities of the likes of Umar and Hajjaj as administrators can also not be underestimated. By giving the caliphate the governmental infrastructure, Umar and his successors not only enabled it to make good on the resources it had won through war and to continue to expand in virtually all directions, they also provided it with the structural integrity and resilience to not fragment when it was faced with the internal conflicts of the Fitnas.

The outbreak of hostilities on the murder of Uthman proved to the Arabs that, much like Heraclius had found, building and maintaining a world empire on the back of religion could have its drawbacks. While the victory of Mu'awiya over Ali in 661 had confirmed the dynastic prominence of what would become Sunni Islam, those Shi'ites who believed in the right of Ali and his descendants to inherit the caliphal throne, along with the Kharijites and other schismatic branches, would continue in their opposition to the Umayyad dynasty even after their military defeats during the First and Second Fitnas. However, despite this religious factionalism, such was the grip of Sunni Islam at the centre of the caliphate that, even when the Umayyad dynasty was driven to the western fringe of the Islamic world by the Third Fitna, it did nothing to alter the religious affiliation of the caliphate. The Abbasid Revolution, despite having the support of Shi'ites keen to place an Alid on the caliphal throne and of Iranians looking for more of a say in caliphal politics, ended up as nothing more than a change of Arab dynasty.

The End of the Ancient World

Given the sheer size, scale and duration of their titanic two-decade-long struggle in contrast to the largely sterile affairs in the past, Heraclius and Khusro will have firmly believed that they were fighting for the future of their world. Indeed, in many ways the war of 602–628 was to be a fitting crescendo to four centuries of intermittent Romano-Persian warfare: the two power-houses of the Ancient World bludgeoning each other almost into mutual submission. Little did they know that the future belonged to neither of their respective empires. Battered and bruised from their epic finale, the Romans and the Persians were relatively easy pickings for the emergent armies of Islam. The subsequent spread of teachings of the Prophet and the geo-political changes it caused were the most obvious changes to have affected the world by the mid-seventh century. However, the defeat of the Persian Empire and the humbling of the Romans by the Islamic caliphate have also been seen as the final giving way of Antiquity to the period of cultural and economic decline known as the Dark Ages, which had seemingly descended over western Europe at the collapse of the Roman Empire there in the late-fifth century.

However, the very idea of these 'Dark Ages' is being increasingly dismissed. It can hardly be said to be a dark time for the ever-expanding realm of Islam, especially when it played as big a role in the preservation of many classical works and teachings as the Roman remnant that became known as the Byzantine Empire. In some ways, the coming of Islam improved more cultural outlets than its Roman predecessors, particularly in the realm of religious philosophy where the aura of tolerance allowed Christian scholars to read Aristotle and comment on the actions of the church without fear of reprisal from imperial authorities attempting to impose doctrine. Certainly, a civilisation that brought workers from across its empire to produce such marvels as the Dome of the Rock in Jerusalem, the Great Mosque of Damascus and eventually Baghdad itself could not be described as being culturally dark. Because of such achievements, it is becoming more frequent for historians to speak of how relatively 'Light' these supposed Dark Ages really were, even in Western Europe.[5] So detached from the post-Roman Mediterranean has the term become that it has taken on a more scientific meaning in academic circles as a way to describe a period of time that is poorly illuminated by historical or archaeological records.

However, this does not mean that the period following the supplanting of the Romans by first the Germanic tribes and then the Slavs and Muslims was not one of great economic, social and cultural change. Perhaps the most important change was the transition of focus from the Mediterranean to the Middle Eastern landmass. From the network of Roman cities – Constantinople,

Antioch, Alexandria, Carthage and Rome itself – linked by the sea, the centre of the early medieval world shifted to the caliphal capitals at Medina, Damascus and later Baghdad. Of these cities and others such as Basra, Kufa, Fustat, Toledo and Cordoba, few were anywhere near the sea, while several large sea ports such as Palestinian Caesarea fell into permanent decline. This was due to the pastoral way of life that the Arabs brought with them from the Arabian oases. While it did not greatly affect the settled agriculture and urbanisation of many of the areas they conquered, the Arab persuasion towards land-based trade and their initial misgivings about the high seas led them to complete the revitalisation of the caravan routes across Central Asia to the Chinese markets that had begun during the intensified Romano-Persian fighting of the sixth and seventh centuries.

Therefore, the importance of land links and the continued Roman presence on the waves, later taken up by Italian city states like Venice, Genoa and Pisa, saw to it that the ship, so long the backbone of trade, was gradually replaced at the top of the trading hierarchy by the camel as the primary mode of commercial transport throughout much of the Middle East and southern Mediterranean. Even when the Muslims did take to seaborne trade, it was not with the Mediterranean. Instead, with the foundation of Baghdad, Islamic trade would sweep down the Tigris and Euphrates, through Basra, and into the Persian Gulf to travel to the ports of the Indian subcontinent, Indonesia and south-east China. It has been argued that this 'eastward pull' of Abbasid trade was as much the salvation of Europe as the Greek fire of the Roman navy or the Frankish army of Charles Martel.[6]

In the realm of religion, along with the latest resurgence of paganism in the form of the Avars, Slavs, Bulgars and Khazars, Islam had broken Christianity's centuries-long dominance over the Mediterranean. However, Islam had an even greater impact than simply the vast area into which it was spread by conquest – from India and China to the Atlantic, Sahara and Pyrenees. By redirecting and weakening the power of the Romans and influencing the religious policies of Constantinople, particularly over Iconoclasm, the faith established by the Prophet enabled the Papacy to grow in authority not just on its own Italian doorstep but further abroad amongst the Christian kings of Western Europe. This in turn would encourage the internal schism within Christianity that would evolve into the Catholic and Orthodox division that still exists to this day.

Militarily, it is normally assumed that the victories of the Arabs, Turks and Avars brought about the final decline of the infantryman as the main fighting force on the battlefield; a decline supposedly in effect since the defeat of the Roman emperor Valens by the Visigoths at the Battle of Adrianople in 378. However, much like the 'Dark Ages', this establishment of the 'cavalry age' in warfare is something of a misnomer. Arab infantry had played a perhaps understated but no less important part in the major Arab victories over the Persians and Romans during the 630s and 640s and, without the platform it was able to provide against the infantry of Heraclius and Yazdgerd, the elite cavalry squadrons of Khalid, Iyad and Qaqa would not have been able to deal the devastating blows they were able to. Disciplined infantry forces of the Franks and Romans were also able to repel and defeat Muslim cavalry forces in head-on battle. Even more than a century later, the Muslims themselves were still deploying infantry at the core of their armies. The Umayyad Syrian army in particular, probably in reaction to its battles with the Romans and Armenians, was a heavy exponent of the spear wall. Perhaps most poignantly, at the Battle of the Zab on 25 January 750 the Abbasids would achieve victory thanks in large part to an infantry spear wall improvised by the dismounting of their cavalry.

These changes were to be long lasting and even the extended bloodbaths of the Crusades were unable to reverse this trend. Indeed, the eastward shift in the economy would remain in place until the west was able to make good on its population boom in the early centuries of the second millennium CE, while the cultural and political balance would perhaps not be fully redressed until after the Renaissance. The horse would face challenges for supremacy on the battle-field from the return of more professional infantry and the rise of gunpowder in later centuries but would remain an important component of any army right through the Industrial Revolution, and would not be completely superseded until the invention of rapid-fire machine guns and the tank. Therefore, while the end of Antiquity may not have led to the spread of a 'Dark Age', these transitions in primary focus from Mediterranean to Mesopotamian hub, sea lanes to camel-laden caravan trade, and infantry to cavalry demonstrate that while the eighth century was not necessarily a darker world than the seventh century it was most certainly a different one; one with a severely chastened and truncated Roman Empire, without a Sassanid Persian Empire and bestrode by a triumphant Islamic caliphate.

Notes

Introduction
1. Wiesehöfer (2001), 154–164; Daryaee (2009), xvii–xix on Sassanid sources.
2. For the physical evidence, the *Approaching the Ancient World* series has provided some general overviews with Bagnall (1995) on papyri, Bodel (2001) on epigraphy, Howgego (2001) on numismatics and Biers (1992) on archaeology.
3. The most authoritative study of the sources of the seventh century is the quite outstanding work of Howard-Johnston (2010). Various entries in Barchiesi and Scheidel (2010), 1–200 from Bagnall, Bodel, Harries, Hurst, Metcalf and more give a good account of the types of source material surviving from the ancient world, as well as their uses and potential drawbacks.

Chapter 1: The Participants and Their Road to 600
1. Williams and Friell (1999), 191.
2. *CJ* II.7.25[519].
3. Procopius, *Anecdota* XIX.7.
4. Procopius, *De Aedificiis.*
5. *Scriptores Originum Constantinopolitanarum* I.105.
6. Hughes (2009) on the life and career of Belisarius.
7. Jacobsen (2010).
8. Evagrius IV.29 on Ethiopia being the focus of the initial outbreak; Evans (2001), 160 suggests as far south as Kenya, Uganda or the Congo.
9. Procopius, *BP* II.23.1.
10. Noethlichs (1996), 10, 151–153 n.64–68 on the estimates of Jewish population in the Empire; Wasserstein (1996), 309–314 against the usual total of nearly 7 million.
11. Jones (1964), 950.
12. *CTh* XVI.8.24[418].
13. Murdoch (2003).
14. Procopius, *BP* I.13.21–29, 18.5; *BG* VII.29.3; Marcellinus Comes 95.
15. Jones (1964), 1449; Treadgold (1995), 63.
16. Agathias V.13.17.
17. Theophanes, *Chronographia* 251.24–27; Cedrenus, 690.14–15; Treadgold (1995), 64.
18. Mauricius, *Strat.* III.8, 10.
19. Mauricius, *Strat.* XI.
20. Vegetius I.20; Procopius, *BV* IV.2.1–2; IV.3.4–6.
21. Mauricius, *Strat.* XII B.
22. Mauricius, *Strat.* XII B 1–6.
23. Mauricius, *Strat.* XII B.9.
24. Procopius, *BV* III.11.3–4; IV.5.13; *BG* VII.5.13–14.
25. Jones (1964), 666.
26. Procopius, *Anecdota* XXIV.21–26.
27. Treadgold (1995), 96.

28. *CTh* VII.20.4[325]; 22.8[372].
29. Procopius, *Anecdota* XXIV.13–14.
30. Southern and Dixon (1996), 37.
31. *CJ* I.27.2 §8[534].
32. Whitby in Cameron (1995), 89.
33. The numerous works of Walter Scheidel tackle many of the problems faced with any study of the population of Late Antiquity.
34. Dio LXXX.3; the fact that the westernised form of the name 'Ardashir' was 'Artaxerxes,' a name used by three Achaemenid Kings of Kings, might give further credence to this claim.
35. *Chronicle of Arbela* VIII; Dio LXXX.3; Hormizdagan was probably somewhere near Isfahan on the road to Hamadan; coins of Vologaeses VI were minted at Seleucia perhaps as late as 229 but this is somewhat suspect and was of no real threat to Sassanid power.
36. Boyce (1979), 29.
37. Boyce (1979), 1.
38. Wiesehöfer (2001), 200.
39. Wiesehöfer (2001), 200.
40. Judaism, Buddhism, Hinduism, Manichaeanism and various branches of Christianity are recorded.
41. Wiesehöfer (2001), 169–170.
42. Tabari I.897.
43. Daryaee (2009), 54–55.
44. Daryaee (2009), 39–40.
45. Procopius, *BP* I.19.1; 20.9; Menander Protector fr. 19ff.
46. Harris (1980), 118; (1999), 65 on between a fifth and a sixth of the gross population being slaves; Scheidel (1997c), 158 suggests a slave population of about 10 per cent.
47. Wiesehöfer (2001), 199.
48. Tabari I.964.9.
49. Plutarch, *Crassus* 27.2.
50. Daryaee (2009), 45.
51. Ammianus XXV.1.11–14.
52. Ammianus XXV.1.11–14.
53. Mauricius, *Strat.* XI.1.
54. Ammianus XXV.1.11–14.
55. Ammianus XXV.1.18; Mauricius, *Strat.* XI.1.
56. Mauricius, *Strat.* XI.1.
57. Ammianus XIX.5; XX.6; Mauricius, *Strat.* XI.1; Wiesehöfer (2001), 198.
58. Procopius, *BP* I.13.23; 14.1; 15.1, 11.
59. Theophylactus Simocatta V.9.3–4.
60. Dio LXXX.4.
61. Lactantius, *De Mort. Pers.* 5
62. Garnsey and Saller (1987), 8.

Chapter 2: The War of the Usurper and the Revolt of Heraclius
1. George of Pisidia, *Heraclias* II.6–11; Theophylactus Simocatta, 4; Theophanes, *Chronographia* I:290; Nikephoros, *SH* 3; Cedrenus I:708.
2. Bury (1889), II.206; Pernice (1905), 7; Ostrogorsky (1963), 72ff.
3. Olster (1993).
4. Gregory the Great, *Registrum Epistolarum* XIII.31, 38.
5. Theophylactus Simocatta, *Hist.* III.1.1.
6. Sebeos, *Hist.* ch.6–7.

7. Epiphania may well have been from Cappadocia, as John of Nikiou, *Chron.* 106.2, 109.27 suggests that Heraclius the Younger had Cappadocian origins although the term 'Cappadocia' can be applied to a large geographic area from eastern Anatolia to the borders of Mesopotamia so a link with Armenia is not irreconcilable. It could also be that Heraclius was born in Cappadocia but had little or no genetic link to Cappadocians.

8. Charles Cawley's website *Medieval Lands* provides an excellent summary of 'territories in the medieval western world and the royal and noble families which ruled them' with that of Heraclius found at http://fmg.ac/Projects/MedLands/BYZANTIUM.htm.

9. Kaegi (2003).

10. Fredegarius IV.65.

11. Leo Grammatikos, *Chron.* 147.

12. Fredegarius IV.65.

13. John of Nikiou, *Chron.* 107.10.

14. John of Nikiou, *Chron.* 106.1–6.

15. Nikephoros, *SH* I.

16. Kaegi (2003), 37.

17. Despite Heraclius the Elder's sharing in this declared consulship, he played little role in the rebellion itself. He was to die shortly after word of Heraclius' victory had reached Africa, probably due to his more advanced years and possibly illness, although the date is unknown.

18. John of Nikiou, *Chron.* 107.5.

19. Kaegi (2003), 45–48 presents the possible routes taken by Heraclius around the Mediterranean and the evidence for and against; John of Antioch, *FHG* V.38.

20. John of Nikiou, *Chron.* 109.26.

21. John of Nikiou, *Chron.* 110.4–7; Kaegi (2003), 51; *Chron. Pasch.* 700–701; John of Antioch, *FGH* V.38.

22. Theophanes, *Chron.* AM 6102; John of Nikiou, *Chron.* 110.9.

23. Nikephoros, *SH* 2.

24. Kaegi (2003), 51.

25. Olster (1994), 73; 93 on urban unrest and Jewish-Christian clashes continued across the Levant.

Chapter 3: It Has Come to the Triarii

1. Kaegi (2003), 61; Nikephoros, *SH* 3; Zonaras XIV.14.

2. Sebeos. *Hist.* 108–111.

3. *Vie de Theodore de Sykeon* c.153; Theophanes, *Chron.* AM 6103.

4. Nikephoros, *SH* 2.

5. Sebeos. *Hist.* 114, ch.34.

6. Sebeos. *Hist.* 115, ch.34.

7. Qur'an, *Sura* 30.1–3.

8. Agapios, *Kitab al-Unvan* PO8: 450; Ps-Isidore, *Continuationes* 335.

9. Strategius VIII.5–6.

10. Howard-Johnston (2010), 164 n.2 provides the evidence for the later dates from Flusin (1992), II.154–158.

11. Faulkner (2002), 294–361 on the seven-month Roman siege of 70 CE.

12. James (2010), 20–27 on the use of burning sulphur and bitumen.

13. Sebeos, *Hist.* ch.24.

14. Reich in Geva (1994), 111–118.

15. Howard-Johnston (2010), 422.

16. Sophronius, *Anacreontica* 18.85–88; George of Pisidia, *In rest. S.Cruciis* 25–26; Theophylactus Simocatta V.7.8–7; Eutychius c.270; Howard-Johnston (2010), ch.5 on anti-Semitism in the sources of the mid-seventh century and how it could twist the retelling of the event.

17. Kaegi (2003), 79; Foss (1979), 103 on an earthquake at Ephesus in 614 which will have played further into the idea of divine wrath.
18. *Chronicon Paschale* 707–709 on the letter to Khusro.
19. Theophanes, *Chron.* AM 6105; 6109.
20. Nikephoros, *SH* 6–7.
21. Lilie (1985), 34; John of Nikiou, *Chron.* 109.18; Isidore of Seville 129; Fredegarius, *Chron.* IV.33.
22. Nikephoros, *SH* 8; *Chron. Pasch.* 708 also suggests that Heraclius wrote to Khusro II explaining that he meant to return to Africa without assuming imperial power.
23. Theophanes, *Chron.* AM 6113; Nikephoros, *SH* 11; George of Pisidia, *Heraclias* II.35–61; Cameron (1976).
24. *Chron. Pasch.* 713–714 on Heraclius and Martina being married by March, 624; Garland (1999), 52–65.
25. Anastastius the Sinaite c.40 on the plague reaching Africa.
26. Kaegi (2003), 101.
27. *Chron. Pasch.* 706; Hendy (1985), 494–499; Grierson (1951); (1953) also suggests that a mint was opened at Seleucia Isauricae near the main battle front to help pay the soldiery.
28. *Chron. Pasch.* 711; Nikephoros, *SH* 12.4–8.
29. Theophanes, *Chron.* AM 6112.
30. George of Pisidia, *Exped. Pers.* I.163–238.
31. George of Pisidia, *Exped. Pers.* II.165–169.
32. George of Pisidia, *Exped. Pers.* III.144–152.
33. George of Pisidia, *Exped. Pers.* III.30–304.
34. Mauricius, *Strat.* XI.1.
35. Vegetius III.6
36. George of Pisidia, *Exped. Pers.* III.179–304; Haldon (1984), 95–100; 105–107; 116–118.
37. Kaegi (2003), 117.
38. The exact date is disputed, with 617 and 619 also suggested (Kaegi (2003), 119 n.59).
39. George of Pisidia, *Exped. Pers.* III.311–340; Theophanes, *Chron.* AM 6113; Fine (1983), 34–59; Nikephoros, *SH* 10.
40. Nikephoros, *SH* 13.
41. Kaegi (2003), 120.
42. Theophanes, *Chron.* AM 6111; Theodore Synkellos, *Analecta Avarica* 302.28–35.
43. George of Pisidia, *Heraclias* I.157–158.
44. Sebeos, *Hist.* 123 ch.38.
45. Tabari, V.320–321.
46. Haldon (1999), 27–33; Dennis in Laiou and Mottahedeh (2001), 31–39; *contra* Kolbaba (1998), 194–221; Whitby (1998), 191–208.
47. The emperor Julian took between 65,000 and 95,000 men on his doomed expedition in 363 (Ammianus XXIII.3.5; Zosimus III.12.5–13.1; Jones (1964), 684; Elton (1996), 210–211); Anastasius sent a 52,000-strong army against Kavadh I in 502 (Joshua the Stylite 54).
48. Sebeos, *Hist.* 124 ch.38 on 120,000; Haldon (1997); (1999); Howard-Johnston (1999), 1–44 on the smaller estimates.
49. Theophanes, *Chron.* AM 6113.
50. George of Pisidia, *Heraclias* II.162–166; Sebeos, *Hist.* 124 ch.38; Theophanes, *Chron.* 308.
51. Sebeos, *Hist.* 124 ch.38.
52. Theophanes, *Chron.* AM 6114.
53. The chronology of 625 is somewhat muddled with Zuckerman (2002a) going against the more established view of Stratos (1968–1980).
54. Sebeos, *Hist.* 124 ch.38.
55. Theophanes, *Chron.* AM 6115.

56. Theophanes, *Chron.* AM 6115.
57. Theophanes, *Chron.* AM 6115.
58. Mauricius, *Strat.* XI.1.51–53.
59. Sebeos, *Hist.* 126 ch.38.
60. Theophanes, *Chron.* AM 6116; Eutychius, *Hist.* c.29.
61. Theophanes, *Chron.* AM 6116.
62. Kaegi (2003), 129; Wiita (1977), 99–108.

Chapter 4: The Ram Has Touched the Wall

1. *Chron. Pasch.* 170; Theodore Synkellos, *Analecta Avarica* 300; Nikephoros, *SH* 12.
2. George of Pisidia, *Bell. Avar.* 197–203; Nikephoros, *SH* 13 both thought that the siege of Constantinople was a pre-planned attack by the Persians and the Avars.
3. *Chron. Pasch.* 170–171; George of Pisidia, *Bell. Avar.* 219; Theodore Synkellos, *Analecta Avarica* 300.39 on Avar strength being measured in 'myriads' – tens of thousands; Barisic (1954) on the presence of Slavs; Theophanes, *Chron.* AM 6117 on perhaps 'Gepids' being involved.
4. *Chron. Pasch.* 168–169 on Seismos; Theophanes, *Chron.* AM 6117 on reinforcements; George of Pisidia, *Bell. Avar.* 246–247, 266–293; *Chron. Pasch.* 718.
5. *Chron. Pasch.* 711; Nikephoros, *SH* 12.4–8 on the cancellation of the grain dole in 618.
6. Theodore Synkellos, *Analecta Avarica* 300.35.
7. Theodore Synkellos, *Analecta Avarica* 305.21–26; 302–303.
8. *Chron. Pasch.* 173.
9. Theodore Synkellos, *Analecta Avarica* 306.
10. *Chron. Pasch.* 174.
11. *Chron. Pasch.* 721; *Chron. Pasch.* 175 on 3,000; George of Pisidia, *Bell. Avar.* 329–331 on 1,000.
12. *Chron. Pasch.* 175–178; Theodore Synkellos, *Analecta Avarica* 306–308; Nikephoros, *SH* 13; the taunting by the Persian envoys could be an invention of the literary sources, not only to make the Persians seem too overconfident – as the author will likely have known of the outcome of the war – but also as an explanation for the deplorable treatment of these envoys by the Romans, who had them beheaded.
13. Theodore Synkellos, *Analecta Avarica* 312–313; *Chron. Pasch.* 180–181.
14. *Chron. Pasch.* 725.
15. McCotter (1996); *Chron. Pasch.* 180.
16. Whether Shahin died in the midst of battle, later from a wound or old age or from the wrath of Khusro is unknown. Theophanes, *Chron.* AM 6117 suggesting that Khusro had Shahin skinned and salted could be a distortion of Zoroastrian funerary practices.
17. Nikephoros, *SH* 55; Moses Dasxuranci, *Hist.* II.12; Eutychius 104; Zuckerman (2002b); Theophanes, *Chron.* AM 6117; Brown, Bryer and Winfield (1978), 30 on the possibility that Heraklonas was born in Lazica.
18. The Western Turkic Khaganate was itself an offshoot of the original Turkic Khaganate that had been established in the mid-6th century, stretching across vast tracts of Central Asia from the Caspian to Mongolia and at times beyond. A defeat at the hands of these Turks had led to the appearance of the Avars in Europe. This vast Khaganate descended into a decade of civil war in the mid-580s from which it emerged in two separate parts – the Eastern and Western Turkic Khaganates.
19. The identity of the Turkic Khan that Heraclius dealt with is also not agreed upon. Attempts have been made to equate the Ziebel mentioned by the Roman sources with Yabghu, leader of the West Turkic Khaganate between 618 and 628 but not without criticism.
20. Theophanes, *Chron.* AM 6117; Moses Dasxuranci, *Hist.* II.12; Nikephoros, *SH* 12.
21. Dennis (1998), 99–115.
22. Nikephoros, *SH* 12.51–64.

23. Theophanes, *Chron.* AM 6118; Moses Dasxuranci, *Hist.* II.16; Thomson (1996), 234–235; Zuckerman (2002b).
24. Theophanes, *Chron.* AM 6118; Sebeos, *Hist.* 126.
25. Roch Vehan is known in the Greek sources as Rhazates and Rhahzadh in the Persian.
26. Theophanes, *Chron.* AM 6118.
27. 627 also saw the outbreak of an ecclesiastical dispute in Italy, where Pope Honorius protested against the interference of the governor of Sardinia, Theodore, in church matters on the island and eventually dragged the Praetorian Prefect of Africa into the dispute. 'The outcome is unknown, but it is a reminder that secular and ecclesiastical authorities did not suspend their quarrels for the sake of the struggle against the Zoroastrian Sasanians', (Kaegi (2003), 155).
28. Mauricius, *Strat.* III.14.
29. Theophanes, *Chron.* AM 6118.
30. Tabari V.322–323.
31. Theophanes, *Chron.* AM 6118; the slightly less panegyric Nikephoros, *SH* 14 does suggest that Roch Vehan challenged Heraclius personally.
32. Theophanes, *Chron.* AM 6118.
33. Theophanes, *Chron.* AM 6118 on not only the retrieval of 300 Roman standards lost in the fighting but also 'much aloe and large woodstocks of aloe, of seventy and eighty pounds, and much silk and pepper and many beyond counting number of shirts of charbasia, sugar and ginger and many other sorts of things, and asimon and shirts made wholly of silk, wool carpets and carpets sewn by needle so many that, because of their weight, he burned them because they were too heavy to carry away.'
34. Theophanes, *Chron.* AM 6118.
35. *Chron. Pasch.* 732.
36. Theophanes, *Chron.* AM 6118; Tabari I.1046–1049; 1059–1061.
37. *Acta* 42
38. Theophanes, *Chron.* AM 6118; *Chron. Pasch.* 184 n.486.
39. Eutychius ch.29.
40. Nikephoros, *SH* 15.
41. *Chron. Pasch.* 735–736.
42. Theophanes, *Chron.* AM 6119; Eutychius 29.
43. Nikephoros, *SH* 18.
44. *Chron. Pasch.* 730–731; Tabari I.1043.
45. Sebeos, *Hist.* 127 ch.39; Moses Dasxuranci, *Hist.* II.16.
46. *Chron. Pasch.* 704–705.

Chapter 5: A New Challenger Approaches

1. Hoyland (2001) provides a dry but authoritative look at the history of Arabia up until the revelations of Muhammad.
2. Donner (1981), 11–49 on pre-Islamic Arabia.
3. Hourani (2005), 10.
4. Hourani (2005), 12.
5. Fisher (2011).
6. Kaegi (1992), 52.
7. Brown (2006), 189.
8. Hourani (2005), 15.
9. Brown (2006), 190.
10. Brown (2006), 190–191.
11. Ibn Ishaq, 119.
12. Hourani (2005), 21.
13. Landau-Tasseron in Cameron (1995), 299.

14. Hoyland (1997).
15. Kennedy (2001), 3.
16. Landau-Tasseron in Cameron (1995), 309.
17. Donner in Cameron (1995), 337–360 on the authority of the early Caliphate.
18. Hill in Parry and Yapp (1975).
19. Due to the importance of Arab cavalry, it might be expected that they made use of the stirrup. However, while it was mentioned in the *Strategikon*, this was the first recorded reference to the stirrup and the use of the word σκάλα, meaning 'step' or 'stair', suggests that it was new to the Romans (Mauricius, *Strat*. I.2). The stirrup seems only to have become more widely used after its introduction to Eastern Europe by the Avars. The Persians may have encountered it somewhat sooner due to the presence of Asiatic tribes on their northern frontiers and their connections to China, where the stirrup seems to have been in widespread use by the end of the fifth century CE. Therefore, as they did not produce it independently, it would seem that the Arabs would have had little exposure to the stirrup and the benefits it might have had to light cavalry before their invasions.
20. Kennedy (2001), 171 using Nicolle in Lev (1997), 15.
21. Kennedy (2001), 183–194; Purton (2009), 49; swing-beam technology did not appear in the western world until the late-sixth century with it first being seen at the Avar siege of Thessalonica in 597, and true trebuchets not until the twelfth century, limiting the possibilities of their usage by the Muslims.
22. Landau-Tasseron in Cameron (1995), 310.
23. Brown (2006), 193.
24. Kennedy (2001), 1.
25. Landau-Tasseron in Cameron (1995), 324–334.
26. Prolonged reoccurrences of plague are usually assumed to be one of the pre-eminent factors in the decline in the size of Roman and Persian forces. It is made an all the more attractive explanation by the suggestion that the Justinianic Plague left Arabia and its population untouched (Donner in Maas (2004), 519; Sarris (2002), 173). However, greater Roman and Persian populations would not have been more successful in resisting the Arab Conquests if the social, economic and political infrastructure for recruiting armies had already failed, as had already been proven with the fall of the western half of the Roman Empire to what amounted to a couple of hundred thousand barbarians and their families (Scheidel in Scheidel (2001), 68 n.276).
27. Mauricius, *Strat*. III.8, 10.

Chapter 6: The Islamic Eruption
1. Kaegi (2003), 222.
2. Kaegi (2003), 222.
3. Kaegi (1992), 39–40.
4. Kaegi (2003), 213–220 on Heraclius' attempts to encourage/force some kind of religious unity not only across his empire with the rebuilding of religious sites, forced baptism of Jews and conversion of non-Monothelites, but also beyond its borders with his interactions with the Frankish kingdom and Persian priests.
5. Suda II: 583 suggests 200,000.
6. Kaegi (2003), 224.
7. Kaegi (2003), 218; Theophanes, *Chron*. AM 6123; Nikephoros, *SH* 20.
8. Moses Dasxuranci, *Hist*. II.14.
9. Moses Dasxuranci, *Hist*. II.16.
10. Daryaee (2009), 34–35.
11. Daryaee (2009), 36; Daryaee (1999); (2004).
12. Donner (1981), 177.

13. Donner (1981), 177–178 summarises much of the argument.
14. Donner (1981), 179 n.66 on the attempts to identify the important locations of Khalid's march to Hira.
15. Donner (1981), 187–188 focuses more on the tribes Khalid fought against than the cities and armies he reportedly defeated.
16. Donner (1981), 187.
17. Donner (1981), 97.
18. Kaegi (1992), 41;
19. Tabari I.2107, 2108, 2079; Kufi I.123 on Amr having 6,000.
20. Theophanes, *Chron.* AM 6127; Nikephoros, *Hist.* 20.
21. Kaegi (1992), 39–43 on the forces available to defend Roman Palestine and southern Syria.
22. Kaegi (1992), 83–87 on the events around Areopolis/Ma'ab.
23. Tabari I.2108.
24. Donner (1981), 116; Kufi I.124 has Abu Bakr giving a direct order to avoid cities and open countryside.
25. Tabari I.2122; Ibn al-Athir, Kamil II.408.
26. Donner (1981), 119–127 on the numerous suggested routes that Khalid took; 128–146 on the different chronologies recorded, but rather strangely fails to pick between them.
27. Kaegi (2003), 234.
28. Fredegarius, *Chron.* IV.66 – '150,000 Roman soldiers were slain.'
29. Nicolle (1994), 43.
30. Kaegi (1992), 101.
31. Nikephoros, *SH* 69.
32. Sebeos, *Hist.* 133, 44.143, 44 – 'in return for your acting thus towards me, and not wishing to lay your hand on my life and that of my sons, I shall not set my hand on you or your sons. But go and stay where I shall command you, and I shall have mercy upon you.'
33. However, the idea that the name 'Gaudomelete' applies specifically to the second largest island of the Maltese Archipelago, known in the modern day as Gozo, cannot be completely ruled out.

Chapter 7: 636 – The Year of the Muslim Beast
1. Donner (1981), 130.
2. Baladhuri p.140 – 200,000; Tabari II.598 – 200,000; Ibn Ishaq (Tabari III.75) – 100,000; *Chronica Minora* II p.75 records the battle costing 50,000 Roman lives.
3. Kaegi (1992), 131 – 15–20,000.
4. Baladhuri p.140, Ibn Ishaq (Tabari III p.74) – 24,000; Donner (1981), 133, 135, 221 – 20,000–40,000.
5. Nicolle (1994), 64.
6. Kaegi (1992), 119.
7. The identity and even the nationality of Buccinator, recorded as Qanatir in Muslim sources, is disputed. It was long held that he might have been a Slavic prince commanding a contingent of Slavs in the Roman army. However, his conflict with George has led some to believe that he shared Armenian heritage with his fellow commander, which brings personal, familial and even religious dimensions into their dispute. The word 'buccinator' has military connotations, being the Latin name for the person who played the brass instrument known as a *buccina*, which was used in the Roman camp to announce changes in the watch and other movements.
8. Theophanes, *Chron.* AM 6126 on the dissension within the Roman ranks.
9. Haldon (2008), 59.
10. Kaegi (1992), 139.
11. Eutychius 279.
12. Michael the Syrian, *Chron.* XI.6.

13. Donner (1981), 192.
14. *CHI*, IV.8.
15. Howard-Johnston (2010), 467 n.20 follows Ps-Sebeos and Moses Dasxuranci in dating the Battle of the Bridge to a Persian counter-attack in 637.
16. Donner (1981), 192–195 on the size and composition of the Muslim force.
17. Donner (1981), 199.
18. Donner (1981), 203 n.174 gives some of the sources for the Persian army.
19. Muruj II.312 suggests 90,000.
20. Tabari I.2261–2264; Kufi I.173.
21. Donner (1981), 205–209.
22. Donner (1981), 204.
23. Another version of Rustam's death is that he was accidentally crushed by a cache of weapons that fell from a camel that he was taking shelter behind in a sandstorm.

Chapter 8: A Farewell to Syria and Mesopotamia

1. Some chronologies would suggest that the surrender of Jerusalem to Umar only came at the end of the Muslim campaigns in Palestine, with the conquests, of Damascus, Caesarea and even Gaza placed before it.
2. It is possible that the surrender of Beirut took place after that of Caesarea in 640 (Kaegi (1992), 146).
3. Tabari 915 – 'May Allah have mercy upon Abu Bakr. He was a better judge of men than I have been.'
4. Also known as the Lake of Antioch, Lake Amik was drained between the 1940s and 1970s to be used for farmland and then Hatay Airport in 2007.
5. Michael the Syrian, *Chron.* XI.7.
6. The timeline of the Muslim conquest is muddled. Iyad may have conquered the likes of Callinicum and Edessa in 637, in the immediate aftermath of Heraclius' refuting of the Truce of Chalkis, before returning a year later after the defeat of the Christian Arab attack on Emesa to continue the conquest along with Khalid: or there was just a single invasion of Upper Mesopotamia and the southern provinces of Armenia sometime before 640. Kaegi (1992, 181–204) highlights the prominent position of Armenia in the seventh-century Roman Empire and the difficulties of outlining the Muslim campaigns against the Armenian provinces.
7. Khalid's involvement in the raid on Armenia is by no means certain. It is possible that the attributing of the presence of a 'Khalid b. al-Walid' in this raid and the subsequent probing of northern Anatolia was due to the service of his son, Abd al-Rahman b. Khalid b. al-Walid, the later governor of Emesa.
8. Beck (1990) reviews the history of alcohol as an antiseptic.
9. The Battle of Mu'ta can hardly be claimed as a victory, although, for the period that Khalid commanded the Muslim army, he did rescue it from a total disaster.
10. Akram (2004) on Khalid's life and career.
11. Amwas was long identified as the Biblical Emmaus, where Luke 24:13–15 records that Jesus of Nazareth first appeared after his resurrection; however, doubt has been cast upon this identification given the distance of this Emmaus, also known as Nicopolis, from Jerusalem – the Biblical Emmaus was recorded as being 7 miles from the holy city, while Amwas is 18 miles away. It is possible that the Biblical Emmaus was destroyed during the Bar Kokhba revolt of 132–136 CE, leaving later scholars to identify Amwas as the original.
12. Kaegi (1992), 175.
13. Donner (1981), 154.
14. Donner (1981), 155.

15. That the capture of a bridge behind enemy lines repeatedly appears in the records of Muslim battles may give rise to the idea that it was used almost as a literary *topos*, calling into question the authenticity of these retellings.

Chapter 9: Stealing Roman Bread and Persian Heart

1. Despite its age, Butler (1902) remains one of the best works on the Muslim invasion of Egypt.
2. Butler (1902), 208.
3. Herodotus II.141; III.1.13; Procopius, *BP* II.22.6.
4. Jones (1964), 1438 gives a table of the forces of Egypt recorded in the *Notitia*; Treadgold (1995, 50) uses Jones' establishment, with some corrections, to suggest that Egypt contained 16,500 infantry and 9,000 cavalry, while the Thebaid had 10,000 infantry and 12,500 cavalry; the section regarding the military forces of Libya/Cyrenaica is missing from the surviving manuscripts of the *Notitia* with Treadgold (1995, 50) suggesting perhaps 13,000 men under the *dux Libyarum*.
5. Butler (1902), 228 n.1.
6. Butler (1902), 233.
7. Pliny, *NH* VI.31 suggests that the Tigris and Euphrates may have had at one time separate outlets into the Persian Gulf.
8. The surrender of Tustar and further retreat of Persian armies left the Muslims in control of the vast agricultural area that surrounded the Karun river. The most famous part of that system is the Band-e-Kaisar – the Dam of Caesar – a combined bridge and dam of the Karun, reputedly conceived and built by Roman captives from the Battle of Edessa in 260CE, and which is now a UNESCO World Heritage Site.
9. Donner (1981), 217.
10. The suggestion that some Persian infantry was chained together could suggest that some of the 'volunteers' were far from willing to serve in the army.
11. The exact date of the Battle at Nahavand is not certain but the precursory moves to the battlefield, the dispositions, the Muslim frontal assaults and then the decisive attack seem to have taken place throughout December of 641 and into the early days of 642.
12. The West Turkic Khaganate was either in the course of breaking up by this time or had already done so. This would have given Yazdgerd more recruiting options but at the same time would have presented less of an overall threat to the Arabs.

Chapter 10: Three Deaths, Two Gods, One Winner

1. Kaegi (2003), 300–301 counts thirteen different major crises faced by Heraclius throughout his career, ranging from civil war, the premature death of Eudocia and some of his children, the abortive rebellion of Athalarichos, repeated fiscal crises, the Persian, Avar and Muslim invasions, the failure of Monotheletism, the succession crisis to his own failing health; Nikephoros, *SH* 27 on Heraclius' urinary problems; Lascaratos, Poulakou-Rembelakou, Rembelakos and Marketos (1995) on epispadias, although the chances of this are reduced by his numerous children.
2. Kaegi (2003) mentions it on several occasions.
3. Kaegi (2003), 314.
4. Haldon (1993), 1–67; (1999), 71–74.
5. Gibbon (1788), V.46.
6. Kaegi (2003), 315.
7. Ostrogorsky (1956), 99.
8. Nikephoros *SH* 29.
9. Haldon (1997); (1999); Treadgold (1995); (1997).
10. Herrin (2007) gives an overview of the Byzantine Empire; Haldon (2008) describes many of the wars of the Byzantine Empire.

11. Madelung (1997) gives a good account of the accessions of Abu Bakr, Umar, Uthman and Ali and the establishing of the Umayyad dynasty.
12. It is not firmly established whether it was Utba, al-Mughira or Abu Musa.
13. Hormuzan was soon murdered by a son of the dead caliph.
14. As well as semi-autonomous regions such as Armenia, there appear to have been twelve provinces with Arabia divided into Medina and Mecca; Iraq into Basra and Kufa; Palestine into Aylya and Ramlah; Egypt into Upper and Lower Egypt; Persia into Azerbaijan, Fars and Khurasan, and Syria a province by itself.
15. Madelung (1997), 113–140.
16. Madelung (1997), 140.
17. Madelung (1997), 148–149.
18. Madelung (1997), 267–269; 293–307.
19. Despite a general massacre, the Umayyad family survived the Third Fitna and by 756 its last remaining members had made their way to Muslim Spain where they established the Caliphate of Cordoba, which dominated the Iberian Peninsula for the best part of three centuries before collapsing into anarchy in the early-11th century before its final dissolution in 1031.
20. The Tang dynasty had established hegemony over the Tien Shan, the Pamir mountains and the Tarim Basin in the form of the Anxi Protectorate, also known as the 'Protectorate General to Pacify the West', in the aftermath of the breakup of the Turkic Khaganate in the first half of the seventh century.
21. Either Taizong, who ruled from 627 to 649, or Gaozong, who ruled from 650 to 683.
22. Lipman (1997), 29.
23. Gibbon (1788), V.51 n.38.
24. What is now known as Xi'an, the capital of Shaanxi province of China, was the capital of not just the Tang dynasty but also the Zhou, Qin, Sui and Han and is the home of such diverse elements as the Terracotta Army of Qin Shi Huang, the terminus of the ancient Silk Road and the Lantian Man discovered in 1963.
25. Daryaee (2004), 59–79 on the chronology of the late Sassanids; Wahram's campaigns may form the basis of the Middle Persian poem 'On the Coming of the Miraculous Wahram.'
26. Daryaee (2009), 38.

Chapter 11: The Feast Continues: From the Atlantic to the Indian Ocean

1. Cyrenaica and Tripolitana equate largely to the Mediterranean coast of modern-day Libya, whilst Tunisia covers much of what was Africa province.
2. Pringle (1981), 46.
3. Diehl (1896), 562.
4. Diehl (1896), 559–560.
5. The Romans under Scipio Aemilianus had destroyed Carthage in 146 BCE only to rebuild it again just over a century later.
6. The exact origins of Tariq are unknown. It is largely thought that he was a freed slave of Musa but where he was from is much disputed. Suggestions range from an Arab from Kindah, a North African Berber, a Persian from Hamadan, a Christian Goth to even a converted Jew.
7. This had been established largely by the conquests and assassinations of Clovis of Tournai in the late-fifth and early-sixth centuries, but by the early-eighth century the Merovingian kings had dwindled in power to short-lived puppets at the whim of the Mayor of the Palace.
8. Mastnak (2002), 99–100; Barbero (2004), 10.
9. Paul the Deacon LIV.
10. The events of the Third Fitna actually meant that Pepin attacked the Muslim enclave of Septimania as an ally of the Abbasid caliph after Hispania had fallen to the fleeing Umayyads. Charlemagne's campaigns across the Pyrenees were also part of this Frankish-Abbasid alliance against the Umayyad caliphate of Cordoba.

11. This was the first of three battles of Balajar with the Muslims winning engagements there in 723 and 732.
12. Haldon (1997), 64; Treadgold (1997), 325.
13. Carey (2012) on the intervening centuries before Manzikert.

Epilogue
1. Brown (2006), 200.
2. Holland (2012) gives a thought-provoking discourse on the development of Islam in the seventh century.
3. Kennedy (2001), 6.
4. Brown (2006), 194.
5. Wells (2008); Wickham (2009).
6. Brown (2006), 202.

Bibliography

Primary Sources

Acta of St Anastasius the Persian (Franklin, C.V., translation, 2004).

Agapios, *Kitab al-Unvan* (Vasiliev, A.A., translation, 1910–1912).

Agathias, *De imperio et rebus gestis Iustiniani* (Frendo, J.D., translation, 1975).

Ammianus Marcellinus (Hamilton, W., translation, Penguin Classics, 1986).

Anastasius the Sinaite (Nau edition, 1902).

Baladhuri, *Futuh al-Buldan* (de Goeje, M.J., translation, 1866).

Cassius Dio, *Historia Romana* (Cary, E., translation, Loeb Classical Library, 1914–1927).

Cedrenus, *Historiarium Compendium* (Bekker, I., edition, 1838).

Chronica Minora (Mommsen, T., edition, Teubner, 1892).

Chronicle of Arbela (Kroll, T., translation, 1985).

Chronicle of Zuqnin/Pseudo-Dionysius of Tel-Mahre, *Chronicle* (Witakowski, W., translation, 1997).

Chronicon Paschale (Whitby, M. and Whitby, M., translation, Translated Texts for Historians, 1989).

Codex Iustinianus (Krueger, P., translation, 1914).

Codex Theodosianus (Pharr, C., translation, 1952).

Eutychius, *Annals* (Breydy, M., translation, 1985).

Evagrius Scholasticus, *Historia Ecclesiastica* (Whitby, M., translation, Translated Texts for Historians, 2000).

Fredegarius, *Chronicle* (Wallace-Hadrill, J.W., translation, 1960).

George of Pisidia, *Bellum Avaricum* (Tartaglia, L., translation, 1998).

—— *De Expeditione Persica* (Tartaglia, L., translation, 1998).

—— *Heraclias* (Tartaglia, L., translation, 1998).

—— *In rest. S.Cruciis* (Tartaglia, L., translation, 1998).

Gregory the Great, *Registrum Epistolarum* (Ewald, P. and Hartmann, L., edition, 1887–1899).

Herodotus, *Histories* (de Selincourt, A., and Marincola, J., translation, 2003).

Ibn al-Athir, al-Kamil fi-l Ta'rikh (Tornberg, C.J., translation, 1965).

Ibn Ishaq (Guillaume, A, translation, 1978).

Isidore of Seville, *Historia Vandalorum* (Mommsen, T., edition, Teubner, 1892).

John of Antioch (Mariev, S., translation, 2008).

John of Nikiou, *Chronicle* (Charles, R.H., translation, 1916).

Joshua the Stylite, *Chronicle* (Trombley, F.R., and Watt, J.W., translation, 2000).

Kufi, *Kitab al-futuh* (Muhammad Ali al-Abbasi and Sayyid Abd al-Wahhab Bukhari, translation, 1968–1975).

Lactantius, *De Mortibus Persecutorum* (Creed, J.L., translation, 1984).

Leo Grammatikos, *Chronographia* (Bekkeri, I., edition, 1842).

Marcellinus Comes, *Chronicon* (Croke, B., translation, 1995).

Mauricius, *Strategikon* (Dennis, G.T., translation, 1984).

Menander Protector, *Historia* (Blockley, R.C., translation, 1985).

Michael the Syrian, *Chronicle* (Palmer, A., translation, Translated Texts for Historians, 1993).

Moses Dasxuranci, *History of Albania* (Dowsett, C.J.F., translation, 1961).
Muruj al-dhahab (de Meynard, B., translation, 1861–1917).
Nikephoros, *Short History* (Mango, C., translation, 1990).
Notitia Dignitatum (Jones, A.H.M., translation, 1964).
Paul the Deacon, *Historia Langobardorum* (Foulke, W.D., translation, 1906).
Pliny the Elder, *Natural History* (Bostock, J., and Riley, H.T., translation, 1855).
Plutarch, *Lives* (Perrin, B., translation, Loeb Classical Library, 1923).
Procopius, *Anecdota* (Williamson, G.A., translation, Penguin Classics, 1967).
—— *De Aedificiis* (Dewing, H.B., translation, Loeb Classical Library, 1940).
—— *De Bello Gothico* (Dewing, H.B., translation, Loeb Classical Library, 1919).
—— *De Bello Persico* (Dewing, H.B., translation, Loeb Classical Library, 1914).
—— *De Bello Vandalico* (Dewing, H.B., translation, Loeb Classical Library, 1916).
Ps-Isidore, *Continuationes Isidorianae Byzantia Arabica et Hispana* (Mommsen, T. edition, 1961).
Scriptores Originum Constantinopolitanarum (Preger, T., Teubner edition, 1907).
Sebeos, *History* (Thomson, R.W., translation, 1999).
Sophronius, *Anacreontica* (Gigante, M., translation, 1957).
Strategius (Garitte, G., translation, 1974–1975).
Suda (Adler, A., translation, 1928–1938).
Tabari (Yar-Shater, E., translation, 1985–1999).
Theodore Synkellos, *Analecta Avarica* (Sternbach, L., translation, 1900 and Cameron, A., translation, 1979).
Theophanes, *Chronographia* (Mango, C., and Scott, R., translation, 1997).
Theophylactus Simocatta, *Historiae* (Whitby, M., and Whitby, M., translation, 1986).
Vegetius, *De rei militari* (Milner, N.P., translation, 1993; Reeve, M.D., translation, 2004).
Vie de Theodore de Sykeon (Festugiere, A.-J., translation, 1970).
Zonaras, *Epitome* (Banchich, T.M., and Lane, E.N., translation, 2009).
Zosimus, *New History* (Ridley, R.T., translation, 1982).

Secondary Sources
Akram, A.I., *The Sword of Allah: Khalid bin al-Waleed – His Life and Campaigns*, Karachi (2004).
—— *Muslim Conquest of Persia*, Rawalpindi (2009).
Al-Tel, O.I., *The First Islamic Conquest of Aelia (Islamic Jerusalem): a Critical Analytical Study of the Early Islamic Historical Narratives and Sources*, Dundee (2003).
Bagnall, R.S., *Reading Papyri: Writing History*, Ann Arbor (1995).
Ball, W., *Rome in the East: the Transformation of an Empire*, London (2000).
Barbero, A., *Charlemagne: Father of a Continent*, Berkeley (2004).
Barchiesi, A. and Scheidel, W. (eds), *The Oxford Handbook of Roman Studies*, Oxford (2010).
Barisic, F. 'Le siege de Constantinople par les Avares et les Slaves en 626', *Byzantion* XXIV (1954) 371–395.
Beck, W.C., 'Disinfection from antiquity to the present', *The Guthrie Journal* 59 (1990), 191–195.
Biers, W.R., *Art, Artefacts and Chronology in Classical Archaeology*, London (1992).
Bodel, J. (ed.), *Epigraphic Evidence: Ancient History from Inscriptions*, London (2001).
Boyce, M., *Zoroastrians: Their Religious Beliefs and Practices*, London (1979).
Bravmann, M.M., *The Spiritual Background of Early Islam: Studies in Ancient Arab Concepts*, Leiden (2009).
Brooks, E.W., 'On the Chronology of the Conquest of Egypt by the Saracens', *ByzZ* IV (1895), 435–444.
Brown, P., *The World of Late Antiquity*, London (2006).
Brown, T.S., Bryer, A. and Winfield, D. 'Cities of Heraclius', *Byzantine and Modern Greek Studies* 4 (1978), 15–38.

Bury, J.B., *A History of the Later Roman Empire from Arcadius to Irene, 395 A.D. to 800 A.D.*, 2 Vols., London (1889).

Butler, A.J., *The Arab Conquest of Egypt*, Oxford (1902).

Cameron, A., *Circus Factions: Blues and Greens at Rome and Byzantium*, Oxford (1976).

Cameron, A. (ed.), *The Byzantine and Early Islamic Near East III: States, Resources and Armies*, Princeton (1995).

Cameron, A. and Conrad L.I. (eds), *The Byzantine and Early Islamic Near East I: Problems in the Literary Source Material*, Princeton (1992).

Carey, B.T., *Road to Manzikert: Byzantine and Islamic Warfare 527–1071*, Barnsley (2012).

Casey, P.J., 'Justinian, the Limitanei and Arab-Byzantine relations in the Sixth Century', *JRA* 9 (1996), 214–222.

Collins, R., *The Arab Conquest of Spain, 710–97*, London (1989).

—— *Visigothic Spain, 409–711*, London (2004).

Conrad, L.I., *History and Historiography in Early Islamic Times: Studies in Perspective*, Princeton (1994).

Daryaee, T., *The Fall of the Sasanian Empire and the End of Late Antiquity: Continuity and Change in the Province of Persis*, Ph.D Thesis, UCLA (1999).

—— *The Fall of the Sasanians*, Nashr-e Tarikh-e, Iran (2004).

—— *Sasanian Persia: The Rise and Fall of an Empire*, New York (2009).

Debevoise, N.C., *A Political History of Parthia*, Westport (1970).

Dennis, G., 'Byzantine Heavy Artillery: The Helepolis', *Greek, Roman, and Byzantine Studies* 39 (1998), 99–115.

—— 'Defenders of the Christian People: Holy War in Byzantium', in Laiou, A.E. and Mottahedeh, R.P. (eds), *The Crusades from the Perspective of Byzantium and the Muslim World*, Washington (2001), 31–39.

Diehl, C., *L'Afrique Byzantine. Histoire de la Domination Byzantine en Afrique (533–709)*, Paris (1896).

Dols, M.W., 'Plague in Early Islamic History', *Journal of the American Oriental Society* 94 (1974), 371–383.

Donner, F.M., *The Early Islamic Conquests*, Princeton (1981).

—— 'Centralized Authority and Military Autonomy in the Early Islamic Conquests', in Cameron, A. (ed.), *The Byzantine and Early Islamic Near East III: States, Resources and Armies*, Princeton (1995), 337–360.

—— *Narrative of Islamic Origins: the beginnings of Islamic historical writing*, London (1998).

—— 'The Background to Islam', in Maas, M. (ed.), *The Cambridge Companion to the Age of Justinian*, Cambridge (2004), 510–533.

Edwell, P.M., *Between Rome and Persia: the Middle Euphrates, Mesopotamia and Palmyra under Roman Control*, London (2008).

Elton, H., *Warfare in Roman Europe AD 350–425*, Oxford (1996).

Evans, J.A.S., *The Age of Justinian: The Circumstances of Imperial Power*, London (2001).

Faulkner, N., *Apocalypse: The Great Jewish Revolt against Rome AD 66–73*, Stroud (2002).

Fine, J.V.A., *The Early Medieval Balkans: A Critical Survey from the Sixth to the Late Twelfth Century*, Ann Arbor (1983).

Fisher, G., *Between the Empires: Arabs, Romans and Sasanians in Late Antiquity*, Oxford (2011).

Flusin, B., *Saint Anastase le Perse et l'histoire de la Palestine au début du VIIe siècle*, 2 Vols, Paris (1992).

Foss, C., 'The Persians in Asia Minor and the End of Antiquity,' *EHR* 90 (1975), 721–743.

—— *Ephesus After Antiquity*, Cambridge (1979).

Frye, R.N. (ed.), *The Cambridge History of Iran Vol. IV*, Cambridge (1975).

—— *The Golden Age of Persia: the Arabs in the East*, London (1993).

Garland, L., *Byzantine Empresses: Women and Power in Byzantium AD 527–1204*, London (1999).

Garnsey, P. and Saller, R., *The Roman Empire: Economy, Society and Culture*, Berkley (1987).

Geva, H. (ed.), *Ancient Jerusalem Revealed*, Jerusalem (1994).

Gibb, H.A.R., *The Arab Conquests in Central Asia*, London (1923).

Gibbon, E., *The Decline and Fall of the Roman Empire*, 6 Vols, London (1776–1788).

Gnoli, G., 'The Quadripartition of the Sasanian Empire', *East & West* 35 (1985), 265–270.

Greatrex, G., 'Byzantium and the East in the Sixth Century', in Maas, M. (ed.), *The Cambridge Companion to the Age of Justinian*, Cambridge (2004), 477–509.

Greatrex, G. and Lieu, S.N.C., *The Roman Eastern Frontier and the Persian Wars AD 363–628*, London (2007).

Grierson, P., 'The Isaurian Coins of Heraclius,' *NC* ser. 6, 11 (1951), 56–67.

—— 'A New Isaurian Coin of Heraclius,' *NC* ser. 6, 13 (1953), 145–146.

Haldon, J.F., *Recruitment and Conscription in the Byzantine Army c.550–950: A Study on the Origins of the Stratiotika Ktemata*, Vienna (1979).

—— *Byzantine Praetorians: An Administrative, Institutional and Social Survey of the Opsikion and Tagmata c.580–900*, Bonn (1984).

—— 'Military Service, Military Lands and the Status of Soldiers: Current Problems and Interpretations', *DOP* 47 (1993), 1–67.

—— *State, Army and Society in Byzantium: Approaches to Military, Social and Administrative History 6th–12th Centuries*, Aldershot (1995).

—— *Byzantium in the Seventh Century: The Transformation of a Culture*, Cambridge (1997).

—— *Warfare, State and Society in the Byzantine World 565–1204*, London (1999).

—— 'The Byzantine World', in Raaflaub, K.A., and Rosenstein, N. (eds), *War and Society in the Ancient and Medieval Worlds: Asia, The Mediterranean, Europe, and Mesoamerica*, Cambridge (2001), 241–270.

—— *The Byzantine Wars*, Stroud (2008).

Harris, W.V., 'Towards a study of the Roman slave trade', in D'Arms, J.H. and Kopff, E.C. (eds), *The Seabourne Commerce of Ancient Rome: Studies in Archaeology and History*, Rome (1980) 117–140.

—— (ed.), *The Transformation of the 'Urbs Romana' in Late Antiquity*, *JRA Suppl.* 33, Portsmouth (1999).

Hendy, M., *Studies in the Byzantine Monetary Economy c.300–1450*, Cambridge (1985).

Herrin, J., *Byzantium: The Surprising Life of a Medieval Empire*, London (2007).

Hill, D.R., 'The Role of the Camel and the Horse in the Early Arab Conquests', in Parry, V.J. and Yapp, M.E. (eds), *War and Technology and Society in the Middle East*, London (1975), 32–43.

Hinds, G.M., *Studies in Early Islamic History*, Princeton (1996).

Holland, T., *In The Shadow Of The Sword: The Battle for Global Empire and the End of the Ancient World*, London (2012).

Hourani, A. *A History of the Arab Peoples*, London (2005).

Howard-Johnston, J. 'The Two Great Powers in Late Antiquity: a Comparison', in Cameron, A. (ed.), *The Byzantine and Early Islamic Near East III: States, Resources and Armies*, Princeton (1995), 157–226.

—— 'Heraclius' Persian Campaigns and the Revival of the East Roman Empire, 622–630', *War in History* 6 (1999), 1–44.

—— *East Rome, Sasanian Persia and the End of Antiquity: Historiographical and Historical Sources*, Aldershot (2006).

—— *Witnesses to a World Crisis: Historians and Histories of the Middle East in the Seventh Century*, Oxford (2010).

Howgego, C., *Ancient History from Coins*, London (2001).

Hoyland, G.R., *Seeing Islam as Others Saw It: A Survey and Evaluation of Christian, Jewish and Zoroastrian Writing*, Princeton (1997).

—— *Arabia and Arabs: From the Bronze Age to the Coming of Islam*, London (2001).

Hughes, I., *Belisarius: The Last Roman General*, Barnsley (2009).

Isaac, B., 'The Army in the Late Roman East: the Persian Wars and the Defence of the Byzantine Provinces', in Cameron, A. (ed.), *The Byzantine and Early Islamic Near East III: States, Resources and Armies*, Princeton (1995), 125–155.

Jabbur, J.S., *The Bedouin and the Desert: Aspects of Nomadic Life in the Arab East*, New York (1995).

Jacobsen, T.C., *The Gothic War: Rome's Final Conflict in the West*, Yardley (2010).

James, S., 'Death Underground: Gas Warfare at Dura-Europus', *CWA* 38 (2010), 20–27.

Jones, A.H.M., *Ancient Economic History*, London (1948).

—— *Later Roman Empire 284–602*, Oxford (1964).

Kaegi, W.E., *Some Thoughts on Byzantine Military Strategy*, Brookline (1983).

—— *Byzantium and the Early Islamic Conquests*, Cambridge (1992).

—— 'The Battle of Nineveh', *AABSC* 19 (1993), 3–4.

—— *Heraclius, Emperor of Byzantium*, Cambridge (2003).

Kennedy, H., 'The Financing of the Military in the Early Islamic State', in Cameron, A. (ed.), *The Byzantine and Early Islamic Near East III: States, Resources and Armies*, Princeton (1995), 361–378.

—— *The Armies of the Caliphs: Military and Society in the Early Islamic State*, London (2001).

Khorasani, M.M., *Arms and Armor from Iran: The Bronze Age to the End of the Qajar Period*, Tübingen (2006).

King, G.R.D. and Cameron, A. (eds), *The Byzantine and Early Islamic Near East II: Land Use and Settlement Patterns*, Princeton (1994).

Kolbaba, T., 'Fighting for Christianity: Holy War in the Byzantine Empire,' *Byzantion* 68 (1998), 194–221.

Laga, C., 'Judaism and Jews in Maximus Confessor's Works. Theoretical Controversy and Practical Attitudes', *Byzsl* 51 (1990), 177–188.

Laiou, A.E. and Mottahedeh, R.P. (eds), *The Crusades from the Perspective of Byzantium and the Muslim World*, Washington (2001).

Landau-Tasseron, E., 'Features of the Pre-Conquest Muslim Armies in the Time of Muhammad', in Cameron, A. (ed.), *The Byzantine and Early Islamic Near East III: States, Resources and Armies*, Princeton (1995), 299–336.

Lascaratos, J., Poulakou-Rembelakou, E., Rembelakos, A. and Marketos, S., 'The First Case of Epispadias: an Unknown Disease of the Byzantine Emperor Heraclius (610–641 AD)', *British Journal of Urology* 76 (1995), 380–383.

Lev, Y. (ed.), *War and Society in the Eastern Mediterranean 7th–15th Centuries*, New York (1997).

Lewis, D.L., *God's Crucible: Islam and the Making of Europe 570–1215*, London (2008).

Lilie, R.-J., 'Kaiser Herakleios und die Ansiedlung der Serben,' *Sudest-Forschungen* 44 (1985), 17–43.

Lipman, J.N., *Familiar Strangers: a History of Muslims in Northwest China*, Washington (1997).

Luttwak, E.N., *Grand Strategy of the Byzantine Empire*, Cambridge (2009).

Maas, M. (ed.), *The Cambridge Companion to the Age of Justinian*, Cambridge (2004).

Madelung, W., *The Succession to Muhammad: A Study of the Early Caliphate*, Cambridge (1997).

Mastnak, T., *Crusading Peace: Christendom, the Muslim World, and Western Political Order*, Berkeley (2002).

McCotter, S.E.J., 'The Strategy and Tactics of Siege Warfare in the Early Byzantine Period', Ph.D Thesis, Queen's University, Belfast (1996).

Millar, F., *A Greek Roman Empire: Power and Belief Under Theodosius II 408–450*, London (2006).

Nicolle, D., *The Armies of Islam 7th–11th Centuries*, London (1982).

—— *Armies of the Muslim Conquest*, London (1993).

—— *Yarmuk AD 636: the Muslim Conquest of Syria*, Oxford (1994).

—— 'Arms of the Umayyad era: Military Technology in a Time of Change', in Lev, Y. (ed.), *War and Society in the Eastern Mediterranean 7th–15th Centuries*, New York (1997), 9–100.

Noethlichs, K.-L., *Das Judentum und der romische Staat: Minderheitenpolitik im antiken Rom*, Darmstadt (1996).

Noth, A. and Conrad, L.I., *The Early Islamic Historical Traditions: A Source Critical Study*, Princeton (1994).

Olster, D.M., *The Politics of Usurpation in the Seventh Century: Rhetoric and Revolution in Byzantium*, Amsterdam (1993).

—— *Roman Defeat, Christian Response, and the Literary Construction of the Jew*, Philadelphia (1994).

Ostrogorsky, G., *The History of the Byzantine State*, Oxford (1956).

—— *Geschichte des Byzantinischen Staates*, Munich (1963).

Parry, V.J. and Yapp, M.E. (eds), *War and Technology and Society in the Middle East*, London (1975).

Pearson, J.D. (ed.), *A Bibliography of Pre-Islamic Persia*, London (1975).

Pernice, A., *Imperatore Eraclio*, Florence (1905).

Pourshariati, P., *Decline and Fall of the Sasanian Empire: the Sasanian-Parthian Confederacy and the Arab Conquest of Iran*, London (2009).

Pringle, D., *The Defence of Byzantine Africa from Justinian to the Arab Conquest: An Account of the Military History and Archaeology of the African Provinces in the Sixth and Seventh Century*, Oxford (1981).

Purton, P., *A History of the Early Medieval Siege c.450–1200*, Woodbridge (2009).

Reich, R., 'The Ancient Burial Ground in the Mamilla Neighbourhood, Jerusalem', in Geva, H. (ed.), *Ancient Jerusalem Revealed*, Jerusalem (1994), 111–118.

Reinink, G.J. and Stolte, B. (eds), *The Reign of Heraclius (610–641): Crisis and Confrontation*, Leuven (2002).

Rickman, G., Austin, M.M., Harries, J. and Smith, C.J., *Modus Operandi: Essays in Honour of Geoffrey Rickman*, London (1998).

Roth, N., 'The Jews and the Muslim Conquest of Spain,' *Jewish Social Studies* 38 (1976), 146–148.

Rubin, Z., 'The Reforms of Khusro Anūshirwān', in Cameron, A. (ed.), *The Byzantine and Early Islamic Near East III: States, Resources and Armies*, Princeton (1995), 227–298.

Sarris, P., 'The Justinianic Plague: origins and effects', *Continuity and Change* 17 (2002), 175–179.

Scheidel, W., 'Quantifying the Sources of Slaves in the Early Roman Empire', *JRS* (1997), 156–169.

—— (ed.), *Debating Roman Demography*, Leiden (2001).

—— 'Progress and Problems in Roman Demography', in Scheidel, W. (ed.), *Debating Roman Demography*, Leiden (2001), 1–81.

Southern, P. and Dixon, K.R., *The Late Roman Army*, London (1996).

Stratos, A., *Byzantium in the Seventh Century*, 6 vols., Amsterdam (1968–1980).

Thomson, R.W., *Rewriting Caucasian History: The Medieval Armenian Adaptation of the Georgian Chronicles*, Oxford (1996).

Treadgold, W., *Byzantium and its Army 284–1081*, Stanford (1995).

—— *A History of the Byzantine State and Society*, Stanford (1997).

—— *The Early Byzantine Historians*, London (2007).

Wasserstein, A., 'The Number and Provenance of Jews in Graeco-Roman Antiquity: A Note on Population Statistics', in Katzoff, R. (ed.), *Classical Studies in Honor of David Sohlberg*, Ramat Gan. (1996), 307–17.

Wells, P.S., *Barbarians to Angels: The Dark Ages Reconsidered*, New York (2008).

Whitby, M., *The Emperor Maurice and his Historian: Theophylact Simocatta on Persian and Balkan Warfare*, Oxford (1988).

—— 'Greek historical writing after Procopius: variety and vitality', in Cameron, A. and Conrad, L.I. (eds), *The Byzantine and Early Islamic Near East I: Problems in the Literary Source Material*, Princeton (1992), 25–80.

—— 'Recruitment in Roman armies from Justinian to Heraclius (ca. 565–615)', in Cameron, A. (ed.), *The Byzantine and Early Islamic Near East III: States, Resources and Armies*, Princeton (1995), 61–124.

—— 'Deus Noiscum: Christianity, Warfare and Morale in Late Antiquity', in Rickman, G., Austin, M.M., Harries, J. and Smith, C.J., *Modus Operandi: Essays in Honour of Geoffrey Rickman*, London (1998), 191–208.

—— 'Emperors and Armies AD 235–395', in Swain, S. and Edwards, M. (eds), *Approaching Late Antiquity: The Transformation from Early to Late Empire*, Oxford (2004), 156–186.

—— 'Army and Society in the Late Roman World: A Context for Decline?', in Erdkamp, P. (ed.), *A Companion to the Roman Army*, Oxford (2007a), 515–531.

—— 'The Late Roman Army and the Defence of the Balkans', in Poulter, A.G. (ed.), *The Transition to Late Antiquity on the Danube and Beyond*, Oxford (2007b), 135–161.

Wickham, C., *The Inheritance of Rome: Illuminating the Dark Ages 400–1000*, London (2009).

Wiesehöfer, J., *Ancient Persia From 550 BC to 650 AD*, London (2001).

Wiita, J.E., 'The Ethnika in Byzantine Military Treatises', Ph.D. Thesis, University of Minnesota (1977).

Williams, S. and Friell, G., *Theodosius: The Empire at Bay*, London (1994).

—— *The Rome That Did Not Fall: The Survival of the East in the Fifth Century*, London (1999).

Zuckerman, C., 'Heraclius in 625', *REB* 60 (2002a), 189–197.

—— 'The Khazars and Byzantium', in *Proceedings of the International Colloquium on the Khazars* (2002b).

Index

\